# EUROPE ON THE EVE
# OF WAR 1900–1914

## A note for the general reader

*War, Peace and Social Change: Europe 1900–1955* is the latest honours-level history course to be produced by the Open University. War and Society has always been a subject of special interest and expertise in the Open University's History Department. The appeal for the general reader is that the five books in the series, taken together or singly, consist of authoritative, up-to-date discussions of the various aspects of war and society in the twentieth century.

The books provide insights into the modes of teaching and communication, including the use of audio-visual material, which have been pioneered at the Open University. Readers will find that they are encouraged to participate in a series of 'tutorials in print', an effective way to achieve a complete command of the material. As in any serious study of a historical topic, there are many suggestions for further reading, including references to a Course Reader, set book and to two collections of primary documents which accompany the series. It is possible to grasp the basic outlines of the topics discussed without turning to these books, but obviously serious students will wish to follow up what is, in effect, a very carefully designed course of guided reading, and discussion and analysis of that reading. The first unit in Book I sets out the aims and scope of the course.

Open University students are provided with supplementary material, including a *Course Guide* which gives information on student assignments, summer school, the use of video cassettes, and so on.

## War, Peace and Social Change: Europe 1900–1955

*Book I Europe on the Eve of War 1900–1914*

*Book II World War I and Its Consequences*

*Book III Between Two Wars*

*Book IV World War II and Its Consequences*

*Book V War and Change in Twentieth-Century Europe*

Prepared by the course team and published by the Open University Press, 1990

### Other material associated with the course

*Documents 1: 1900–1929*, eds Arthur Marwick and Wendy Simpson, Open University Press, 1990

*Documents 2: 1925–1959*, eds Arthur Marwick and Wendy Simpson, Open University Press, 1990

*War, Peace and Social Change in Twentieth-Century Europe*, eds Clive Emsley, Arthur Marwick and Wendy Simpson, Open University Press, 1990 (Course Reader)

*Europe 1880–1945*, J. M. Roberts, Longman, 1989 (second edition) (set book)

If you are interested in studying the course, contact the Student Enquiries Office, The Open University, PO Box 71, Milton Keynes MK7 6AG.

*Cover illustration:* poster by E. Vulliemin for Peugeot bicycles, about 1900 (reproduced by kind permission of Musée de la Publicité, Paris).

# EUROPE ON THE EVE OF WAR 1900–1914

*Arthur Marwick, Bernard Waites,*
*Clive Emsley and Ian Donnachie*

**OPEN UNIVERSITY PRESS**

Open University Press
*in association with*
The Open University

The Open University

## A318 Course team

Tony Aldgate  *Author*
Kate Clements  *Editor*
Charles Cooper  *BBC Producer*
Henry Cowper  *Author*
Ian Donnachie  *Author*
Nigel Draper  *Editor*
Clive Emsley  *Author*
David Englander  *Author*
John Golby  *Author*
John Greenwood  *Liaison Librarian*

Tony Lentin  *Author*
Arthur Marwick  *Author and Course Team Chair*
Ray Munns  *Cartographer*
Bill Purdue  *Author*
Wendy Simpson  *Course Manager*
Tag Taylor  *Designer*
Bernard Waites  *Author*
Geoffrey Warner  *Author*

Open University Press
Celtic Court
Buckingham
MK18 1XT
England

*and*
1900 Frost Road, Suite 101
Bristol, PA19007, USA

First published in 1990

*British Library Cataloguing in Publication Data*

War, peace and social change: Europe 1900–1955.
  1. Europe, history
  I. Marwick, Arthur, *1936–*   II. Open University, *A318 War, Peace and Social Change course team*   III. Open University
  940

  ISBN 0-335-09305-1 (hardback)   ISBN 0-335-09304-3 (paperback)

*Library of Congress Cataloging in Publication Data*

Europe on the eve of war, 1900–1914 / Arthur Marwick . . . [et al.].
    p.   cm. – (War, peace, and social change; bk. 1)
  Material for an honours-level history course produced by Open University.
  ISBN 0-335-09305-1   ISBN 0-335-09304-3 (pbk.)
  1. World War, 1914–1918 – Causes.  2. Europe – Social conditions – 1789–1900.  3. Europe – Social conditions – 20th century.
  4. Social change.  I. Marwick, Arthur, 1936–  .  II. Open University.  III. Series.
  D511.E79   1989
  940.2'88–dc20                              8923165 CIP

Designed by the Graphic Design Group of the Open University

This book is set in 10/12pt Palatino by Rowland Phototypesetting Ltd Bury St Edmunds, Suffolk

Printed and bound in Great Britain by
Redwood Burn Limited, Trowbridge, Wiltshire.
1.1

# CONTENTS

## Acknowledgements

Grateful acknowledgement is made to the following sources for permission to use material in this book:

**Text**

Holton, S. S. *Feminism and Democracy*, 1986, Cambridge University Press; McMillan, J. F. 'World War I and women in France' and Reid, A. 'World War I and the working class in Britain' in Marwick, A. (ed.) *Total War and Social Change*, 1988, Macmillan; Hardach, G. *The First World War 1914–1918*, 1977, Allen Lane. Copyright © Deutscher Taschenbuch Verlag GmbH and Penguin Books Ltd, 1973, translation copyright © Ross, P. and Ross, B., 1977. Reproduced by permission of Penguin Books Ltd and University of California Press; Marwick, A. *War and Social Change in the Twentieth Century: A Comparative Study of Britain, France, Germany, Russia and the United States*, 1974, Macmillan; Kocka, J. *Facing Total War*, 1984, Berg Publishers; Macartney, C. A. *The Habsburg Empire 1790–1918*, 1969, George Weidenfeld & Nicolson Ltd; Anderson, R. *France 1870–1914*, 1977, Routledge and Kegan Paul; Clark, M. *Modern Italy 1871–1982*, 1984, Longman Group UK Ltd; Sheehan, J. J. *German Liberalism in the Nineteenth Century*, 1978, The University of Chicago Press; Péguy, C. 'Prayer for we others', translated in Cruickshank, J. (ed.) *French Literature and its Background*, vol. 6, 1970, Oxford University Press; Rogger, H. *Russia in the Age of Modernisation and Revolution 1881–1917*, 1983, Longman Group UK Ltd.

**Tables**

Table 3.2: Moeller, R. G. *Peasants and Lords in Modern Germany*, 1986, Unwin Hyman Ltd; Table 3.3: Blum, J. *The End of the Old Order in Europe*, 1978, Princeton University Press; Table 3.4: *An Economic History of Modern France 1730–1914*, 1981, Macmillan; Table 3.6: Hardach, G. *The First World War 1914–1918*, 1977, Allen Lane. Copyright © Deutscher Taschenbuch Verlag GmbH and Penguin Books Ltd, 1973, translation copyright © Ross, P. and Ross, B., 1977. Reproduced by permission of Penguin Books Ltd and University of California Press; Tables 3.7, 3.8 and 3.9: Pearson, R. *National Minorities in Eastern Europe 1848–1945*.

# UNIT 1 INTRODUCING THE COURSE

*Arthur Marwick*

# 1 *THE COURSE TITLE EXPLAINED*

This is the first book in the Open University course A318 *War, Peace and Social Change: Europe 1900–1955*. The first part of the course title brings out that, while, as indicated, there will be discussion of developments taking place in time of peace, particular emphasis will be placed upon the contrasts between 'war' and 'peace', with questions being raised about the significance of war in twentieth-century European history; the first part of the title also indicates that we shall have a special concern with 'social change'. The second part of the title indicates that it is a course in twentieth-century European history up to about 1955. It would have been possible to construct a course which was more simply a general history of Europe between around 1900 and around 1955, much as the textbook by J. M. Roberts, *Europe 1880–1945* (the set book for this course) is a general history of Europe between the two dates contained in its title. Roberts's aim is, within the space at his disposal, to cover anything that is of importance in understanding the development of Europe in the period he is concerned with. Inevitably, he emphasizes certain topics at the expense of others, but he has chosen his topics in order, firstly, to give as fair and comprehensive a coverage as possible and, secondly, because he believes the topics he has chosen to be the most important in explaining the development of modern Europe. Naturally he discusses the two major wars ('total' wars as we shall be calling them in this course), but he does not give any special emphasis to them. Our course (while making great use of Roberts's excellent book as a basic secondary source) *does* give a special emphasis to the two total wars. This is partly because we believe that a history course is more likely to arouse and maintain your interest, and is more likely to be effective as teaching material, if it sets up some central questions and issues to be discussed, and partly because there actually is quite a good case (perhaps greater than Roberts allows) that it is impossible to understand twentieth-century European history without being fully aware of the various implications of the two total wars. You do not have to agree with this proposition: the course encourages debate and argument over it. Indeed, you could say that there is a third reason for designing the course in this way, which is that among historians and students of twentieth-century history everywhere this debate is considered a most important one, as shown, for instance, by the fact that 'war and society' courses now exist in a number of other universities.

As a teaching course, *War, Peace and Social Change* differs in other ways as well from a general textbook such as that by Roberts. In a very skilful way, and at a quite advanced level, Roberts presents his readers with information, ideas, interrelationships, causes, consequences, comparisons and contrasts: he presents a balanced, carefully structured account, involving narrative, analysis and de-scription. But our course encourages you (the student and reader) to be active. It seeks to help you to develop and practise some of the skills of history. It seeks to show you how to discuss important historical issues relevant to the course, how to develop these arguments in properly written essays. It seeks to develop your understanding of the nature of the primary source materials upon which all historical writing is based, and of how to analyse and use such sources. It seeks to help you master many of the problems involved in historical study and to help you understand the significance of the different approaches which have been taken in that study (Marxist and non-Marxist approaches, for instance). Most of this introductory unit will take the form of an elaboration and discussion of the following six aims:

1   To enable students to argue in an informed way over the nature, extent and causes of social change within and across the main European countries c.1900–c.1955, which are defined for the purposes of this course as Russia, Austria-Hungary (up to the aftermath of World War I only), France, Germany, Italy and the United Kingdom; Turkey and the Balkans, and Central European countries will be discussed as relevant. (There will also be references to Scandinavian and other European countries.)

2   To help students to understand the nature of total war and the differences between different kinds of war, including internal and civil war, and to help them to discuss in an informed way the relationship between war and revolution in the twentieth century.

3   To enable students to discuss the causes of the two total wars, evaluating 'structural' (that is to say 'concerning economic and industrial imperatives') forces against other forces such as those of geopolitics, ideology, nationalism and contingency.

4   To enable students to argue in an informed way about the causes of twentieth-century social change, and in particular to evaluate the significance of the two total wars with respect to this change relative to 'structural' (see Aim 3), political and ideological forces, and to enable them also to discuss the relationship of the wars to the major geopolitical changes.

5   To assist Open University students to develop skills learned at Foundation and Second Level in:

(a)   the critical analysis and interpretation of primary source materials, including written documents, as well as literary and artistic materials, film, radio and manifestations of popular culture;

(b)   understanding some of the different approaches to historical study, in particular Marxist/sociological/linguistic approaches on the one side, and 'liberal humanist' ones on the other, and also quantitative and qualitative approaches;

(c)   dealing with such problems as periodization and historical semantics; and

(d)   writing history essays of BA (Honours) standard.

6   To take further students' understanding of the nature of historiographical controversy (a matter first raised in the Foundation course, dealt with further at Second Level) and to enable them to arrive at informed judgements on the issues and debates presented within the framework of the course.

# 2  *THE SIX AIMS OF THE COURSE EXPLAINED*

## 2.1   Aim 1

Essentially this aim serves two purposes: it indicates that a major concern of the course is social change, and it spells out firmly which countries we shall be dealing with.

It is a platitude that history is concerned with both continuity and change. Aim 1 brings out that our emphasis is on change, the idea being to highlight issues for discussion and debate. If one looks rigorously and systematically for change, one will automatically reveal starkly the areas in which there was little or no change. Note that Aim 1 speaks, as does the title of the course, of social change. Here it is time to pause, in order to help you to be sure that you know what is meant by social change.

**Exercise**  Three potentially useful ways of pinning down what is meant by 'social change' would be:

1   to write a direct definition of the term;

2   to write down examples of social change;

3   to identify other types of historical change which are not *social* change.

I now want you to try to do each of these things. I suggest that after a quick shot at a definition you move on to the other two questions. After dealing with them you may find it possible to attempt a fuller answer to the first question. ∎

**Specimen answers and discussion**  For an initial definition you may have said something like: 'social change is change taking place in human societies', or 'social change is change affecting everyday life'. I hope you then went on to give such examples as living conditions, social welfare, social structure, beliefs, customs and attitudes. For other types of historical change I hope you thought of political, constitutional and economic change; perhaps also administrative, technological, scientific and intellectual change and change in international relationships. □

Social change may include, or be related to, some of these, but it is not identical to any of them. I'd offer a definition something like this: 'Change in the institutions, ideas and behaviour of society; change affecting human lives as they are actually lived, change directly affecting everyone in society, or large sections of it.' By that sort of definition, social change is not rigidly distinguished from other sorts of historical change, but is indeed seen as embracing, or being closely involved with, other sorts of historical change. Thus when we say this course is primarily concerned with 'social change', it is a matter of *emphasis* rather than precise content. The replacement of a Conservative government by a Labour government would conventionally be regarded as a political change. But in so far as such a change would also entail a change in the social composition of government (more MPs from a working-class background, for instance), and in so far as it would entail new ideas, about social welfare policy, and so on, it would involve social, as well as political change. Our course will not ignore political developments, but the emphasis will be on their social implications.

Briefly, there is not, in my view, a great deal of value in arguing over what precisely is 'political' and what 'social'. It will be much more useful to you if I now list the ten overlapping areas of social change on which we shall concentrate in this course.

### Ten areas of social change

*1   Social geography*

This concerns population (including, for instance, rises and falls in birthrates), population movements (including from agricultural to urban areas), and the environment in general. It concerns those matters affecting society as a whole which, as the heading suggests, might traditionally be associated with the discipline of geography, that is to say the distribution of people, of town and country, of housing and communications. Such matters are absolutely basic to any study of social change.

## 2    Economic performance and theory

Here we are already into overlap. Economic performance, that is to say the building of factories and the production of commodities, will obviously affect social geography. But here the emphasis is on relative efficiency, productivity, and so on. Also included are questions of the levels of exploitation of science and technology, and the impact of these (very important social questions), and the related question of the nature of work (something which affects very large numbers of people). It can well be argued that upon levels of economic performance depend all other matters such as standards of living and welfare benefits. As indicated, the concern too is with the theories lying behind, or alternatively themselves being affected by, economic activities: for instance, theories of free trade or private enterprise and laissez-faire or, on the contrary, of state regulation and intervention.

## 3    Social structure

This area also is a strong contender for being considered the central one in all questions of social change. It refers to the way in which societies divide up in hierarchical fashion into 'classes', 'estates' or 'social groups'. In the eyes of most non-Marxist historians, 'classes' are a feature of industrial rather than non-industrial societies (of which there were many in Europe before 1914); Marxists accord a special importance to 'class' (as they understand the term) throughout all periods of history.

## 4    National cohesion

As I have just suggested, individual countries divide up into 'estates' or 'classes'. Very many, especially in pre-1914 Europe, divided up into different racial and ethnic groups as well. We shall look at the extent to which different countries were racially or nationally cohesive (or unified), and the extent to which they were divided up ethnically.

## 5    Social reform and welfare policies

This is a very obvious aspect of social change, and probably one of the ones you thought of immediately in answering the first exercise. It covers such matters as Old Age Pensions, Family Allowances, National Health Services.

## 6    Material conditions

Material conditions are central to social life in the most obvious sense of that term. Obviously they are connected to social geography, economic performance and social policies. Specifically they concern housing, diet, nutrition, health and sanitation, and relate also to conditions of work.

## 7    Customs and behaviour

Here we come to an area which would almost certainly have been neglected in traditional accounts of political, constitutional or economic change. We come to the very heart of the most 'advanced' kind of social history. There is, of course, some overlap with material conditions, and even more overlap with my next three headings (particularly 'Women and the family', and 'High and popular culture').

None the less this is a useful heading for fixing attention on such matters as rural folk customs (such as feast days, festivals and important fairs) and questions about what happened to these in urban society, on costume and dress, eating and drinking habits, hours of work and recreation, and attitudes towards such authorities as monarch, lord, church and family.

### 8  Women and the family

Clearly the role and status of women is a very important issue in social change (some would say, the most important one). The heading is not in any way intended to imply that the role and status of women cannot be discussed as a topic completely independent of the family; it simply recognizes that within the period we are studying the role of women was most usually considered in the context of the family. In itself, family history is an important element in the study of social change.

### 9  High and popular culture

Culture, as is well known, is a difficult word with several shades of meaning. Here it is taken to mean what our newspapers often refer to as 'the arts and entertainment', together with leisure activities in general. To avoid direct overlap with 'Customs and behaviour', the emphasis is very much on art, literature, music, film, newspapers and broadcasting. By and large, 'high' culture is the culture of the élite, always a minority in any society.

It is not automatically assumed that 'high' culture is 'better' than 'popular' culture; it is simply recognized that this is the culture which, in the period we are studying, was accorded high status – it includes 'classical' music, and the work of artists and writers considered to be 'great' or, at least, whose work was accorded attention by serious critics. Popular culture, of course, refers to the entertainment and leisure activities of the mass of the people. In itself it has two aspects: (a) culture created *for* the masses (by rich newspaper proprietors, film producers, and so on; (b) culture created *by* the masses (for example, folk songs, traditional village football games and carnivals).

### 10  Political institutions and values

Are we going beyond the boundaries of social change here? One can't in practice discuss 'changes affecting everyone in society, or large sections of it' without considering those political institutions which do, indeed, impinge on ordinary lives: town and village councils, parliaments, and their correlatives, the possession, or non-possession, of the right to vote. Still more important are questions of values: do people accept the pre-conditions of liberal democracy, that the majority have the right to rule, but that the rights of minorities must be respected? Is religious 'truth', or national solidarity, or obedience to the monarchy, ranked more highly than liberal democracy? Is socialism regarded as a high ideal or a sinister threat? These are all important questions intimately related to other aspects of social change.

### Concluding words on the ten areas of social change

We shall be studying politics, as relevant, but the thrust of this course is towards *social* change. Clearly major political upheavals (both revolutions in government, and those changes in national frontiers which we shall term 'geopolitical changes' – that is, changes which are both geographical and political) arising from, or at the very least coinciding with, the two total wars, did affect the lives of whole societies and vast numbers of people. This important aspect is taken up in Aim 4.

It would be widely agreed that in most, if not all, of the ten areas I have just identified, noteworthy changes did take place between the first decade of the century and the 1950s. However, in serious historical study broad generalizations about 'noteworthy' or 'important' changes are not enough. As Aim 1 spells out, this course is concerned with 'the nature and extent of social change', that is to say we have to establish answers about how much social change there was in the different areas, we have to distinguish between areas in which a lot changed, and areas in which perhaps not very much changed.

Having established the basic way in which social change will be treated in this course, I must add that some historians would prefer to define social change in rather broader terms: in terms, indeed, of shifting patterns of dominance, of changing structures of power, of groups and classes overthrowing or replacing or reaching accommodations with each other, of, perhaps, a bourgeois class replacing a landed class and then, say, of the bourgeois class skilfully fending off the claims of a 'rising' working class (more on that later).

### Countries to be studied in this course

The central and inescapable point about the geographical coverage of this course is that it concerns Europe; the focus is on changes across Europe, and on comparisons between the different European countries. There is no emphasis on Britain, but in order to set clear limits somewhere, there is an overwhelming emphasis on what would usually be agreed to be the 'major' European countries. In our case, this means Russia, Germany, Italy, France and Britain. The Austrian Empire (Austria-Hungary) was a major power, until it was pulled apart in World War I; thus it figures prominently in Books I and II. One highly troubled area before 1914, and the location of the actual crisis which brought about war, was the Balkans, where the once triumphant imperial power, Turkey, was in a state of retreat and collapse. The Balkans and Central Europe (largely the states which had formerly made up the Austrian Empire) continued to be sources of international friction and the site of German ambition in the inter-war years: thus, although these countries do not figure consistently in all parts of the course, they do have to be brought in from time to time. The course, in other words, concentrates on those countries which were directly involved in the two world wars of the twentieth century: after all, one of our major concerns is to discuss the effects of these two wars.

**Exercise**    I have listed the ten areas of social change the course deals with. You will be introduced to arguments that the experiences of war had important effects in bringing about changes in most or all of these areas. Yet such arguments could be said to have a fatal weakness if they concentrated solely on the countries engaged in the two wars. What is this weakness? ■

**Specimen answer and discussion**    If it could be shown that neutral countries (for example Denmark in World War I, Sweden in both wars) had shared broadly in the same social changes as the other countries, this might cast doubt on the idea that change was brought by war.

It can indeed be maintained that, in many ways, the Scandinavian countries are models of progressive social change. Thus, although we make no consistent study of the neutral countries, references to them will have to be made. □

Let me make it absolutely clear what your workload responsibilities are: with regard to the main countries identified, you will be expected to read the course units, J. M. Roberts *Europe 1880–1945* (the set book) and *War, Peace and Social Change in Twentieth-Century Europe*, edited by Clive Emsley, Arthur Marwick and Wendy Simpson (the Course Reader); with regard to other countries you need not go beyond the references made to them in the course units themselves. When writing the Tutor-marked Assignments (TMAs), where, of course, there is much additional reading to be done, you can choose which topics and countries you wish to go into in more depth.

## 2.2   Aim 2

The French philosopher Raymond Aron wrote of the twentieth century as 'the century of total war'. We do not need to worry about the precise meaning of the term 'total war': it is widely accepted in both academic and popular usage as being an effective description of the two major wars of the twentieth century, the wars we are concerned with in this course. The implication is that the term does not apply to earlier wars, or to some wars since (for example, the Korean War or the Falklands War): World War I was the first total war. Later you will be asked to read the article on 'Total War' by Ian Beckett in the Course Reader, which brings out that the distinctions between the twentieth-century wars and earlier wars are not as clear-cut as often thought. Nevertheless the essential distinction remains that earlier wars were in essence fought by the armed forces, without civilians (though often affected by the devastation of war) directly participating in the war effort, while total war, the war of mature industrialized societies, entailed direct involvement of civilian populations (because of the need for munitions, the need to organize manpower in the most effective way, and so on) and attempts by governments to control entire nations, rather than purely strategic and military aspects. Thus, total war has been seen as affecting society in almost all its aspects in a way in which previous wars did not: this idea provides a good deal of the subject matter for this course.

We know the dates of the declarations of war by the various powers (the dates vary somewhat for different countries, of course: Italy was not involved in World War I until 1915, Russia in World War II until 1941) and we know the dates of the armistices, and of the peace settlements. We can, therefore, define the periods of what, whatever the qualifications that have to be made, I shall now call the two total wars. But towards the end of World War I in Russia (to take the most striking example), total war developed into revolution, and then into civil war ('Whites' versus 'Reds', with the active interference of the Western powers on the side of the former), and then into a long period of violence and heavy loss of life within Russia, which was certainly not international war, but nor was it really civil war (in the sense of there being two clearly identifiable 'sides' fighting against each other): this phenomenon, in which an indisputably established government was in violent conflict with a section of its own population (basically the 'kulaks', the wealthier peasants) is best described as one of 'internal war'. Thus, you should keep the following categories in mind: international war (as in the Balkan wars which preceded World War I), total war, revolution, civil war, and internal war.

As Aim 2 indicates, this course takes a close look at the relationship between war and revolution. It is common knowledge that the closing stages of World War I in Russia were accompanied not just by the February (ushering in parliamentary government) and October (ushering in Bolshevik one-party dictatorship) revolutions, but also by revolutions in Germany, Austria-Hungary, and Turkey, which if limited in character, certainly brought the end of imperial rule. To Marxists at the time (and to some today) revolution is an inevitable stage in historical development. At the extreme that line of argument would hold the war to have been irrelevant. A less extreme position might be that the war provided the actual crisis which provoked revolution at the precise moment it occurred. An extreme position at the other end would be that it was war alone (or most specifically, failure in war) which brought the collapse of the existing regime, and therefore the revolutionary situation.

**Exercise**    Is there any other element you would expect to find in carrying through a revolution? ■

**Specimen answer and discussion**    There are lots of things one might say, such as conditions of extreme deprivation, possibly a strong sense of national resentment among an oppressed people, but the (arguably) more universal element I was thinking of was a strong revolutionary leadership. □

Again, one can see that as operating independently of war, or one could see the war as giving such leadership its ideal opportunity. You can see how there are a number of different arguments, and your task will be to try to develop a position on the influence, or lack of it, of war with regard to the main revolutions we shall be studying. If we note along the way that the various revolutions I have mentioned so far are all slightly different from each other in character, that must lead to the question of what exactly constitutes a revolution. We will make more elaborate, and more precise, definitions later: here I will content myself with the suggestion that a revolution is more than simply the replacement of one ruler, or group of rulers, by another; it involves a change in the *character* and *values* of the regime – from, say, the principle of monarchical government to that of parliamentary government, from the principle of the autocratic power of an emperor to the principle of the dictatorship of the proletariat, from the principle of multinationality, embodied in one dynasty (as with the Habsburgs in Austria) to the principle of each nation having its own independent state, and so on.

Further questions arise relating back to Aim 1: what are the interconnections, if any, between war, revolution and social change? In Russia, in Germany and in Czechoslovakia (formerly incorporated in the Austrian Empire) there were various social reforms in the years after the war. Were these a direct result of revolution, or of the war, or of both, or of neither? I have mentioned the period of 'internal war' in Russia in the 1920s: was that directly an outcome of the revolution, or of the war, or was it perhaps a calculated decision by Russia's rulers? You can see the sorts of problems we shall be trying to tease out in this course.

## 2.3   Aim 3

This course puts much more weight on social change, and on the debates over the possible consequences of wars, than it does on the causes of the total wars. None the less the juxtaposition in the title of the words 'war' and 'peace' indicates that we do want you to be aware of how, on two major occasions in the twentieth century, 'peace' gave way to 'war'. Unit 6 is wholly devoted to bringing together the arguments about the causation of World War I, and Unit 20 serves a similar function with respect to World War II. But longer term causes of the war are discussed in other units. Aim 3 introduces some words that need explaining: for example, 'structural', 'geopolitical', 'ideological', 'contingency'.

*Structural*

Marxists have long argued that the wars in essence were the inevitable outcomes of capitalist struggle for markets and industrial and commercial supremacy. That is one type of 'structural' argument: political and diplomatic decisions or bungles, for instance, are played down; the wars, it is said, are brought about by much more profound long-term economic, industrial and 'class' forces, that is to say 'structural' factors. Many non-Marxists would give precedence to similar (though not quite identical) arguments, particularly with respect, in the case of World War I, to the expansionist drives said to be inherent in German economic and commercial development in the years before 1914.

*Geopolitical*

More traditional non-Marxist historians have always tended to stress geopolitical considerations: fears in Germany of being encircled by a powerful ring of hostile powers, Russia in the East, Britain and France in the West, and fears in the West of a potential German dominance of (or hegemony over) the European continent. There is a long tradition of maintaining that Britain entered World War I to 'maintain the balance of power'.

*Nationalism*

Few historians have found it possible to discuss the origins of World War I without some reference to the problems of nationalism: Serbia wishing to unite within her frontiers fellow southern Slavs still living within the boundaries of Austria-Hungary, Russia seeing herself as the champion of the Slav populations both inside and outside Austria-Hungary, and various subject nationalities having aspirations themselves towards separate nationhood.

*Contingency*

'Contingency', as I have used it here, means something like 'chance event or occurrence'. Arguably no event occurs completely by chance (all human beings are, and are known to be, mortal; assassins, however crazy, usually have some political purpose). However some events are chancier than others, and may certainly be brought about by a highly unpredictable convergence of longer term forces and immediate circumstances. As is well known, the event which touched off the series of threats and counter-threats, and orders for mobilization, which brought war as an actual fact, was the assassination on 28 June 1914 of the Austrian Archduke Franz Ferdinand and his wife by a Serbian nationalist. It needs no profound historical skills to see nationalism as a deeper force behind this 'chance event'; historical investigation has made clear that powerful persons in Austria-Hungary were only too happy to have an excuse to intimidate or crush Serbia. Yet, had the assassination attempt not taken place, had it failed (as it very nearly did), the way things actually happened would have been different, though how different it is nearly impossible to say.

*Ideological*

'Ideological' in this context simply means 'relating to ideas, beliefs and attitudes'. Among educated liberal opinion in the West there was deep hostility to Russian autocracy and in Britain, at least, some of this sentiment emerged in the form of a generalized hostility towards Russia among the population at large. However, in the event, Britain, as well as France, fought on the same side as Russia. Ideological forces may be thought to be more important with respect to the origins of World War II, when German National Socialist ideology aroused much fear and loathing. Yet one has to tread cautiously in noting that the war began with Germany in alliance with Soviet Russia, and then continued with the Western democracies in alliance with that power. If we consider the broadly shared attitudes and assumptions of European rulers (and probably most of their subjects too) in 1914 we alight on the point stressed by many historians that going to war in support of national interests was a perfectly normal act: this particular 'shared ideology' may be a large part of the explanation of the events of 1914.

*Psychological*

There is another aspect to this sort of approach which might reasonably be termed 'psychological': the argument that there was already in 1914 a widespread expectation of war (possibly a fear of war, possibly a desire for war) which helped to facilitate war as an actual happening.

*Political and diplomatic*

Some historians would still continue to pay a great deal of attention to the detail of political and diplomatic arrangements, particularly the system of interlinking alliances built up before World War I which resulted, it has been argued, in all of the powers being pulled in one after the other in support of their allies.

*Conclusion*

I hope you can begin to see the kind of evaluation of causes, as between different circumstances and trains of causation, that we shall be concerned with. See if you can identify some of the different approaches that individual historians have taken.

**Exercise** Here are a few extracts dealing with the causes of World War I. Read them carefully, then write down with reference to each extract, what causes are being singled out as important, and (if relevant) what alleged causes are being dismissed, trying at the same time to identify the general approach or approaches being followed (structural, geopolitical, and so on).

> *Extract (a)*
> The immediate occasion and the deeper causes largely coincide, for . . . the reasons for hostility among the various nations of Europe were manifold. The relative strengths and the relationships of alliance excluded partial conflicts. The rise of Germany, whose hegemony France dreaded and whose navy menaced England, had created an opposition that claimed to be defensive but was denounced by German propaganda as an attempt at encirclement. The two camps alarmed each other, and tried to soothe their own fears by piling up defensive armaments. The atmosphere grew heavy with multiplied incidents, which spread the conviction of approaching disaster. The explosion finally came in the East, where Russia and Austria were advancing contradictory claims, and where the principle of national sovereignty had ruined the Ottoman Empire and was beginning to undermine the still imposing edifice of the Austro-Hungarian Empire. (Raymond Aron, 'The century of total war', 1954, p.72)

*Extract (b)*

. . . the Great War of 1914 . . . was an outgrowth of the latter-day remobilization of Europe's *anciens régimes* [old regimes]. Though losing ground to the forces of industrial capitalism, the forces of the old order were still sufficiently wilful and powerful to resist and slow down the course of history, if necessary by recourse to violence. The Great War was an expression of the decline and fall of the old order fighting to prolong its life rather than of the explosive rise of industrial capitalism bent on imposing its primacy. Throughout Europe the strains of protracted warfare finally, as of 1917, shook and cracked the foundations of the embattled old order, which had been its incubator. (Arno J. Mayer, *The Persistence of the Old Regime*, 1981, p.4)

*Extract (c)*

The alliance system, for instance, did contain a major danger of escalation; large nations, as has often been pointed out, were likely to be drawn into the quarrels of their lesser allies. Yet, to this one can reply that in the first place, alliances were not that binding in 1914; the Italians certainly did not think so. And one might add that if the alliances had been firmer, if only, let us say, the Austrians had been totally certain that an attack on Serbia meant an attack on Russia, war might never have come that year.

Or there is the problem of imperialism. It is easy enough to show that it contributed to national antagonisms and to the atmosphere of violence in Europe and overseas. Yet when 1914 came some of the first colonial antagonists of former years found themselves fighting on the same side, as in the case of Britain and France, or of Britain and Russia. As for economic rivalries, these greatly added to the ill humor of Europe, but divergent national interests in the field of commerce did not make for armed conflict; in times of crisis, 1914 included, businessmen on all sides were among the strongest advocates of peace . . .

But what is worth saying here is that problem-free ages are a myth, and that all these long-range factors were part and parcel of the mood and the realities of early twentieth-century Europe. This was the world in which the nations and their leaders had to operate, and the truly significant question is how well they did so – in the non-mythical, non-ideal continent they jointly inhabited . . .

How many people, in 1914, were really aware of all the origins of the conflict, immediate and long range, that we abstract in leisure from the documents later? . . . What most of them did feel – and act on – was that here was another crisis, one that contained great risks, obviously, but that might reasonably be expected to end as non-cataclysmically as the diplomatic crises of the past decades had . . . And perhaps, all that one can say in the end is that World War I was a modern diplomatic crisis gone wrong, the one gamble, or rather series of gambles, that did not work out, the one deterrent that did not deter. It happens. (Joachim Remak, '1914 – The Third Balkan War: origins reconsidered', 1971, pp.87–8, 100)

*Extract (d)*

Remak's view of July 1914 as the one gamble that did not succeed overlooks the fact that those who gambled in Germany and Austria did not expect to succeed in avoiding general war.

Thus the search for the fundamental cause of World War I is futile, while the argument that the war simply happened is unhelpful. Is there no exit from the cul-de-sac? a different question may help: not why World War I?

but why not? War was still the *ultima ratio regime* [the ultimate policy of governments]. World War I was a normal development in international relations; events had been building toward it for a long time. There is no need to explain it as a deviation from the norm. In this sense, the question why not? answers the question Why?

More important, it points to what is unexpected about the war and needs explanation; its long postponement. Why not until 1914? . . . Preventive wars, even risky preventive wars, are not extreme anomalies in politics, the sign of the bankruptcy of policy. They are a normal, even common, tool of statecraft, right down to our own day. British history, for example, is full of them; the British Empire was founded and sustained in great part by a series of preventive and pre-emptive wars and conquests. (Paul W. Schroeder, 'World War I as Galloping Gertie: A Reply to Joachim Remak', 1972, p.104) ■

**Specimen answers and discussion**

*Extract (a)*

The extract begins with the general point that there were manifold reasons for hostility between the nations, which suggests that any special significance that might be attached to the immediate occasion (or contingency – the assassination of Franz Ferdinand) is being dismissed. Then comes the more specific point of the alliance system – with respect to identifying the author's general approach, a diplomatic or political issue. But beyond that (and still more important, it would appear) is the rise of Germany (a 'structural' factor, one could argue) giving rise to French and British reactions, and then the German claim about 'encirclement' (both geopolitical factors). The outcome of this, 'the conviction of approaching disaster' could be described as a 'psychological' factor. Then Aron identifies, if not the 'immediate occasion' of the war, certainly the location of the 'explosion' – and he gives nationalism as the basic cause of this. Here, then, several different approaches to causation (political, structural, geopolitical, psychological) are brought together with the basic fact of nationalism.

*Extract (b)*

One fundamental cause is given here, the determination of the old order to fight to retain its position. This is a 'structural' argument, in fact a Marxist one, though Mayer is highly unconventional in rejecting 'the explosive rise of industrial capitalism' as the prime cause of the war, the view of traditional Marxists.

*Extract (c)*

This extract starts by dismissing the significance of, first, the alliance system (diplomatic and political, or perhaps geopolitical factors), second, imperialism and, finally, economic rivalries (both structural factors, and much stressed by Marxists). The fundamental point being argued is that in any age there is a potential threat of war (no 'problem-free ages') and that there is nothing special about 1914, the real issue being how the statesmen dealt with their 'everyday' problems of crisis management. They had done well for a decade, but then in 1914 their gambles happened to go wrong. This is a very naked statement of the contingency approach.

*Extract (d)*

Schroeder is specially dismissive of this 'contingency' explanation. He is saying that the statesmen were not even trying to avoid war. His is the 'shared attitudes' approach (which might be regarded, I suggested, as an ideological explanation), arguing that war came because statesmen were quite deliberately prepared to go to war on behalf of national interests. The only issue that needs explaining, he claims, is why war didn't come sooner.

It's early days yet, and you may well not have got very close to my answers. But I hope you now have some insight into the sorts of approaches historians can follow. I don't think the final answers being offered are necessarily as different as these short extracts may suggest (save for extract (b), which really is distinctive: there are long extracts from Mayer in the Course Reader which we shall use for intensive study later in Book I). In most cases it's a matter of emphasis rather than fundamentals: in my view, for instance, the basic assumptions of Remak and Schroeder are really quite similar: both draw attention to the actions of politicians, Remak seeing them as 'gamblers', Schroeder regarding them as being governed by purely selfish and callous calculations. □

## 2.4   Aim 4

This aim links with Aim 1 and together the two aims encapsulate what is absolutely essential to this course, historical change and the place of total wars in it. Aim 1 deliberately concentrated on social change, since that is where the major emphasis of the course lies. What I did mention then was that, even if one's main concern is with social change, it would be impossible to ignore the ramifications of geopolitical change. So Aim 4, in its concluding phrase, indicates that we shall be giving careful attention to the redrawing of national frontiers as a result of war, with the disappearance of the Austro-Hungarian Empire (Would this have come about eventually anyway, as a result, in particular, of the forces of nationalism? We must in this course consider all the options with an open mind); the emergence after World War II of Russia as a superpower (Would this have come about anyway? Was it simply a restoration of the position Russia had enjoyed before 1914?). We shall need to give careful consideration to the processes of peacemaking, the actual details of peace settlements (while wars leave certain geopolitical consequences which simply cannot be gainsaid, statesmen of strong character can influence at least the detail of the drawing of boundaries, and the allocation of territories and resources).

Nowhere in this course is it argued that war is the most important, still less the only, cause of major social change: the task is to evaluate the significance of war as against all other possible factors. For convenience these factors can be discussed under three headings: 'structural', 'ideological' and 'political'. Unit 5 goes into more detail, bringing out that these headings are not totally distinct from each other, but explaining the ways in which they may be used. In the major historical debate over whether or not the two total wars were of importance in bringing about social change, the most frequently found line of divide is over the weight to be attached to structural forces. Very many historians, both non-Marxist and Marxist, would contend (and it does indeed seem very difficult to disagree) that the great changes of the twentieth century – higher living standards for the mass of the people, expanded welfare provision, greater (if still circumscribed) freedom and new roles for women, a key position in society for the mass media, and so on – are essentially the product of long-term economic, industrial and technological processes. Some would also stress the importance of such ideological movements as liberalism, democracy and socialism. A relatively small number of historians (though they have been increasing in number in Britain in recent years) put a major emphasis on the importance of individual politicians, political parties, pressure groups or political activists. For example, the setting up of the National Health Service in Britain in 1948 might be attributed basically to the Labour Party's election victory in 1945, or perhaps even to the personality of the then Minister of Health Aneurin Bevan; or, the winning of votes for women in Britain in 1918 might be attributed to the work of activists on behalf of women's suffrage before World War I. The sorts of question this course sets out to explore are: did certain developments come about in the *way they did* and *when* they did because of the experiences of war? Did the necessities of war, as it were, force the hands of politicians at certain times? What exactly is the relationship, with regard to particular issues, between long-term trends (structural and ideological), the pressures of war, and the calculations (or perhaps even eccentricities) of politicians?

I am now going to give you some examples from secondary sources of what historians have written in connection with these issues, in order to see if you can identify the various approaches being taken.

**Exercise**   Comment on each of the following extracts from secondary sources, saying what position they take with regard to the significance of World War I in bringing about historical change relative to the other causes of change (in particular, structural, ideological and political).

> *Extract (e)* (refers to Germany)
> Wars are usually considered as periods of accelerated change, if not as birth-places for new social formations. Certainly World War I had a far-reaching impact on the social fabric in Germany, even though in the end the forces of continuity proved stronger than those of change. However, in socio-economic terms the exigencies of the war appear not to have initiated anything altogether new; rather they resulted in a considerable acceleration of those processes of change in economy and society which had already been under way for a considerable time, but which so far had been moderated by a variety of political and economic factors which under the conditions of the war lost their momentum. (Wolfgang J. Mommsen, 'The social consequences of World War I: the case of Germany', 1988, p.27)

> *Extract (f)* (refers to Britain)
> It seems reasonable to argue that British suffragists might fairly have expected to have gained the vote by 1918 if a Liberal government had been returned in the expected general election. It is even possible that there might have been a limited measure of women's suffrage under a Conservative government. All this must significantly modify those interpretations which stress the advent of war as the decisive factor in the eventual winning of the women's vote. It might even be that the war postponed such a victory. What can be confidently asserted is the importance of women's suffragists' own efforts, especially the efforts of the democratic suffragists, in securing the strong position enjoyed by their cause at the outbreak of war. Women's war work may have been important in converting some former opponents, or providing others with a face-saving excuse to alter their positions. But even before this, the political alliances the democratic suffragists had formed in support of their demand had ensured that women would have to be included in any future reform bill. (Sandra Stanley Holton, *Feminism and Democracy*, 1986, p.130)

*Extract (g)* (refers to France)

Contrary to popular belief, the war had not led to exciting new opportunities for women in the world of work. Both the war and the demobilisation involved distortions and disruptions which sometimes obscured the broader pattern, which is best discerned by comparing pre-war figures with the census data of 1921 and 1926. Overall, *fewer* women were employed in industry than in 1906. More than a quarter of a million women disappeared from the textile industry between 1906 and 1921 – a drop of 18 per cent. The clothing industry *shed nearly* 55 000 women workers in the same period, and another 162 000 between 1921 and 1926. Domestic service lost 86 000 women between 1911 and 1921, with another 12 000 following suit over the next five years. At the same time as women were abandoning jobs in the traditional 'feminine' sectors, they began to be taken on in newer industries such as chemicals, electricity, and light engineering, and in the tertiary sector . . . The tertiary sector employed 344 000 women in 1906; 855 000 in 1921; and 1 034 000 in 1936 (by which latter stage it accounted for nearly a quarter of the entire female work force outside of agriculture). The war, therefore did not increase the number of women at work but formed part of a process whereby women were redistributed in the labour force.

The drift away from older occupations into new jobs was clearly visible before 1914. The trend towards the tertiary sector was especially marked and had its roots in pre-war technological change and in the expansion of the bureaucracy. The numbers of state schoolteachers tripled between 1866 and 1936; likewise employees at the Ministry of Posts. Fewer than 410 000 civil servants in 1866 had become more than 600 000 in 1906 and over 900 000 in 1936. Women gained particularly from the invention of the typewriter, the telegraph and the telephone and from the advent of the big department stores and the multiplication of banks. In 1866 they formed only 25 per cent of employees in the commercial sector: by 1911 this had risen to 40 per cent. The feminisation of office work was well under way when World War I broke out. Likewise, at the higher level of the professions, the decisive battles to open up careers for women in, say, medicine and law, had been fought and won before 1914. Julie Chauvin became the first woman to graduate from the Law Faculty of the Sorbonne in 1890, while some 578 female students were registered to read medicine in 1914. Professional women were still a long way from achieving equality with men (in 1929 there were still only a hundred women enrolled at the Paris Bar) but World War I was not a turning point in their struggle. (James F. McMillan, 'World War I and women in France', 1988, pp.9–10)

*Extract (h)* (refers to Britain)

. . . how are we to explain the important legislative and political changes which occurred in its [World War I's] immediate aftermath? Here it seems the answer is that Arthur Marwick was quite right when he drew attention to the importance of the 'military participation ratio'. That is, the larger the proportion of the population which is involved in a national war effort the more likely it is to be accompanied by major social reforms, or, to re-state it in other terms, the further down the social hierarchy this involvement goes the more egalitarian the social consequences are likely to be. Whatever the objections to Stanislav Andreski's original formulation of this idea (that he stressed the military aspects too much, or that his use of the word 'ratio' implies an unwarranted degree of precision) the emphasis on the social and political consequences of mass participation is a valid one. Put in the crudest terms, this is because of the demand for labour: even if that labour was of much the same type and quality as before war broke out the removal of large numbers of young workers into the armed forces and the increased demand for labour in war industries would strengthen the position of the less advantaged and less powerful groups in the nation . . .

Understanding the impact of World War I on British society in terms of an improved bargaining position for the working classes offers an explanation of why the war had significant social consequences even though it affected the quality of social relationships so little. (Alastair Reid, 'World War I and the working class in Britain', 1988, pp.21–3)

*Extract (i)* (refers to Europe in general)
There are turning-points in history whose significance is at once economic, social and political. That the Great War undoubtedly qualified as such was already recognized by contemporary observers, a view which the intervening years have done nothing to change. On the other hand certain structural elements in the international economy were at most only temporarily, and never more than superficially, affected by the Great War . . .

Least of all did the Great War crystallize the inner social tensions in the industrial capitalist nations. On the contrary, being an imperialist war, it brought the proletariat's class consciousness more nearly into accord with their objective class condition than had previously been the case. Where the ruling classes sought to reduce increasing pressure by means of concessions, there might appear to be a trend towards the harmonization of class relations. This forms the point of departure for the theories evolved by Andrzejewski [Andreski] and others to the effect that a positive correlation exists between the mobilization of large masses for war on the one hand and, on the other, social change tending towards the harmonization and stabilization of social relations, as exemplified in the 'welfare state'.

The foregoing is explicitly based on the British experience which in no way admits of generalization. On the Continent, the critical year 1917 had already demonstrated that, under increasing pressure from the 'left', a bourgeois society might react, not with concessions, but equally well and even for preference, with a move to the 'right'. Looked at in this way, the rise of fascism after the First World War is not surprising, although it may at first be distasteful to see 'liberalism' and 'fascism' ranged alongside each other as alternative forms of bourgeois rule. In conclusion, attention should once more be drawn to the fact that the exacerbation of social tensions gave rise to the socialist October revolution in Russia and hence to the polarization of the world economy into a socialist and capitalist camp. The Russian Revolution and its consequences, whose epoch-making significance largely escaped contemporary observers outside Russia and the revolutionary labour movement, is now perhaps generally acknowledged to be the most important consequence of the First World War. (Gerd Hardach, *The First World War, 1914–1918*, 1987, pp.283, 293–4)

*Extract (j)* (refers to Britain, France and the USA)
The women's success story in the First World War is well known: in Britain women over the age of thirty, who were themselves householders, or whose husbands were householders, were given the vote in 1918, and the various states of the Union granted votes for women throughout that, and the two following years; in each country including France, there was a spate of legislation affecting the social position of women. It is important to be clear first of all how much these successes depended on the participation in the war effort, not of women, but of men. It was this,

obviously, which provided the first employment opportunities for women; and, in the end, it was because a drastic reform in the franchise for men was being contemplated in Britain, so that those men who had never had the vote, or who had actually lost their residence qualification by going out to fight, might be rewarded for their part in the war effort, that the question of women's suffrage also became a pressing issue. Although voting rights for women in France were widely predicted as early as 1915, French women did not get the vote at the end of the war. Partly this was because traditional attitudes about the roles of the sexes were stronger in rural, Catholic France. But two other factors, particularly significant with regard to this question of *participation*, are also relevant: *all* French *men* already had the vote, so in this case there could be no question of men's efforts helping to open the door for women; and, secondly, the French labour movement, being weaker than the British, was less able to push anyway. A third point brings the United States into the comparisons and contrasts: it was in the United States first, then in Britain, that the Women's Rights movements were strongest before the war. Due weight must be given to the unguided forces of change: yet in history, as elsewhere, those are helped who help themselves.

But once all differences are stated, the process by which women's participation in the war effort brought considerable social, economic and political gains can be traced in a very straightforward manner. The first issues to stress this time are again strengthened market position and the desire of governments to offer rewards for services rendered. But two further changes are also critical: the increased sense of their own capacity and increased self-confidence on the part of women themselves; and, on the other side, the total destruction of all the old arguments about women's proper place in the community, which both men and women had previously raised against any moves towards political and social equality for women (in France both changes appear only in a much weaker form). In the political story what is most striking in Britain and the United States is the way in which one after another all the old leading opponents of the idea of votes for women recant, and declare that since women have played such a vital part in the national effort, of course they must be allowed to share in the politics of their country. However, political rights are only one side of the story. Women also gained a measure of economic independence. And, whatever the intentions of law-makers, they had gained a new self reliance and new social freedoms. (Arthur Marwick, *War and Social Change in the Twentieth Century*, 1974, pp.76–7) ∎

**Specimen answers and discussion**

*Extract (e)*

Quite clearly and explicitly this passage gives overriding priority to long-term forces ('forces of continuity') and it is clear that what is intended here is what I have called 'structural forces' ('processes of change in economy and society which had already been under way for a considerable time').

At the same time Mommsen does fully recognize that World War I 'had a far-reaching impact': however, he sees this impact in terms of 'acceleration' of existing structural forces, rather than in terms of the initiation of anything new.

I will just add that I find something unsatisfactory about the notion of 'acceleration', a metaphor drawn from the physical sciences. Beware of such metaphors: they may possibly *describe* what is happening, they certainly do not explain it. If it is true that wars accelerate existing trends (and this has to be demonstrated), then we need to know *why* this happens. Some suggestions will be made during this course.

*Extract (f)*

This extract stresses the importance of political forces, in particular the efforts of the women's suffragists *before* the war. It is also suggested that in ordinary circumstances a Liberal government, or perhaps even a Conservative one, would in any case been have inclined to concede a measure of women's suffrage. So, perhaps ideological forces are being stressed as well: a general 'democratic' trend towards extending the franchise, particularly in the direction of women. In this passage, the war is not seen as at all important: indeed, it is even suggested that the war may have postponed votes for women.

*Extract (g)*

This passage denies that the war had any effect on employment opportunities for women: what is stressed is the long-term structural process 'whereby women were redistributed in the labour force'.

*Extract (h)*

The author of this extract recognizes that the war itself did have important consequences though he puts limits on these by saying that 'the quality of social relationships' was altered little (by this he means that people did not suddenly become equal with each other, women with men, workers with employers – which is certainly true enough). He draws attention to an explanation that is related entirely to the war itself, not to structural, ideological or political factors. As he mentions, it is an idea which I have used myself and which I originally got from the sociologist, Andreski. The idea is an important one and you will find it cropping up quite often in this course (though you do not, of course, have to agree with it). Basically it is that when under-privileged groups (for example, the workers, or women) participate in the war effort, this very participation tends to improve their social position: in essence, as Reid puts it, they have 'an improved bargaining position'. I will just add here that I personally, as Reid suggests, dislike the full phrase 'military participation ratio': I prefer to talk simply of 'participation', arguing that such participation, generally in domestic industry, rather than in the military effort in the narrow sense, does produce social gains for the participants.

*Extract (i)*

While recognizing that the war had economic, social and political significance, essentially the author of this passage stresses that structural elements were basically unchanged. As I hope you noted, the approach is Marxist, referring to such other long-term structural factors as the inner 'social tensions' held to be inherent in capitalist society, and the advance of 'the proletariat's class consciousness' nearer to congruence with 'their objective class condition'. (Incidentally, it could be noted, with regard to our earlier discussion of Aim 3, that the causation of the war is seen as structural; it is an 'imperialist war'.) Hardach then goes on to refer to the military participation theory we have already encountered (he gives the original Polish version of Andreski's name), but comments that if it is relevant at all, it applies only to Britain. In traditional Marxist vein he argues that under pressure from the Left a bourgeois society is quite likely to react with a move to the Right. Thus, he suggests, rather than progressive social change, a main consequence of World War I was fascism. His general line is the Marxist one of the increased social tensions provoked by war resulting in polarization: on the one side, fascism, and on the other, Soviet Russia, in his view 'the most important consequence of the First World War'.

*Extract ( j )*

This clearly gives weight to the significance of the war, contrasting with the views of Holton and McMillan, and chiming in with those of Reid. (Note, incidentally, that there are references to the United States as well as to France and Britain – when you are doing your work for this course you will have to ignore such references.) Like Reid the passage makes the argument about 'strengthened market position', but also adds that governments themselves desired to reward those who had participated in the national effort, and that through their war work women gained an 'increased sense of their own capacity and increased self-confidence'. It also maintains that women's war work brought about 'the total destruction of all the old arguments about women's proper place in the community'. This is much too extreme a comment, as I would now confess, though I would maintain that a significant number of opponents of votes for women did change their views because of women's war work. The passage reveals the important factual point that women in France, unlike those in Britain, did not actually get the vote at the end of the war. Obviously this is very important in any general assessment of whether wars tend to bring change or not. The passage brings in other long-term and short-term forces. It suggests that traditional attitudes (ideological forces, we might call these) played a part in preventing French women from getting the vote. It is also pointed out (a matter of contingency, or immediate political circumstances) that the participation at the battle front of men who had not previously had the vote meant that there had to be franchise reform anyway – this, it is being said, provided the *occasion* for votes for women as well. Finally, like Holton, the author does point to the importance of the women's movement itself ('those are helped who help themselves'). □

That has been just a brief scattering of different ways in which historians have addressed the question of the relationship between war and social change. If you read each author in full, paying attention to all of their qualifications and detailed arguments, I think you would find that their overall accounts do not clash as much as they may seem to do at first sight. Good historians who have done their work well will generally agree on the main developments; their differences are essentially matters of emphases within the complex of forces which bring about social change.

## 2.5   Aim 5

Our first four aims have been concerned with content, what problems you will be discussing, what countries you will be studying, and so on. Now we turn to the other important dimension of the course (and the one which would not be treated in a straightforward textbook, such as the book by Roberts), that of methods and skills.

### Aim 5(a)

Absolutely fundamental to all serious historical study is the question of the critical analysis and interpretation of primary sources; it is a simple truism that without primary sources there could be no history. A historian producing a learned article or a major new historical work goes to find the sources in archives, libraries, and so on, as indeed does a PhD student. You as an undergraduate will, of course, simply be studying the extracts from various primary sources which we have selected for you. None the less the principles are essentially the same, and I now want to discuss with you the sort of documents exercise we will be setting you in order to test whether you have mastered these principles. What we will give you will be a substantial extract from one of the documents, usually at least a paragraph in length, and we will set this question:

> Comment on the following extract, saying what the document is, setting it in its historical context, commenting on specific points in the text, and summing up the extract's historical significance for the study of war, peace and social change, 1900–1955.

In the *Introduction to History* in the Open University's Arts Foundation Course I set elementary documents exercises very much in the abstract but, of course, no real working historian tries to interpret a document without already knowing a good deal about the historical context. It is from your general reading in the course that you will be able to say clearly what the document is, and more importantly, give the historical context (that is, what circumstances brought it into being, how it fits in with other aspects of the topic it is related to, and so on). In order to interpret a document fully, historians need to be sure that they have fully understood any particular phrases, and also that they understand the full significance of particularly important ones. We ask you, again calling upon your general reading, also to go through these activities. The most important task is summarizing the historical significance of the document – that, of course, always depends on what subject is being studied: here we ask you, naturally enough, to pin down the significance with regard to some aspect of the topics studied in our course. Given the background knowledge which is needed, it would be unfair to expect you at this stage to do a full commentary on a document. None the less, it would be fruitful if now you did begin to think about the sort of response you might make.

**Exercise**   I want you to jot down any thoughts you have about writing a commentary on the extract that follows. My specimen answer will actually take the form of a fully rounded exam answer to this kind of question. Here I will give you a little bit of the contextual information which normally you would have to acquire from your wider reading in the course. As a break from the other exercises you have been doing, this one concerns World War II.

In March 1944, more than two months before D-Day, France was under German occupation, against which clandestine warfare was being waged by various resistance groups. After the Liberation many Resistance leaders participated in the first Liberation government, which was responsible for a number of economic and social reforms, including votes for women, nationalization of the leading banks and insurance companies, the coal mines, many major companies (for example Citroën), and also welfare legislation. Resistance groups included right and centre elements as well as socialist and communist ones; however, many historians have argued that there is a connection between the struggles of the Resistance against the rule of the Nazis and those who collaborated with them, and social reform after the war.

Now attempt a commentary on the extract that follows (observing the rubric for an exam question set out above):

> United as to the goal to be attained, united as to the means required to achieve this goal, the speedy liberation of the country, the representatives of the movements, groups, parties and political tendencies joined together

in the CNR, proclaim their decision to remain united after the liberation . . .

In order to promote essential reforms:

(a)   Economic plan:

– the establishment of a true economic and social democracy, involving the expulsion of the great feudal combines of economics and finance from the direction of the economy;

– a rational organization of the economy assuring the subordination of private interest to the general interest and freed from the direction of employment instituted in the image of the fascist states;

– an increase in national production in accordance with the plan to be issued by the state after consultation with everyone involved in such production . . . (Programme of the National Council of Resistance [CNR], 15 March 1944) ∎

**Specimen answer**  This is an extract from the Programme of the National Resistance Council which, as the extract itself tells us, joined together various different resistance groups, which from other sources we know to have been right-wing and centrist, as well as socialist and communist. As is clear from the way the programme is phrased it is intended as a statement of policies to be followed by government immediately 'the speedy liberation of the country' has been achieved. At the time when the programme was issued, France was still under German occupation, though there was optimism at this stage of the war that German power was on the wane. In fact the Allied landings were just over two months away, so one could say that this very precise statement of reforms was being issued in good time for the expulsion of the Germans and creation of an independent French government. In sum, the document is a programme for peace, promulgated in the later stages of the war.

The necessities of war and the overriding need to defeat the common enemy, and perhaps also the sense of having shared, whatever one's own political opinions, in common dangers for a common cause, are the mainspring behind the declarations of unity, which open the document and are clearly intended as its keynote. The intention was almost certainly genuine, though it has to be noted that once the enormous danger was over, and once the country was faced with the problems of reconstruction, political unity began to break up. The next part of the extract sets out 'essential reforms': obviously the feeling was that the France which had collapsed in 1940 had been much in need of reform. The first reform in part reflects the belief held by Centre and Left that France in the 1930s had been run by a 'wall of money', 'the 200 families'. The use of the word 'feudal' is noteworthy – *France must modernize*. It is a moot point whether the Liberation government achieved 'true economic and social democracy', but certainly the great combines *were* nationalized as stated here. The second reform develops the idea of combining private enterprise and the idealistic notion of 'rational organiz-ation' (always argued for by socialists and communists); it also reflects the current experience of control of labour in the fascist 'image'. The idea of central planning is developed in the third proposed reform. The emphasis on *increased* production may represent the view of more traditional and conservative elements, but also, again, the widespread feeling that pre-war France had been commercially stag-nant (recent research has shown that this was not entirely true). Consultation with the workers indicates, in a remarkable way, the consensus achieved in the Resistance: hard-line left-wingers traditionally envisaged a total take-over by the workers. Post-war France was marked very much by rigorous economic planning and, to a much lesser degree, worker participation.

Thus much of what is proposed here was put into practice. The significance of the document is that it shows the experience of war (specifically of Resistance) engendering ideas of consensus on behalf of progressive economic and social planning. Because of the prestige of the Resistance, and because of the feeling that defeated France had been a flop, many of these proposals were put into practice after the Liberation.

**Discussion**   I don't expect you to have achieved anything like that, many of the points I make simply being unknown to you at this stage. But I hope you see now how all information (some of it from the document itself) is incorporated in a systematic analysis. Note the precise use of *brief* quotations from the document itself. □

### Aim 5(b)

You may well, at the first reading, have found this aim the most daunting and off-putting of all. Let me just set out again what this aim is. It is to develop your skills in:

> understanding some of the different approaches to historical study, in particular Marxist/sociological/linguistic approaches on the one side, and 'liberal humanist' ones on the other, and also quantitative and qualitative approaches.

Is this really necessary? you may cry. Yes, in the age in which we now work and study it is, I believe, profoundly necessary. History, as a central discipline in the humanities, has for long been subject to influences from both the social sciences and from the other arts disciplines.

Often these influences can be used entirely beneficially in an *ad hoc* 'pick and mix' fashion, but sometimes they involve all kinds of hidden assumptions which are not always clearly understood by the historians who use them, nor by the readers who read their books. In subjects such as literature, art history and media studies, and in reviews in newspapers and journals, it is difficult to avoid some contact with approaches carrying such labels as 'critical theory', 'cultural theory', 'linguistic theory', 'linguistic materialism', 'discourse theory'. On the whole the books which historians continue to publish, aimed at making substantial contributions to historical knowledge, eschew all of these approaches. I do myself. So again, you may feel bound to expostulate, why on earth does this stuff have to be brought in here? Well, a further reason is that if, as historians and history students, we are going to continue to ignore developments which certainly have had profound influences in other disciplines, we must be able to state clearly why we are doing this, why we feel such approaches are entirely irrelevant to historical study. But the most important reason (which I have already partially hinted at) is that in your reading for this course you are almost bound to encounter some of these approaches; it is therefore important that you should be able to recognize and evaluate them – that is, be able to decide what use, if any, to make of them.

I have crammed together an enormous mouthful – Marxist/sociological/linguistic approaches – 'on the one side', posed against 'liberal humanist' (the quotation marks are highly deliberate) on the other. Until now in this introductory unit I have simply referred to the distinction between 'Marxist' and 'non-Marxist' approaches. But the phrase 'non-Marxist' is scarcely exact in counterbalancing the phrase 'Marxist/sociological/linguistic'. One might speak of 'empirical' or 'pragmatic', or simply 'traditional' approaches. However, the first of these terms might well be objected to by the proponents of the first set of approaches, while the second two are not altogether fair to the approach they are purporting to describe (there is nothing 'traditional', for instance, about the most up-to-date computer-based statistical methods). It would be the contention of most of the proponents of the second type of approach that their methods are systematic, subject to constant improvement, and as objective as it is possible to be (of most, but not all: there are 'liberal humanists' who argue, regrettably in my view, that historical writing inevitably depends on the political and personal views of the writer – the very case that those within the Marxist/sociological/linguistic tradition make against traditional history). The term 'liberal humanist' is one of several (another is 'positivist') used by upholders of the Marxist/sociological/linguistic approaches, and is intended as a criticism, 'liberal humanism' being reckoned a value particularly prized by the bourgeoisie. For that reason the label has to be kept in quotation marks, but it does otherwise seem quite a convenient one for what is in effect that approach pursued by the overwhelming majority of historians in the Western countries and therefore, of course, by the majority of historians you will be studying in this course.

The major qualification to that statement is that you will certainly encounter historians who are Marxist, but who have not ventured into cultural or linguistic theory. Some Marxist historians, in their approach to historical study, seem to come as near to the 'liberal humanists' as they do to the cultural theorists: the classic example is the English historian E. P. Thompson, whose famous article 'The poverty of theory' was in many respects a thoroughgoing defence of empirical historical methods; however, Thompson is undoubtedly a Marxist in his understanding of historical processes and his approach to class and class consciousness. There are not, then, two totally opposed schools, but there are, I believe, two distinct approaches or tendencies. A more pompous way of describing them would be *nomothetic* (seeking general laws and theories) and *idiographic* (studying unique, individual cases). I'm not entirely happy with the terms myself, but if you prefer to look at it that way what I mean is the distinction between approaches that stress general laws and theories (Marxist/sociological/linguistic) and approaches that do not ('liberal humanist'). Let me now try to unpack this cumbersome phrase 'Marxist/sociological/linguistic'.

*Marx, history and Marxism*
That Karl Marx (1818–83, son of a Rhineland lawyer, but domiciled for many years in London) made a major and enduring contribution to historical thinking is beyond dispute. What distinguishes those who fall on one side or the other of the broad division of approaches which I have postulated is the key question of whether one regards Marx as one among several who have contributed to the development of historical studies (for example, Leopold von Ranke, 1795–1886, the Prussian protagonist of documents-based history; Marc Bloch, 1886–1944, and Lucien Febvre, 1878–1956, founders of the French *Annales* school which sought to incorporate the discoveries of the social, and indeed the natural sciences within history; and Fernand Braudel, 1902–85, the leading post-1945 figure in this school) or whether one takes the fundamental conception of society and of historical processes, first clearly enunciated by Marx, though, of course, contributed to and modified by many others, as having a primary validity over and above all other contributions to historical study. It is not easy, particularly in a very limited space,

to give an accurate and fair account of, so to speak, the absolute irreducible essence of this conception (that is to say, the fundamental convictions which distinguish those on this side of the 'divide' from those on the other). Marxism has been subject to many revisions and qualifications over the years, the very developments of cultural theory and linguistic materialism having been in large measure responses of those who, deeply committed to the essence of the Marxist conception, have perceived the inadequacies of many of Marx's formulations. I am therefore going, in very schematic fashion, to give a list of key points in the Marxist conception of society and historical processes, starting with ones which remain at the heart of the various theories derived ultimately from Marxism, and proceeding to ones which many in that tradition would now repudiate.

1    All societies divide into 'classes' (whether these 'classes' are 'real' in the sense that one could actually count up the number of families and individuals in each one, or simply 'abstractions' in the historical process, is a subtlety which need not detain us here), and these classes are necessarily, if only they could always perceive their own true interests, in constant conflict with each other. There is always one dominant class, and one or more subordinate classes or groups. What is presented, then, to use the jargon of today, is a 'conflict model' of society.

2    Through one or more devices it is possible for the dominant class to conceal the realities of conflict and thus maintain its dominant position (these 'devices' need not necessarily be seen as part of a deliberate strategy by the dominant class but may be conceived of as arising 'spontaneously' from the nature of dominance relationships). The main device is 'ideology' (in the specialized 'Marxist' or 'critical' definition of this term which differs from the way I have used 'ideological' simply to mean 'relating to ideas, beliefs and attitudes'). 'Ideology', in the Marxist definition, is a collection of ideas and beliefs purporting to be true of society as a whole, but in fact really only representing the interests of the dominant class (for example, ideas that the rich have an inherent right to rule over the poor, that everyone should believe what the churches tell them, that everyone has their proper station in life or, slightly more subtly, that if people will only work hard they too can become rich). 'Ideology', in the Marxist critique, is essentially untrue, but serves to conceal, or prevent, the conflict which is otherwise inherent in society. Some cultural theorists speak of 'dominant ideology' for what I have just described, and recognize the 'alternative ideologies' of those classes or groups who are resisting the dominant class. The Italian Marxist Antonio Gramsci (1891–1937), writing from prison in the 1930s (he was a highly courageous opponent of Mussolini), developed the notion of 'hegemony' (again in a special-ized sense of the term). The thought is similar. The bourgeoisie (or a fraction of the bourgeoisie) win the active consent of the masses for the hegemony over society of ideas and beliefs which support the continuing rule of the bourgeoisie: the disciples of Gramsci study novels, films, radio programmes, paintings, and indeed all the sources historians might use (which is why all of this *is* relevant to us) from the point of view of the manner in which they allegedly contribute to this hegemonic domination.

3    At the heart of historical processes lies the principle of the 'dialectic'. The notion of the dialectic can be traced back to Plato, and lay at the heart of the philosophy of history of the German philosopher Georg Hegel (1770–1831), who was one of the most profound influences on Marx. The principle of the dialectic is, in effect, a rephrasing in philosophical language of the notion that at

the heart of society lies conflict. It postulates that within every society there is 'thesis' and 'anti-thesis', dominant idea and countervailing idea (this was Hegel's formulation), or the existing mode of production and emerging mode of production (this was Marx's fundamental formulation), or dominant ideology and alternative ideology (a notion favoured by many contemporary cultural theorists).

4   History as 'process' unfolds in a series of stages. At the time when he was writing (mainly in the middle, and in the third quarter of the nineteenth century) Marx believed that the stage of capitalist society in which the dominant class was that of the capitalists or bourgeoisie had been reached, the capitalists having overthrown feudal society dominated by the aristocratic class. Marx believed that the next stage in history would come when the working class, or *proletariat*, overthrew the bourgeoisie. For those who continue to adhere to this line of thought, we are still today stuck in the capitalist stage (it having been prolonged by ideology, hegemony, and so on, and by the diffusion – real or illusory – on what is generally held to be the American model, of prosperity to the masses). Views seem to differ as to whether the working class can still be seen as having the special destiny in the historical process of bringing about a better society in the future.

5   Marx insisted that a class was defined by its relationship to the dominant mode of production (that is, land in feudal society, capital in capitalist society). In modern society the two great classes are the capitalists, who own the dominant mode of production, and the working class, who own nothing but their labour. The reality of society, particularly in the twentieth century, appears rather more complex. Some Marxists speak of a person's 'objective class position', that is to say the 'real' position, despite appearances to the contrary. Thus, to take a possible example (which not necessarily all Marxists today would agree with), a bank clerk may appear to be middle class, but in so far as, if this is true, he actually owns nothing more than his labour power, then he is 'objectively' working class. Marx made a distinction between a class 'in itself' and a class 'for itself'. A class 'in itself' is an aggregate of persons 'objectively' in the same relationship to the dominant mode of production, but not yet conscious of their true class interests. A class becomes 'for itself' when it begins to organize in pursuit of these class interests. Individuals are 'class conscious' if they act consciously in the 'objective' interests of their class (that is if, say, they form trade unions, or vote for a socialist political party).

6   Marx believed that the unfolding of the process of history came about through revolutions. The English bourgeoisie overthrew the aristocracy in the civil war of the seventeenth century; the French bourgeoisie did the same thing in the revolution of 1789. The triumph of the working class will come through revolution against the bourgeoisie. Revolutions of this last sort have been noticeable by their absence (leaving aside the question of whether 1642 and 1789 really represent what Marxists say they do). Much Marxist writing concentrating on the period we are studying is devoted to explaining why revolutions which ought to have taken place didn't actually do so. Whether cultural, linguistic and discourse theorists believe in the inevitability, or even the likelihood, of revolution is not usually very clear: their emphasis on ideology should entail a belief that if only ideology did not exist then, recognizing their true interests, the working class would carry through a revolution, but one often gets the impression that ideology has come to assume an independent existence, the assumptions which gave rise to the concept in the first place being conveniently forgotten.

### Weber, sociology and history

Many historians (including members of this course team) stress the differences in the theories of Karl Marx and Max Weber (1864–1920), the pioneer German sociologist, and Bernard Waites does exactly that in the Appendix to this unit, which you should read immediately on completing this section. But if one is dealing in terms of two broad traditions of historical study, it seems to me perfectly reasonable to put Marx and Weber together in the *nomothetic* tradition. Weber did make a number of independent contributions to historical and social study which can be, and indeed have been, separated out from the central conception of historical and social processes entailing a 'conflict model' of society and absorbed into general historical thinking (for example, the concept of bureaucracy, or that of 'disenchantment', actually better translated as 'de-magification', as a feature distinguishing pre-modern societies from modern ones). While Marx saw class as an overriding category, Weber made a distinction between, in particular, class, which was purely economic, and status, which expressed a person's position on a separate social hierarchy. It is doubtful whether this distinction has ever proved particularly useful to historians. But the important consideration here, in my view, is that one can speak of a Marxist/Weberian tradition in which, of course, much Marxism is jettisoned, but in which Marxist concepts of 'the bourgeoisie', 'revolution', 'class conflict' and 'ideology' are retained, and which, in turn, has led in our own time into all kinds of sophisticated studies of the mass media and of cultural practices and phenomena. All of this is of particular relevance to us in connection with the way in which social change is defined. Such writers as, for example, Mayer and Maier (both in the Course Reader) tend to treat social change in the broad manner I identified on page 11.

### Critical theory, cultural theory and linguistics

The detail of the historical evolution of these different approaches need not detain us here. Critical theory, in its origins, is associated with the Frankfurt school of Marxists, established in the 1920s, and seeking to adapt what they termed 'vulgar Marxism' to the complexities of real life. Independently, there came in the 1930s the contributions of Gramsci already mentioned, which were taken up by the 'New Left' Marxists of the 1950s. There were other inputs out of which cultural and literary theory developed, still holding to at least the first three of the essentials of Marxism listed above.

For the intellectual world as a whole, however, the most striking developments after 1945 were in the realm of linguistics (and, to a rather lesser degree, in anthropology). In linguistics, to put matters in the crudest way, there was a search for the 'structures', not readily apparent, but which, it was believed, underlay the immense variety of different languages. At the same time, 'structural anthropology', fired by analogous objectives, came to the attention of scholars in other fields. Many disciplines, including that of history in the hands of many members of the *Annales* school, were pervaded by the notions of 'structuralism'. In that structuralism postulated the existence of structures not readily evident from traditional empirical processes, it was found a congenial bedfellow by many Marxists, since it is a fundamental tenet of Marxism that much in bourgeois society is not what it seems, and that it takes Marxism to perceive the true realities of dominance and conflict. Within its own jurisdiction the advances in linguistics were significant. But the school of structural linguistics (with Roland Barthes a leading figure) began to make enormous claims for language and communication in general. At its most extreme, it was argued that nothing had a real existence outside language. Now, at first encounter this may seem so absurd as not even to be worth considering. But in fact the idea is an extremely rich, and ultimately highly seductive one (it is because of the very appeal, and indeed genuinely stimulating quality, of many of these new developments that we, as students of history who do not wish to bury our heads in the sand of tradition, must pay some heed to them). Think for a moment about what you know, or think you know, about World War II. Almost all of it comes from what you have read, or what you have seen in films, or on television (all forms of communication count as language in contemporary linguistic theory), does it not? If you are as old as I am, no doubt you will have personal recollections from having lived through the war. But hold on a minute: in the entire perspective of the war, your direct personal recollections will be limited to particular locations. What you think you know about the wider war in Africa, or in Europe, for example, or even about bomb attacks on other cities in this country, will actually have come from words spoken to you, or heard on the radio, or from film images seen. After a little thought, one can see how truly omnipresent and potent all forms of communication (language) are.

From this, contemporary linguistic theorists have argued that language is the most potent instrument of power. They posit that embodied in any piece of communication is one or more 'discourse'. (This simple word, which originally meant 'the unit longer than a sentence', is now being used in a highly technical way; the leading protagonist of 'discourse theory' was the French philosopher Michel Foucault, 1926–86.) Different social groups, different interests, different attitudes to life and society, each, so the theory maintains, has its own discourse. In all forms of communication we see different discourses competing with each other, and from time to time, certain discourses taking over, dominating others.

**Exercise**   Does this concept remind you of anything said earlier in this section? ∎

**Specimen answer and discussion**   It is really a kind of abstracted version, is it not, of the first point I made about the essentials of Marxism? We have the same basic idea of conflict, except this time, instead of one class directly establishing dominance, it is a question of certain discourses establishing dominance.

Many discourse theorists prefer to deny that there is any knowable real world out there beyond language itself, which language represents or reflects: all we can ever encounter are the representations or interpretations – never 'society' or 'the world' itself. Therefore they also deny that history, in the sense of a 'systematic body of knowledge about past societies', exists. 'History' is simply a collection of narratives, embodying different discourses, absolutely as subjective as those narratives called novels. (The defence against this assertion, of course, is contained in the sort of disciplined historical methodology exemplified in this course. You should be aware of both the attack and the defence.) What is always implied is a world, or society, of conflict, with dominance being exercised by one group over others. For most discourse theorists, 'ideology', in the Marxist or 'critical' sense, is an indispensable concept.

All of this comes together in the label 'linguistic materialism'. Marxism itself is sometimes referred to as 'the materialist conception of history' since 'vulgar Marxism' postulated material circumstances (the modes and conditions of production) as the prime movers in history. Critical theory, cultural theory, and literary theory all have rather obvious and open affiliations to the essential tenets of Marxism; it is important to be clear that, for all their seeming sophistication and alleged dependence upon the entirely independent discipline of linguistics, linguistic theory, discourse theory, and linguistic materialism all take as, usually unspoken, assumptions the essential and enduring features of Marxism.

Now that does not mean that they are necessarily wrong, and certainly not that they should be ignored. It can be argued that through all this refinement, and through this openness to structuralism and to linguistics, a whole new, more rigorous, more accurate, science of the humanities has evolved. □

### 'Liberal humanist' approaches

What are, or should be, the responses of 'liberal humanists'? Again, for the sake of simplicity and clarity, let me set these out once more in the form of a schematic list.

1     It is sometimes said that to the 'conflict model' which has been at the heart of all of the approaches I have just discussed, the 'liberal humanist' opposes a 'consensual model' of society. Disabuse yourselves of this trivialization immediately: it springs from the simple-minded notion that all academic issues can be resolved into either/or stances (the dialectic again rearing its pretty head) and from confusing the range of ideas held by 'liberal humanists' with the somewhat restricted ideas of the conservative functional sociologists, whose concern is indeed with the way in which societies maintain their cohesion and stability. Most 'liberal humanists' would recognize that there is a great deal of conflict, dissidence, and indeed violence within all societies. What they do not do is neatly package these elements along class lines, so that every protest, every incident of violence, is taken as proving the existence of *class* conflict; conflict, 'liberal humanists' would usually insist, can arise from a multiplicity of causes, and can indeed co-exist at times with relative harmony among social classes, and *sometimes* with genuine consensus over national values and objectives.

2     I have already mentioned E. P. Thompson. There can be no question that E. P. Thompson, and many other Marxist historians who share his general outlook and convictions, see their major professional objectives as historians as adding to historical knowledge, finding out what happened, and why. In doing this, they share with most 'liberal humanists' a belief in the profound value, even necessity, of historical study: to put it in a nutshell, without an understanding of the past we can have no hope of understanding the present, or of beginning to grapple with its problems. Through the labours of historians of a generally 'liberal humanist' disposition an enormous amount has in fact been discovered about the past, so much so that it is possible, for example, for the distinguished French historian Marc Ferro to write a book on *The Use and Abuse of History*, contrasting what we actually do know about the past of such countries as South Africa, or Iran, with the biased and mythical way in which the history of these countries is actually taught in their schools. But for the dedicated work of 'liberal humanist' historians, employing the basic principles of historical study which, in part, it is the task of this course to impart, we wouldn't even know the amount of history which we do know. Now if this is contrasted with, say, the labours of discourse theorists and the practitioners of linguistic materialism, whose openly expressed aim is to reveal the discourses, and the conflict between discourses, allegedly embodied in all pieces of communication, we immediately come up against the obvious conclusion that, however interesting and stimulating these labours are in themselves, they are not going to add much of significance to our knowledge of the past. In fact, a leading exponent of the theories of ideology and discourse, J. B.

Thompson, has admitted (*Studies in the Theory of Ideology*) that results so far from the application of discourse theory have been 'very disappointing'. It is possible to recognize the sincerity of those who wish to develop the more rigorous, and more accurate science which I referred to a few paragraphs ago, while doubting whether such a pursuit actually adds anything of genuine importance to historical knowledge, as distinct from simply repeating *a priori* prejudices about dominance, conflict, and so on. Apply discourse theory to the causes of World War I, or to the relationship of war and social change and, frankly, you won't get very far.

3    The retort from the other side, of course, always is that the 'liberal humanists' are captives of their own class position, that they have themselves swallowed the dominant ideology, and that they fail to accept the realities of dominance and conflict because to do so would disrupt the comfortable complacency of their own class position. The 'liberal humanists'' first response would be that the best way of resisting subjective influences (even if these can never be totally eradicated) is to practise the rigorous and systematic methodology of history as an academic discipline. Their second response would be to ask how their critics can be so sure that they have managed to resist the subjective influences bearing on them, how they can be so sure that they have found the key to true reality. This point has indeed been acknowledged by one of the leading figures in contemporary Marxism, Jürgen Habermas: but acknowledging the existence of the problem is not the same as solving it. Sometimes it would seem that the answer is no more than that it is better to have some kind of systematic, overarching theory than to have no such theory at all. Part of the reasoning here is that without theory, a discipline is not fully academically respectable. To that there are at least two responses. The first is that history, even without such theory, is a difficult and intellectually challenging enough discipline to earn fully its position of academic respectability. The second is that when the theory is actually wrong (and 'liberal humanists' would point out that Marxism, even in all its complex and subtle refinements, hasn't been terribly successful in its explanations, let alone its predictions), it is far better to do without it.

4    Some of the areas in which 'liberal humanists' find Marxism, linguistic materialism, and so on, to be wanting are those of class, ideology (and hegemony) and revolutions. There are differences of opinion, of course, as to the salience of class in (to stick to the subject matter of this course) twentieth-century Europe. Those who believe that a most important characteristic of twentieth-century European societies is the way in which they divide up into different classes, do not thereby accept all the assumptions that Marxism loads on to the concept of class. Classes are distinguished from each other, most certainly, by the amount of wealth, the access to positions of power, and the lifestyles enjoyed by those who belong to them; but classes can share common ideas and attitudes, and need not necessarily be in conflict with each other. Individuals can be *aware* of belonging to a particular class (that is, they can be 'class-aware') without being 'class-conscious' in the Marxist sense of the term. Marxists would concede that all of this might *appear* to be so, but that is only because of the workings of ideology. However, 'liberal humanists' tend to believe in the scientific principle of 'economy of explanation'. Why go for a convoluted explanation, for which there never seems to be any hard evidence, when you can go for the simple and straightforward one which does seem to fit the evidence? The working class is said by cultural theorists to enjoy certain films, allegedly instruments of the dominant

ideology, simply because of the workings of cultural hegemony: why might it not be that they enjoy such films because in fact these films embody values which appeal directly to them? It is probably not worth labouring the point about revolutions: on the whole, they haven't taken place on anything like the scale predicted, so why, the 'liberal humanist' asks, produce complicated explanations in order to preserve the theory that revolutions ought to take place, instead of just dropping the theory?

*Conclusion*
In highly condensed fashion, I have tried to summarize the two broad sets of approaches. As a 'liberal humanist' myself, my own sympathies, I fear, have been all too plain. But there is in fact no 'party line' in this course and, indeed, several units in this course are written by colleagues who take up a very different stance from mine. If you can make effective and well-reasoned use of any of the approaches touched on here, please do so. Now read the Appendix to this unit by Bernard Waites.

**Exercise**      There is one approach to the study of history (and other subjects) which has very much come to the fore during the 1970s and 80s which I have not even mentioned. What is that? Can it be fitted into one or other of the two broad sets already outlined? ■

**Specimen answer and discussion**      Feminism. It is broadly true that feminism in academic work has tended to be associated with Marxism, cultural theory and linguistic approaches, above all in that it has tended to operate within a framework postulating the existence of both capitalism and the new concept of patriarchy (male dominance), and has found the concept of ideology useful in explaining the apparently wide acceptance of masculinist ideas. Some feminists have also been attracted to the notion of certain discourses being clearly reflective of male authority and dominance. But it is certainly not inevitable that feminist approaches should be incompatible with 'liberal humanism'. The crux is probably whether feminism is regarded as in itself a new kind of history replacing all other kinds, or whether it is seen as offering new perspectives and new insights, while essentially using the tried and tested methods of 'liberal humanist' history. □

**Exercise**      1      You have already encountered two examples of Marxist analysis. What were they, and how helpful did you find them?

2      What approach does this passage exemplify (give examples of phrases peculiar to this approach)? What is the passage actually saying?

> In the summer of 1923, a British film titled *Maisie's Marriage* (co-written by Marie Stopes and directed by Walter Summers) became the target of a number of attempts at censorship. Institutional practices of film censorship are always obliged to assume as their object individual films – texts, representations with specific boundaries: and yet in any actual instance of censorship there is usually more than this at stake. Certainly in the case of *Maisie's Marriage*, the content of the film does not alone provide sufficient explanation either for the excessive efforts at censorship directed at it, nor for the consequences of those efforts, many of which were unforeseeable and some indeed the very opposite of what had been intended.
>      *Maisie's Marriage* became an object of censorship by virtue of its implication, at a particular historical moment, within a certain set of

discourses and power relations, which penetrate the text and yet also exceed it. These include discourses and practices of film censorship, but also involved in the constitution of *Maisie's Marriage* as censorable are the operations on the one hand of the film industry and on the other of contemporary debates around sexuality and birth control. Each of these – censorship, the film industry, discourses on sexuality – constructs the film differently, and each is caught up in a struggle over the conditions under which the film was to enter the public domain. Each, too, inscribes different interests and power relations, some of them operating in contradiction. (Annette Kuhn, 'The "Married Love" Affair', 1986) ■

**Specimen answers and discussion**

1    The two examples are Mayer on the causes of World War I, and Hardach on the consequences of World War I. Both have the merits of clarity. If you accept the Marxist assumptions and language, they provide forceful points which are relatively easy to grasp. You will only be able to make a proper evaluation of their helpfulness when you have had the opportunity to work out your own position more fully.

2    The approach exemplified is discourse theory. The key phrase is 'implication . . . within a certain set of discourses and power relations'. Also the notion that each discourse 'constructs the film differently' and is 'caught up in a struggle'. Seeing everything as a matter of competing discourses, discourse theorists are for ever talking about 'what is at stake'.

The passage is actually saying that in itself *Maisie's Marriage* is so unshocking as not to have warranted the objections of the censor, that there were other factors outside the film. (These factors, as we soon learn, were the controversies already aroused by Marie Stopes and her book *Married Love*.)

As a matter of fact the entire article provides much valuable historical information and is used quite fully in Book II, *World War I and its Consequences*, where there is a discussion of the effects of World War I on manners and morals as represented in the film *Maisie's Marriage*, extracts from which are on video cassette 1. But my own feeling is that the introduction of discourse theory adds nothing, save for a lot of unnecessary confusion. □

*Summary of discussion of 'nomothetic' and 'idiographic' approaches*
Lest there be any confusion, let me summarize the objectives of this discussion.

1    As a well-educated person you should be aware of the approaches widely prevalent in other arts disciplines and, in particular, understand how the word 'discourse' is used.

2    You should understand why many practising historians (both Marxist and 'liberal humanist') find discourse theory irrelevant to their work.

3    You should be aware of the different assumptions embodied in the different approaches taken by historians you will be encountering in this course, for example, Hardach, Mayer and Tim Mason (Marxist), Maier and Kocka (Marxist/ Weberian), Roberts (a not unusual mix of strong 'liberal humanism' with, in his rather bare treatment of class, a vestigial Marxist/Weberian approach).

4    In discussing (later in this course) War and the Arts, War and Popular Culture, and so on, you should be aware that many writers in these areas adopt a cultural theory (for example, Paddy Scannell on radio in World War II) or a discourse theory approach (for example, Annette Kuhn).

Let me add, in case there is confusion on this point too, that it is a well-known characteristic of the various theorists I have mentioned that they argue vociferously with each other. Of course, if you are concerned with the detail of the different theories, there are differences between, say, Foucault and Gramsci, as between Marx and Weber. All I am suggesting is that they belong together in one tradition which, whatever overlaps and borrowings there have undoubtedly been, is different from the 'liberal humanist' (or, if you prefer, 'idiographic') one.

*Quantitative and qualitative approaches*

You cannot but be aware of the all-pervasive influence in our own day of the almighty computer. Actually, the desire to give a firm statistical underpinning to historical analysis was expressed considerably in advance of the arrival of efficient and relatively compact 'adding machines' (a development, incidentally, that can be attributed to the military needs of World War II). It was in the inter-war years that the French historian Lefebvre (not to be confused with Lucien Febvre, though in fact the *Annales* school took up the cause enthusiastically) enunciated the principle *il faut compter* (one must count). In Britain a similar cry was taken up by Sir John Clapham and other economic historians. Many of the calculations historians need to do require no more than simple addition, subtraction, multiplication and division, an ability to calculate percentages, and an understanding of the distinction between an average and a mean (the mean height of soldiers in the British army in World War I will give you a height representative of the *majority* of soldiers: an average could be affected, say, by there being a number of exceptionally tall soldiers, and might be quite misleading as to the height of the majority). A minority of historians began making extensive use of computers in the 1960s: the great expansion came in the 1980s thanks to gigantic advances in micro-electronic technology.

Only two requirements are laid upon you:

1    Where precise numbers are available, and relevant, use them. Rather than: 'large numbers of Frenchmen were killed at Verdun', give a precise statistic (and, if relevant, relate this statistic to the total army, or total French population, so that, expressed perhaps as a percentage, it has a clear, sharp meaning). Rather than: 'an overwhelming majority voted Labour in 1945', check the figures and you'll find this widely believed statement isn't actually true – the percentage of those who actually cast a vote who voted Labour was 47.8 per cent (39.8 per cent voted Conservative, 20 per cent did not bother to vote at all). We will be providing you with a few statistical tables (of wage rates, welfare acts passed, trade union membership, and so on). If, for instance, one is going to argue that wars stimulate trade union membership, or reduce living standards, it is best to present hard figures.

2    Be sensitive to what statistics cannot do, as well as to what they can do. Be aware of their limitations, and (for certain types) of the inherent margins of error (for instance, public opinion polls in 1988 still admitted to a margin of error of 3 per cent either way). Any extended discussion of structural factors (employment trends, population, economic growth, and so on) will require the citation of statistics (remember the extract from James McMillan on French women's employment). But when it comes to ideological, psychological and so many of the other forces and issues which are of such importance in historical study, statistical approaches are often quite irrelevant. In short, much history continues to be 'qualitative' rather than 'quantitative' in character, and rightly so. Count where you can, but other kinds of judgement will be required from you as well.

**Aim 5(c)**

Periodization simply refers to the way in which historians divide history up into, say, 'The Renaissance', 'The Eighteenth Century', 'The Revolutionary and Napoleonic period', 'The Victorian period'. This is partly done for convenience, but also, more importantly, because historians (or rather, some historians) feel that they can distinguish particular characteristics which do give a 'period' genuine unity. But there are no absolute rules governing the selection and definition of historical periods. In our course, we wanted, at the outer limits, to include both the origins of World War I and the consequences of World War II. We also, as with the listing of the countries to be included, wanted to set firm limits on what ground we were asking you to cover. Clearly some of the deeper origins of World War I go back well before 1900 and, quite certainly, the consequences of World War II do not suddenly cease to have any effect in 1955. The period covered by your set textbook, J. M. Roberts, *Europe 1880–1945*, is different at both ends. If you glance inside the book at the list of other volumes in the same series, you'll see that the choice of dates by Roberts was at least partly dictated by a need to fit into the series.

**Exercise**   However, on the back cover there is an attempt to pin down the sixty-five years, 1880–1945, as constituting a coherent period. What is the essence of this period as stated on the back cover? ■

**Specimen answer**   It is the period of 'the apogee of European power'. It is the period when Europe's political and economic domination of the globe came to a climax – and then crumbled. □

If you look at Roberts's table of contents you will see that he does not break his main period up explicitly into a number of smaller periods. His book steadily moves forward, mixing narrative with analysis and description: chapters 1–8 cover the period before 1914, only chapter 9 deals with World War I, then chapters 10–15 deal with the inter-war years, with just chapter 16 dealing with World War II. We, on the other hand, have divided our course up into five separate books, the first four suggesting a kind of periodization: Europe before 1914; World War I; between two world wars; World War II and its aftermath.

Such sub-periodization might well be considered excessive; but it does parallel the very strong sense that many ordinary people in the twentieth century have had of each of the total wars being a historical watershed. It is one of the functions of a serious academic course to examine carefully such popular ideas, which may well turn out to have little real foundation. Certainly the lines of critical change will vary in different parts of Europe. For example, the break between pre-1914 and post-1918 probably was quite sharp in those parts of East and Central Europe where there was both a change in regime and a new contact with Western ideas and behaviour. Pause just for a moment to reflect on your own (for the moment preliminary) notions on periodization. Is it your impression that the inter-war years were a very different era from the years before 1914, or that the years after 1945 were very different from those before 1939? By the end of the course your thoughts should have been refined and clarified.

'Semantics' means 'concerned with the meaning of words'. In raising the question of 'historical semantics' I am drawing attention to the problem we have in historical study with certain words which have quite complex meanings, or which are often used in rather different ways by individual writers.

**Exercise**      I have already given one central explanation for the way in which certain words are used differently by individual historians. What is that? Mention two key words which are used in different ways. ∎

**Specimen answer**      The different usage arises from whether the historians are in the Marxist or liberal-humanist tradition. Two key words are 'class' and 'ideology'. □

When you encounter these words in your reading try to be clear whether they are being used in a Marxist or non-Marxist sense. Be clear in your own usage as well: if you find yourself reaching for phrases like 'class conscious' and 'class conflict' think carefully whether you intend the full range of Marxist assumptions which go with such terms. If you're not clear about this go back and read what was said in the previous section.

Among the most abused terms in historical writing are 'bourgeois' and 'middle class'. On any common-sense reckoning, the 'middle class' ought to be the class in the middle, that is to say between the upper class above, and the working class below. On this reckoning it is, in the twentieth century, a highly miscellaneous class, ranging from elementary school teachers, small shopkeepers, and clerical workers at the bottom to successful business and professional people at the top. If you're secure in your Marxist theory, fine. But always be clear *how* you are using such terms, and *who* exactly you mean by them.

For effectively the whole of the period we are studying, every European country except Britain had a substantial peasant class. Disabuse yourself immediately of any connotations the word 'peasant' may have in colloquial English. In fact the nearest translation for the French *le paysan* or the German *der Bauer*, always rendered as 'peasant', is really much more like 'farmer', but that term can suggest very different sets of attitudes and values. At the core of the peasantry were the small landowners cultivating their own soil. Many were no more than landless agricultural labourers, some were quite prosperous; there were many degrees of dependency in between. Generalization of this sort is always risky, but on the whole they can be characterized by a deep attachment to the land, and an intense pride in their roots and in their shared lifestyle. It is salutary, and perhaps even helpful (for potential tourists!) to note that any dish in Germany with the label *Bauer* in it will be large, rich and satisfying.

I have already said something about total war. A similar sounding word which also first came into use in 'the century of total war' is 'totalitarian' (*totalitario* in Italian). One of the earliest recorded uses in England occurred in November 1929 when *The Times* wrote of a 'reaction against parliamentarianism . . . in favour of a "totalitarian" or unitary state, whether Fascist or Communist'. Broadly the term connotes a state which attempts to control all aspects of political and social life in the interests of one political philosophy or ideology and which suppresses all dissent. Parliamentary government implies the existence of at least two competing political parties, totalitarianism indicates the existence of only one. Political scientists have developed more refined definitions which you will encounter later. Whether both the Fascist and National Socialist regimes (of Mussolini and Hitler, respectively) and the Soviet regime should be characterized as totalitarian is a matter of considerable argument. It is also said that 'totalitarian' is a rather outmoded word, belonging to the era of the Cold War. In this course we have used the phrase 'one-party dictatorship' to cover the three regimes just mentioned.

Now, finally, consider this collection of words: 'nation', 'country', 'society', 'state', 'government', 'power'. Several of these words have more than one meaning, and most overlap in meaning. The word 'power', as in the phrase 'the great powers', is usually used with reference to a country in its international aspect and implies a combination of strong and efficient government, a relatively stable society, and a strong economy. It is the word 'state' which has had most attention in recent years, in part because of Marxist arguments that the state is simply an expression of the power of the dominant class. Wilhelmine, Weimar and Federal West Germany were all divided into a number of separate 'states', as of course was the Federal United States of America. That is a particular usage of the word 'state'. In its more general sense the word connotes the entire apparatus of decision making, administration and, as necessary, coercion within an individual country. One can, in parliamentary democracies, make a distinction between *governments*, which may change with elections, and the *state* which only changes with a thorough-going revolution. You will most often meet the term in this course in such phrases as 'state control', or 'the extension of state powers'. Examples are state control of, say, the coal mines or new state regulation governing the sale of alcoholic liquor. It is not just one government doing these things; all relevant agencies of the state are involved in the control or regulation. Bernard Shaw's aphorism may be useful here: 'the government has no more right to call itself the state, than the smoke over London has the right to call itself the weather'. It is of course the allegation against totalitarianism that it merges together government, state and large sectors of society as well.

The essence of the semantic issue is that it is not possible to rule absolutely that words must be used only in a certain way. Words do shift in meaning; you have to be clear at any particular time which meaning is intended.

### Aim 5(d)

This sub-aim concerns assisting you to develop the skills of writing history essays of BA (Honours) standard. The writing of history is the critical activity of the historian. The historian who spends years in the archives, making the most exciting discoveries, but who never communicates them to his colleagues or the wider world, is not really contributing much to historical knowledge. An undergraduate essay, of course, is somewhat different from the research-based writings of a professional historian. Still, as I have already suggested, the basic principles are the same. Thus, one of the most important activities of the student of history is the writing of history essays. These should demonstrate the following skills:

●   the ability to *find* and *select* relevant material, basically from secondary sources, though also probably using the volumes of extracts from documents which we are supplying you with – thus, in a rather elementary way, an exercise in 'research';

●   the ability to address precise problems and to develop balanced and well-substantiated arguments, presented in a coherent and well-organized essay, written in English prose of an acceptable standard, and setting out quotations, references and bibliography in the approved manner.

The only truly effective way of learning how to write history essays is by actually writing them and then having them thoroughly criticized and commented upon by your tutor. For students on this course, that is what will happen. The writing of essays is not simply, or even mainly, a means of assessing you: it is a means of helping you to develop important historical skills. Here I can do no more than offer a few tips on the skills itemized above, and offer you one exercise designed to help with the crucial problem of planning and organizing your essays.

For each essay you have to do you will be given a reading list of up to about a dozen books. If you are aiming to do a really decent essay, it is important that you collect as wide a range of evidence and opinions as you can. It is not expected that you will read the whole, or even necessarily a large part of any one book. It is important to learn to get quickly from each book just what is relevant to your particular essay topic: to do this make use of the table of contents and the index. Develop the skill of skimming pages very quickly, stopping to give full and careful attention every time you come across something that relates directly to the essay you are writing. When you first start you may, quite understandably, have some difficulty in being sure what is going to be directly relevant to the essay and what is not. You may have to read around the subject a bit to begin with. But force yourself to start thinking as early as possible about the sorts of argument you will be wanting to make; it's actually easier and lazier to do a lot of general reading to no great purpose than to do the hard thinking that is necessary in order to begin to plan out what you will need for your essay and what you will not need. The more thought you put in (after doing any necessary preliminary reading), the less likely you are to take loads of notes which will in the end turn out to be useless.

It's not necessary to take notes on cards; practically any sort of paper will do, provided it is loose, so that you can shuffle your pages around in organizing the plan of your essay. The one golden rule is to take notes on one side of the paper only, so that there is no risk of overlooking something when you do come to plan out the essay. Be sure to note carefully where exactly you are taking each piece of information or quotation from (author, title, date of publication and page reference). Be completely clear whether you have taken a direct quotation from the book, or simply your own summary.

By the later stages of your 'research', ideas and arguments relative to the precise question you are dealing with should be beginning to form. But, in any case, go through all of your notes carefully. Then, on a separate blank sheet of paper, work out a plan, and a plan that is not simply a despairing set of arbitrary headings, but a plan that will enable you steadily to develop coherent arguments directly relevant to the topic set. If you number each section of the plan, you can then attach numbers to your notes, indicating where in the essay each idea or piece of information will fit in.

The first thing to do with an essay (or, for that matter an exam) question is to read it very carefully to make sure you understand exactly what is being asked. Often there may be more than one question requiring to be answered, there may be several issues needing to be resolved, there may be problems of definition. Often it may be best to start by breaking the question down into separate components (what social classes are involved, which countries, what topics or debates, and so on). You should attempt this before you start on your reading ('research'), though further reading may reveal complexities in the question not apparent at first sight. You should not attempt to draw up a plan until you have done a fair amount or preferably all of your reading.

**Exercise**   Imagine you are writing an essay on: 'In what ways, if any, did the experiences of World War I increase the political rights and raise the consciousness of women in Britain and France?'

1   There are actually four components to this question, which immediately give

rise to four separate questions which need to be answered. Identify (a) the four 'components', then (b) the four questions.

2    What matters of definition have to be settled and what other issues, implicit in the question as a whole, have to be discussed before you can attack the essay question satisfactorily as a whole? ■

**Specimen answers and discussion**

1(a)    The four components are: women in Britain, women in France, political rights, and consciousness.

1(b)    The questions are:

What effects, if any, did the war have on the political rights of British women?
What effects, if any, did the war have on the political rights of French women?
What effects, if any, did the war have on the consciousness of British women?
What effects, if any, did the war have on the consciousness of French women?

2    You need to explain 'political rights', that it means the right to vote, and the right to be elected to parliament or national assembly. You also need to explain 'consciousness', that it means self-confidence, women's belief in their own capacities, and a willingness to speak up for themselves.

Before it is possible to answer the question as a whole, you would need to establish whether political rights *were* increased (a) in Britain, (b) in France, and in the same way whether consciousness *was* raised. Where you did feel that you could detect changes you'd have to ask how far they came about for other reasons (structural, political, and so on) rather than the war. All this has to be sorted out if you are to give a clear, balanced answer to the question 'In what ways, if any . . .' In this essay it would be difficult to avoid the disagreements between different historians and you'll certainly have to explain clearly where you stand as between the different views. □

**Exercise**

Now let us draw up a plan. This is a slightly artificial exercise since there isn't time here for you to do all the necessary reading. However we can simulate some of the preliminary reading if you, first, re-read the relevant extracts set out in the exercise you did in connection with Aim 4 (particularly extracts (f) by Holton, (g) McMillan and (h) Marwick), and then read the following extracts.

*Extract (k)*
The calling of this Speaker's conference [on franchise reform] had been a response to political problems created by the war. Though it had been agreed to suspend party-political conflicts at the beginning of hostilities, this truce was constantly an uneasy one. At any time the government might have found itself called upon to seek a new mandate at a general election. Even after the formation of an all-party government in May 1915 the dissolution of parliament was repeatedly extended with the agreement of the opposition, but only for short periods at a time. In the event of a general election being called, the voting registers themselves promised to become the focus of considerable dispute and unrest. With the dislocations that attended the war, these registers no longer recorded the possible electorate at all adequately. In particular, men overseas on active service would effectively have been disenfranchised. Moreover, many presently hazarding life and limb at the front had never been enfranchised at all. These issues became particularly contentious with the extension of compulsory military service in May 1916. Arthur Henderson, the Parliamentary Labour Party leader, who had joined the all-party government formed the previous year, used the occasion to raise once

more the general issue of franchise reform, including women's suffrage, in cabinet. He was supported in this by another minister, Sir Robert Cecil, the leader of the Conservative women's suffragists in parliament. Meanwhile other Unionists like Sir Edward Carson were waging a vociferous campaign for the 'soldiers' vote'. Franchise reform, then, had again become a live issue in 1915, and a pressing one by early 1916. The government attempted a series of initiatives during this period to resolve the more immediate issue of the voting disqualification of men at the front, but all were rejected in the House of Commons. The setting up of an all-party Speaker's conference in the autumn of 1916 was intended to resolve this impasse by identifying a compromise programme of franchise reform that would be acceptable to all sides.

While these debates had focused only on how to protect the rights of existing voters, especially the troops at the front, women's suffragists had kept merely a watching brief. But once it became clear that some more fundamental reform might come under consideration, campaigning for votes for women began anew. This campaigning was, of course, to take place in a quite different context to that of the prewar period. The war had brought significant changes to women's lives. The most central of these was the extension of work opportunities, temporary though most of it proved to be. Women had been given a prominent place in the war effort, first in keeping going existing services and industries, but perhaps even more significantly in the massive manufacture of munitions required in twentieth-century warfare. Many, like the women's suffragists' former arch-enemy, Asquith, used such developments to explain their change of heart on votes for women. It remains a matter of dispute whether such longstanding male prejudice was significantly undermined or only put aside for practical reasons during this time. But certainly there were a number of well-publicised 'conversions' to women's suffrage among prominent public figures in the war years, while the rationale of many of the old antisuffragist arguments was effectively undermined by wartime requirements. Modern warfare needed the mass mobilisation of women as well as men for its execution. Ironically, the ideology of separate spheres lost much of its former legitimacy as women provided essential support in this way . . .

When the Speaker's conference report was published it advised full adult suffrage for men on a residential qualification. It then recommended a measure of women's suffrage based on age and property qualifications. Women over thirty or thirty-five should be qualified to vote if they or their husbands were on the local government register, then based on an occupier franchise. As we have seen, suffragists had themselves advised MPs on such a means of limiting the women's vote. Nonetheless it was to be a source of further discord among suffragists. It was pointed out that the young women munition workers, for example, would be excluded by such a franchise. Democratic suffragists in the North Riding and Manchester federations made use of their remaining EFF [Election Fighting Fund] resources to begin a campaign against such limitation of votes for women. The National Union leadership subsequently agreed to run similar campaigns wherever there were munition works. Yet all their parliamentary advisers stressed the danger of the full adultist [that is, all women over 21] demand. Consequently Mrs Fawcett advised working to lower the age limitation but to take care not to upset the whole basis of the compromise that had been achieved. On these grounds the National Union executive resolved to welcome the Speaker's report, while expressing the hope that the House would improve on the recommendations. (Sandra Stanley Holton, *Feminism and Democracy*, 1986, pp. 144–5, 148)

*Extract (l)*

By the end of the war working-class women, as we have seen, had gained far more than a limited right to vote. For years now, in their menfolk's absence, many had reared a family, and found in the responsibility a new freedom. Women were more alert, more worldly-wise. Yet the liberty won, some felt they would have to fight hard to retain once the warriors returned. But with surprise they discovered that husbands, home again, were far less the lords and masters of old, but more comrades to be lived with on something like level terms. Women customers in the shop commented on this change time and again. Life had broadened in scope; a certain parochialism had gone for ever. Food illiterates – husbands who had left home the bane of a wife's existence over what they could and could not eat – came back permanently cured; their taste, often enough, widened by army food. Customers remarked on it with amusement and relief – 'They'll try anything now!' Boys in their war-time waywardness warned by mothers of what would happen when the ruler of the house returned were often surprised to find father good-humoured, indifferent to minor misdeed, understanding, even; a human being, not a tin god. Grown children, remembering the authority that clothed him in pre-war years, felt indignant at the liberties now bestowed upon the 'spoiled' younger end. Disciplines steadily eased all round. The gulf that had stood so long between parent and child began to narrow at last.
(Robert Roberts, *The Classic Slum*, 1971, p.174)

*Extract (m)*

The continuing exclusion of married women from the world of work suggests that the revolution in social attitudes forecast for the post-war years was as chimerical as the revolution in job opportunities. The non-appearance of any new deal for women in respect of their lack of civil and political rights points to the same conclusion. Despite all the rhetoric and confident predictions of the war years and their immediate aftermath, married women continued to be denied the right to full legal capacity and all women were denied the right to vote. A few minor changes in the law, such as the temporary right to assume the paternal power (1915) or the right to guardianship of orphans (1917) did not alter the more important fact that, in the eyes of the law, married women were treated as persons unfit to act in their own right. The Civil Code still obliged wives to be obedient to their husbands, to reside where they chose to live and to recognise their full control over the children. Full legal capacity came only in 1938.

Nor did French women become fully-fledged citizens of the Republic. The auspicious vote in the Chamber in 1919 notwithstanding, French women did not receive the right to the suffrage until after World War II. The bill passed by the Chamber was thrown out by the Senate in 1922. Arguably, far from emancipating women, the war was 'actually a setback for the women's suffrage movement in France'. [This quotation is identified by McMillan in a footnote; it is from a book on women's suffrage in France by S. C. Hause and A. R. Kenney, 1984.] It cut short a campaign which had been building up promisingly on the eve of the war and dispersed its leading figures and organisations. In the words of Hause and Kenney:

> The war also buried women's rights under a host of other problems to which politicians accorded primacy, such as economic recovery or the diplomacy of French security. Such problems created a national mood in which the foremost desire seemed to be a return to the halcyon days of a

lost *belle époque* rather than to further the transformation of French
society.

(James F. McMillan, 'World War I and women in France', 1988, pp.11–12)

1    How does extract (l) differ from extracts (k) and (m)? What is it?

2    Now try to draw up at least two (and preferably more) plans for the essay, that
is to say list and number the main headings (and, if you like, sub-headings) for the
different sections and paragraphs of your essay, keeping in mind how each
section will link with the next one. If you do manage more than one, please say
which plan is the best and explain why. ■

**Specimen answers
and discussion**

1    *Extract (l)* is a primary source, an autobiography in fact (the give-away is the
personal reminiscence 'women customers in the shop': you wouldn't find that in
secondary sources like extracts (k) and (m).

2    *Example I* (This is the very barest of plans, arising out of our earlier discussion.)

1    POLITICAL RIGHTS IN BRITAIN
Definition, then account of what happened with evaluation of the significance
of war as against other factors.

2    POLITICAL RIGHTS IN FRANCE
Definition, then account of what happened with evaluation of the significance
of war as against other factors.

3    CONSCIOUSNESS IN BRITAIN
Definition, then account of what happened with evaluation of the significance
of war as against other factors.

4    CONSCIOUSNESS IN FRANCE
Definition, then account of what happened with evaluation of the significance
of war as against other factors.

5    CONCLUSION

*Example II* (This is a more elaborate version of Example I which gives definite space
to the other issues raised in our earlier discussion.)

1    INTRODUCTION
1(a)  Explanations of political rights and consciousness.
1(b)  What actually happened and the historians' debate. (Significant political
rights in Britain, effectively none – despite Assembly vote whose significance is
calculated differently by McMillan and Marwick – in France. Some debate
among historians over raising of consciousness – you'd have to offer some firm
conclusions for each of Britain and France.)

2    LONG-TERM FORCES TENDING TOWARDS POLITICAL RIGHTS AND HIGHER
CONSCIOUSNESS IN BOTH BRITAIN AND FRANCE
2(a)  Long-term change in women's role in the economy.
2(b)  Ideological forces and the women's movement.

3    POLITICAL RIGHTS IN BRITAIN
3(a)  Discussion of the significance of the women's suffrage movement.
3(b)  Discussion of actual course of events during war evaluating contribution
of war experience as against other factors. Firm conclusion stated. (Did war
actually obstruct women's rights?)

4  POLITICAL RIGHTS IN FRANCE

Depending on what line you'd established in 1(b) you'd say: (i) war had no effect; (ii) war obstructed women's rights; (iii) war had some effects (that is, removing prejudice in National Assembly). Again state a firm conclusion.

5  CONSCIOUSNESS IN BRITAIN AND FRANCE

5(a) Discuss arguments of, for example, Roberts, Holton and Marwick. Your conclusions here will depend on how highly you rate these, but remember also to refer as necessary to points made in 2, in order to offer a careful evaluation.
5(b) Similar discussions for France, bringing out any comparisons and contrasts if there are any.

6  CONCLUSION

Can be very brief since you will have been producing arguments and conclusions as you worked your way through.

*Example III* (This example puts heavy emphasis on the questions raised by the essay being matters of historical debate.)

1  THE HISTORICAL DEBATE
1(a)  The various views on the war and political rights in Britain and France.
1(b)  The various views on the war and consciousness in Britain and France.

2  DEVELOPMENTS IN BRITAIN, 1914–c.1921 (RIGHTS AND CONSCIOUSNESS)
Discussion of different factors: your conclusions.

3  DEVELOPMENTS IN FRANCE, 1914–c.1921
Discussion of different factors: your conclusions.

4  CONCLUSION

*Example IV* (This is a variation on Example III.)

1  THE ARGUMENT THAT WAR DID NOT HAVE ANY EFFECTS OR WAS NEGATIVE IN ITS EFFECTS
1(a)  Political rights in France.
1(b)  Political rights in Britain.
1(c)  Consciousness in Britain.
1(d)  Consciousness in France.

2  THE ARGUMENT THAT WAR DID HAVE POSITIVE EFFECTS
2(a)  Political rights in France.
2(b)  Political rights in Britain.
2(c)  Consciousness in Britain.
2(d)  Consciousness in France.

3  CONCLUSION

*Example V*

1  LONG-TERM FORCES POSSIBLY AFFECTING POLITICAL RIGHTS AND CONSCIOUSNESS (BRITAIN AND FRANCE)

2  POLITICAL FORCES POSSIBLY AFFECTING POLITICAL RIGHTS AND CONSCIOUSNESS (BRITAIN AND FRANCE)

3  EFFECTS OF WAR EXPERIENCES POSSIBLY AFFECTING POLITICAL RIGHTS AND CONSCIOUSNESS (BRITAIN AND FRANCE)

4  CONCLUSION

Many variations on these basic examples would be possible. Very probably you thought of other basic models. I hope anyway you came up with at least one reasonable attempt.

I don't know whether you did manage to distinguish between your best plan and other possible plans (quite a difficult task). Of my five plans I think Example II is best, in that it leaves room to explore all the different issues involved in the question sufficiently. It would be perfectly possible to write good essays based on the other plans (provided that the various ramifications were gone into along the way), but in so far as they are rather basic and simple, I'd see them as plans for exam answers rather than for the more expansive and detailed format of an essay. A good plan is vital, but naturally the standard of the essay will finally depend on how well you write it up. □

There is not, obviously, scope for highly original work in an undergraduate essay, where you're drawing most of your information and ideas from other people's books. Still, you will usually find that the books we have recommended do not directly address the question you have been asked or the topic you have been set. The task for you is to use what you have found out in order to deal with the precise matter of your essay. Alternatively, or additionally, the books may present rather different interpretations of matters vital to your essay. Now, one of the requirements I mentioned was for a 'balanced' argument. This means that you must consider all relevant information and arguments, though in the end you must make it clear what line or conclusion you are opting for. It is here that the requirement for being 'well-substantiated' becomes particularly important. Explain why you are opting for one line of argument rather than another; at all times cite reasons and evidence for your contentions.

The great test to apply to an essay is to check each individual sentence and to ask of it what contribution it is making to your overall argument. Satisfy yourself on this point with each single sentence. Do not leave in sentences that do not, as it were, 'pull their weight'. Beware of sentences beginning 'It is interesting to note that . . .': this nearly always means that you're not really very clear what the significance of the point you are about to make is in your general argument, but that you vaguely thought you ought to stuff it in anyway. Quite often it is not a matter of dropping a sentence that doesn't seem in itself to be contributing much; sometimes you need to add another sentence or phrase bringing out how what you are saying contributes to the development of your overall argument.

Don't overload your essays with direct quotations, certainly not long ones. Remember that the phrase 'scissors and paste' when applied to an essay, is a very severe criticism, implying that all you have done is pasted together bits and pieces from different books without really working out any coherent argument of your own. Quotations from primary sources are, of course, more to be welcomed than quotations from secondary sources. Be sparing with the latter and check carefully to see whether a direct quotation is really necessary. Often you can convey the information or opinion in your own words, simply making a reference to the secondary source. In all quotations the golden rule is to quote the minimum amount necessary to make your point. Be sure that the point is clear to your reader. Don't just leave a quotation to 'speak for itself'. Just as you have to justify each sentence that you write, you have to justify every quotation that you make.

References are not for show, but to serve the highly functional purpose of indicating to the reader where you have got a particular point or quotation from.

Bibliographies are there to give a general sense of the sources on which your work is based. The vital question that readers should always be asking, whether they are students reading a book by an academic, or an academic reading an essay by a student, is 'how does he or she know that?' The good historian always satisfies his or her readers on that point (and that, of course, is the primary function of references or footnotes).

Good writing comes easier to some people than to others. It's a matter on which people are often sensitive: there is no substitute for careful correction by a tutor. Unfortunately face-to-face discussion and correction is not generally possible within the Open University situation. My own procedure when I used to discuss badly written sentences face-to-face with individual students was to ask them to explain to me directly what it was they were trying to say. If you're not clear in your own mind what it is you're trying to say, then you will not write a clear sentence. So that is the first point to think about. Sometimes, however, students can express verbally perfectly clearly and simply what it is they are intending to say. The lesson here is always to aim at simplicity. Don't feel that because you are writing a university essay you have to aspire to some highfalutin or elaborate style. Be very careful with long words. Don't just use them because you like the sound of them or think they will sound good. Be absolutely sure that you really do know what their correct meaning is. There are lots of platitudes and clichés in historical writing which historians who ought to know better often use themselves. One can't, therefore, make too much of a fuss about this. I also recognize that for students who have difficulty in keeping their writing going at all, it is often helpful just to fall back on well-worn, if often rather meaningless, phrases (it is for this very reason that serious academics, fearful sometimes of 'drying-up' themselves, make use of such phrases). Still, avoiding clichés and tired phrases is an objective well worth aiming for even if, like most of the rest of us, you can't always live up to it. The secret of dealing with this one actually is not to worry too much about tired phrasing and clichés in the first draft, but to make a big effort to get them out, or replace them with something more elegant when you go through again polishing up your arguments and your style.

Here are examples of the kind of weary phrase I am thinking of: 'spectrum of opinion', 'climate of ideas', 'tool of analysis', 'frontiers of knowledge', 'spectre of defeat'. Worst, of all, in my view, is the routine use of 'dramatic', which presumably ought to mean something like 'with the force and emotion of a drama': but in standard, unthinking, historical writing, we seem never to have a rise in prices, nor a fall in stocks, never a religious revival nor a political recovery, but each must be 'dramatic'. Whenever you feel yourself reaching for this word, ask whether 'big', 'large', 'major' or 'significant' might not better serve your purpose.

The use of metaphor can greatly enhance historical writing. But the exaggerated use of metaphor can often indicate that a student is really trying to cover up for the fact that he doesn't have anything very clear or straightforward to say. The protracted metaphor is usually to be distrusted: the causes of a war may, if the writer has a liking for particularly hackneyed metaphors, be equated with a long fuse leading to a powder keg, or to runaway trains set on a collision course, but it will be unwise to force every single circumstance or development to fit the metaphor.

**Exercise**        Say what, if anything, you find wrong with this short extract from a secondary source:

> 'All the cards in the hand of France's post-liberation destiny', says Mr. R. Mathews in his *The Death Of The Fourth Republic*, 'had been dealt by April 1945; it only remained for time to play them'. Such a view, though exaggerated, does contain a modicum of truth. ∎

**Specimen answer**        First of all, it seems to me, the metaphor within the quotation from Mr R. Mathews
**and discussion**        is high-flown and not really terribly helpful. Presumably it means that everything which governed the history of France from April 1945 until the end of the Fourth Republic (in 1958) was already settled before April 1945. Once spelled out, the idea, which for a moment did sound quite striking, seems rather absurd. Surely there were other developments of importance after April 1945 – Marshall Aid, the onset of the Cold War, to mention but two of the best known. The comment by the principal author seems even more feeble. What precisely does it mean to say that a judgement is 'exaggerated', and precisely how much is a 'modicum'? What the main author is trying to convey is something like this:

> Many of the circumstances which determined the history of France from the Liberation to the end of the Fourth Republic were already settled by April 1945, though these circumstances alone are not sufficient to explain what happened in the years which followed.

Instead, the author reached for the lazy approach of sticking in an apparently striking (but actually rather silly) quotation from another author, tacking on to it a rather weary qualification. It is always best to work out for yourself exactly what you mean, then to say it in the simplest and most direct way. □

## 2.6   Aim 6

Historiography is the study of the way history is written, of the different kinds of interpretations and arguments that historians put forward.

**Exercise**        We have already encountered two major historiographical debates. Say what these were, and mention some of the main points made in the two debates. ∎

**Specimen answer**        One debate is over the origins of World War I. The main views emerging from the extracts we discussed were:

●   that a complex of long-term and short-term factors knitted closely together to bring about the war;

●   that the war was fought by the traditional upper class in order to safeguard its position;

●   that the war was essentially caused by the failed gambles, or by the cynical attitudes, of the politicians of the time.

The other debate is over the consequences of World War I. We looked at:

●   two extracts (one Marxist) stressing the effects of long-term structural forces over those of war itself;

●   two extracts arguing that the war had little or no effect on the changing position of women;

- two extracts which did suggest that the participation element in war was an important factor for social change.  □

**Exercise**   You might say, as many people have said, that if historians themselves can't come to some agreement, why should anyone else study history. Can you see any value in historiographical debate and controversy of this sort?  ■

**Specimen answer**   It can clarify issues. It can force historians on different sides of the argument to reconsider their own arguments. It can enforce a re-examination of the evidence or a search for new evidence. As long as historians don't simply dig themselves into entrenched positions, historiographical debate can actually further historical knowledge.  □

It is historical knowledge we are concerned with, not the relatively minor details of which historians said what. Still you do have to be aware (particularly when you come to write your own essays) that no history book is a neutral repository of knowledge. To a greater or lesser degree historians will be taking up a particular position: you will have to take this into account when seeking out information for your essays. You have already learned something of my own attitudes, and you can learn more from what Beckett says about me in his article on total war in the Course Reader. You may well therefore, in reading my units in this course, want to be on guard in case I tend to exaggerate the effects of war. It is pretty clear, on the other hand, from the period Roberts chooses to study, and from the layout of his chapters (only one chapter each to the two wars), that he does not see war as a particularly potent influence for change. You might want to bear that in mind too. To know your history, sometimes, it is important too to know your historian.

# 3   CONCLUSION: THREE THEMES

The aim of this unit has been to give you a clear idea of what is involved in this course. There are twenty-nine units still to go and obviously at this stage you cannot really have learned anything of any significance about the issues we shall be discussing. None the less, in order to return from the questions of how one writes and studies history to the questions of content, I am going to present here three themes which form another way of summarizing what in essence the course is about. At the end of the course there will be a whole unit on each of these themes, designed to sum up for you the material we will have covered by that time. The themes are:

1   The nature and causes of war
2   The processes of change
3   The impact of total war

The following questions relate to each of these themes.

## 3.1   The nature and causes of war

**Exercise**   1   Comment on this statement, saying whether you agree or disagree with it, and why. Try to suggest what approach to history the statement might represent.

'Societies are constantly at war; it is impossible to say when war ends and peace begins.'

2   Attempt to answer this question:

'Were the causes of World War II very different from the causes of World War I, or were there many causes common to both wars?' (We, of course, are concerned only with the European aspects of World War II.) ■

**Specimen answers and discussion**   1   World War I was preceded by the Balkan wars, and succeeded by civil and internal war. Within societies there was much conflict. A Marxist approach might well argue that war, in the form of class war, was in operation continuously. On the other hand, there were firmly dated declarations of war and peace settlements, which do separate out war from peace. More critically, the two world wars were characterized by enormous devastation and loss of life. This, one could reasonably argue, does quite distinctively single them out from periods of peace.

2   I don't know how much you felt able to say on this one. There is the argument about German expansionism and ambitions being the causes of both wars. There is the rather obvious point of wars being caused because of the willingness of powers to use war as an instrument of policy. It has been said that World War I came about because everybody prepared for war and then stumbled into it, whereas World War II was caused because the Western powers weren't sufficiently prepared to resist Hitler. Maybe you simply contented yourself with the idea that in the causation of all wars there are structural, geopolitical, ideological, and diplomatic and political factors. For detailed analysis you'll have to wait until Unit 20. □

## 3.2   The processes of change

**Exercise**   Just one question this time:

'In the period of the course, roughly from around 1900–1955, which has been greater, social change or geopolitical change?'

(I'll comment on this after I have asked a question on the third theme.) ■

## 3.3   The impact of total war

**Exercise**   Here also there is just one question:

'By 1955 women in practically all of the European countries had the vote, the old empires had gone, all governments claimed to recognize the interests of the masses, all countries had advanced welfare legislation. Would these circumstances have been roughly the same had there been no total wars?' ■

**Specimen answers and discussion**

*Theme 2*     If your concern is with change that affects the lives of ordinary people, you will probably come down on the side of social change. But even there, it is not as simple as all that. The extent to which the Poles, the Yugoslavs and the Czechoslovaks got nation states of their own at the end of World War I was of considerable importance to them. The division of Europe into East and West at the end of World War II is obviously also of profound general significance. The emphasis of this course, as you know by now, is on social change, and I think it is reasonable to argue that this is what is most important; but we must not ignore the geopolitical changes.

*Theme 3*     Well, as I hope you will have already gathered, the answers will depend on how one estimates long-term structural and ideological forces, as against what happened during war (the effects of participation, for instance). ☐

Let us wait and see how far the answers you give to questions of this sort differ, or remain broadly the same, after you have worked your way through this course.

## References

Aron, R. (1954) 'The century of total war' in Lee, D. E. (ed.) (1958) *The Outbreak of the First World War. Who was Responsible?*, Boston, Heath.

Ferro, M. (1984) *The Use and Abuse of History, or How the Past is Taught*, Routledge and Kegan Paul.

Hardach, G. (1987) *The First World War, 1914–1918*, Allen Lane (first published in 1973).

Hause, S. C. and Kenney, A. R. (1984) *Women's Suffrage and Social Politics in the French Third Republic*, Princeton University Press.

Holton, S. S. (1986) *Feminism and Democracy: Women's Suffrage and Reform Politics in Britain, 1900–1918*, Cambridge University Press.

Koch, H. W. (ed.) (1984) *The Origins of the First World War*, Macmillan.

Kuhn, A. (1986) 'The "Married Love" Affair', *Screen*, vol.27, no.2, March–April.

McMillan, J. F. (1988) 'World War I and women in France' in Marwick, A. (ed.) (1988).

Marwick, A. (1974) *War and Social Change in the Twentieth Century: a Comparative Study of Britain, France, Germany, Russia and the United States*, Macmillan.

Marwick, A. (ed.) (1988) *Total War and Social Change*, Macmillan.

Mayer, A. J. (1981) *The Persistence of the Old Regime*, Croom Helm.

Mommsen, W. J. (1988) 'The social consequences of World War I: the case of Germany' in Marwick, A. (ed.) (1988).

Reid, A. (1988) 'World War I and the working class in Britain' in Marwick, A. (ed.) (1988).

Remak, J. (1971) '1914 – The Third Balkan War: origins reconsidered' in Koch, H. W. (ed.) (1984).

Roberts, J. M. (1989) *Europe 1880–1945*, Longman (first published in 1967).

Roberts, R. (1971) *The Classic Slum: Salford Life in the First Quarter of the Century*, Manchester University Press.

Schroeder, P. W. (1972) 'World War I as Galloping Gertie: a reply to Joachim Remak' in Koch, H. W. (ed.) (1984).

Thompson, E. P. (1978) *The Poverty of Theory and other essays*, Merlin.

Thompson, J. B. (1984) *Studies in the Theory of Ideology*, Cambridge University Press.

# APPENDIX TO UNIT 1

*Bernard Waites*

The ideas of Karl Marx, 1818–83, defy easy summary for intrinsic and extrinsic reasons. To touch briefly on the latter; most of Marx's writings were unpublished in his lifetime and certain important works were not widely available in the West until after 1945. The task of systematizing Marxism was undertaken not by Marx, but by his life-long Collaborator Friedrich Engels, 1820–95, and Karl Kautsky, 1854–1938, the leading theoretician of the German Social Democratic Party before 1914 and a very influential figure in the Second International (1889–1914). It was they who coined the terms 'historical materialism' and 'dialectical materialism' to refer to Marxism as an intellectual system. Many would argue that they foisted on to Marxism ideas which are incompatible with Marx's own writings. For a long time, Engels' *Anti-Duehring*, a polemical work published in 1875, was the source to which Marxists looked for guidance on materialism as a philosophical doctrine and for instruction in dialectics. Engels regarded dialectics as both a natural process of evolution and as a form of thought that reflected and sought to comprehend change in nature and society. The dialectical laws of nature were, in his view, the negation of the negation (that is, the logical idea that the sum of two negatives is a positive) and the transformation of quantity into quality. He wanted to make social-historical science co-extensive with natural science and his 'scientism' greatly influenced Marxism in the Soviet Union.

Marx explicitly claimed in *Capital* to have uncovered 'the natural laws of capitalist production' which, he thought, worked themselves out 'with iron necessity', so he can certainly be charged with 'scientism'. But there is no evidence that Marx believed in the dialectics of nature and in his philosophical writings of the 1840s he rejected a strictly materialist interpretation of human consciousness. His epistemology or theory of knowledge occupies a middle position between the classical materialist view of consciousness emanating from matter and the idealist view of the world as the creation of consciousness. The materialist view leads to a passive conception of thought as mere receptivity to sense data; Marx insisted that consciousness was practical activity. In other words, human thought was a form of action which transformed the objects which it perceived. Actuality was not an external, objective datum, but something shaped by human agency. The dialectics of nature, such as Engels propounded, are quite incompatible with Marx's philosophical position because for Marx consciousness was the essential medium of dialectical change. We have no reason to believe that he ever abandoned the humanist vision – put forward in his early writings – of man in a dialectical relationship with nature which he transforms in the process of making history; nature is for Marx a social category.

We have, therefore, to make a distinction between Marx's own ideas and the intellectual system of 'dialectical materialism' which became the official doctrine of the Soviet Union and that actually owes more to Engels, G. V. Plekhanov (1856–1918) and Lenin.

Marx's writings synthesized three different traditions: German philosophy, British political economy and French socialism. The first shaped his general theory of history and the method he brought to bear on the analysis of society. He was led to the second by his theory of history in which labour is identified as the human essence and the conditions of production as the determining element of social and political forms. Economics provided Marx with the concepts to anatomize production and identify what he regarded as the immanent tendencies in nineteenth-century capitalism which would lead it to beget its own negation, socialism. Although he wrote very little on what the future socialist society would be like, his conversion to communism in 1844, while in Paris, was crucial to his intellectual development because it defined the purpose of his studies and major writings. They were intended to provide the theory for the revolutionary transformation of class-divided society and the inauguration of socialism.

These three major strands in Marx's thought can be individually considered under the following headings:

- theory of history;
- theory of capitalist development;
- theory of class division and revolutionary transformation.

## Theory of history

Marx's first vocation was philosophy, but the tradition of philosophy in which he was schooled was closely allied with history. As a student at the University of Berlin he came to know the philosophy of Georg Hegel and associated with a group of left-wing philosophers known as the 'Young Hegelians'. Both Hegel's dialectical method of reasoning and speculative philosophy of history permanently influenced Marx.

Hegel's method is barely intelligible; he appears to have believed that the process or movement of thought reproduces the flux of existence. Just as natural entities develop out of something very different (such as the oak from the acorn) so the categories of thought have the potential to self-develop in the same way. The dynamic of this dialectical process of development, for Hegel, was that all finite things and concepts are charged with negativity, the capacity to be what they are not. The movement of an idea from thesis, through its antithesis to a final synthesis exemplifies this dynamic which Hegel regarded as a mainspring of both reason and reality. As one commentator puts it: 'Dialectics is a process in a world where the mode of existence of men and things is made up of contradictory relations, so that any particular content can be unfolded only through passing into its opposite' (Marcuse, *Reason and Revolution*, 1955, p.66).

Hegel believed that, because reason is the sovereign of the world, human history is a rational process. Its rationality was displayed in the cultural progression of mankind from lower to higher civilizations, characterized by different modes of thought. These modes of thought corresponded approximately to the intellectual evolution of the human individual. They ascended from sensuous consciousness (in which the mind does not experience itself as separate from the world) through understanding (at which stage the mind distinguishes between itself and different objects and analyses them separately) to reason (where the mind retains the distinctions made in understanding but also fathoms the underlying unity of the world of which it is part). These ascending modes of thought entailed greater self-awareness brought about by the externalization or expression of the mind in culture (as, say, an artist expresses himself in painting).

Now Hegel knew that civilizations had often been widely separated by time and space and an explanation for their cultural progression could not be found in direct, continuous contact between them. A purely religious account was provided by reference to God's Providence, but Hegel believed this religious account could be re-stated in philosophic terms. Cultural progress, he asserted, manifested the presence and self-development of a transhistorical being, a world spirit. This spirit developed through the different modes of thought outlined above and its destined purpose was to realize itself – or develop its full potential – in freedom.

Hegel knew, too, that the history of the world is not a theatre of happiness; it has been punctuated by violence and the collapse of civilizations. How could this be explained? The culture of past epochs initially served, thought Hegel, as vehicles for the expression of human creativity and the development of the world spirit. But after a certain point the culture of an epoch became a stifling restraint on spiritual development. Existing political, social and cultural forms were torn asunder and spirit was at war with itself. When it restored its unity in a new culture this simultaneously sustained the achievements of and abolished the old.

We have here an image of spiritual development in stages whose chief breaks correspond to the forms of thought. In the initial, sensuous stage, spirit is in unthinking community with nature and God; in the process of development it alienates itself from nature (sees nature as something different, strange) and God; in the final stage it restores a rational community with God and nature.

Marx never entirely abandoned Hegel's method of reasoning (he attempted in the opening chapters of *Capital* to deduce the main economic categories from one another in a manner inspired by Hegel's *Logic*) nor Hegel's rhetoric. Moreover, although he discarded the spiritual premises of Hegel's image of history, his own historical vision had a similar form: history was a matter of humanity's progressive self-realization; it moved in stages; its destined end was emancipation. But Marx believed that the first necessity in any theory of history was to recognize that humans had to produce their material life of eating, drinking, clothing themselves, and so on, before they were able to 'make history'. Production was, for Marx, the primordial historical act and the productive forces (of skill, technology, science and so on) were the prime movers of history.

Hegel had seen the different social and political forms in history as expressions of the human mind. Marx reversed the procedure. As he put it in *The German Ideology* (1846), an early statement of his theory of history:

> In direct contrast to German philosophy, which descends from heaven to earth, here we ascend from earth to heaven. That is to say, we do not set out from what men say, imagined, conceived, in order to arrive at men in the flesh. We set out from real, active men, and on the basis of their real life process we demonstrate the development of the ideological reflexes and echoes of this life process.

Out of the struggle to wrest a living from nature and augment their production arose the division of labour, initially, Marx thought, between man and wife. The further development of the productive forces required a structure of economic relations whose nexus was the ability to command the labour of others and extract from them that part of their production which was surplus to the needs of subsistence. Since the dissolution of tribal communism, Marx argued, all economic structures had had this basically antagonistic character. The economic structure was stabilized by political and legal forms, and justified by prevailing ideas. Epochal historical changes occurred, Marx believed, when the productive forces could no longer develop within the existing structure of economic relations; from being a fertile matrix for their growth, this structure had turned into a sterile integument.

The correspondences between Hegel's and Marx's visions of history have been well brought out by G. A. Cohen in this pair of sentences:

> For Hegel: *History is the history of the world spirit* (and derivatively, human consciousness) *which undergoes growth* in self-knowledge, *the stimulus and vehicle of which* is a culture, *which perishes when it has stimulated more growth than it can contain.*
> For Marx: *History is the history of* human industry, *which undergoes growth* in productive power, *the stimulus and vehicle of which is* an economic structure, *which perishes when it has stimulated more growth than it can obtain.* (G. A. Cohen, *Karl Marx's Theory of History*, 1978, p.26)

Marx's vision of history was given its clearest theoretical statement in the Preface to *A Contribution to the Critique of Political Economy* (1859) – which is not to say these pages are free from ambiguities. Here, too, we are told of the epochal stages in the progress of the economic formation of society which are designated 'the Asiatic, the ancient, the feudal, and the modern bourgeois methods of production'. The present, capitalist economic structure was, for Marx, both the most productive and, in some respects, the most antagonistic of all modes of production. It was not overtly antagonistic because a free market in labour was one of its central institutions. Political force was not turned directly to economic purposes, as in previous historical epochs. But it was, Marx believed, the economic structure and the historical epoch in which the alienation of labour was most generalized. That is to say, under capitalism most people give up control of their own labour power when they enter a labour contract (they 'alienate' something of themselves in a legal sense) and the products of their own labour appear as foreign, even hostile objects. Marx believed that capitalism would be superseded by an economic structure which restored human autonomy. He envisaged, therefore, a dialectical pattern of historical change: history began with primitive communism where humans had not learnt to assert their individual autonomy; it moved into a phase of class-divided societies in which individuality did develop but labour was increasingly alienated; and culminated in a social form which would preserve individual autonomy but restore community.

## Theory of capitalist development

Marx was far from being an entirely speculative thinker and was averse to utopianism. Most of his writings are of a technical character and combine a high degree of abstraction with great empirical detail. (This style of presentation is very evident in *Capital 1* which takes an 'unreal' model of a closed capitalist economy, in a state of equilibrium, and then 'illustrates' its workings by reference to the economic history of Britain.) These writings fall into a tradition of economic analysis that goes back to the eighteenth-century physiocrats, although unlike his predecessors he saw his task as interpreting the social process as a whole rather than extracting its unambiguously economic phenomena. His attitude towards this tradition – which we now call classical economics – was ambivalent. On the one hand it was a science which would reveal the 'natural laws' of the capitalist economy and provide a scientific grounding for his view that this economy was morally wrong and should be superseded. On the other, the tradition of political economy was an ideology because it misrepresented – as timeless universals – basic features of a capitalist economy (such as private property) which Marx insisted were historically determined.

Marx's indebtedness to the tradition was most evident in his belief that labour was the sole source of the values at which commodities exchanged in market societies. This labour-input theory of value had been previously formulated by David Ricardo (1772–1823) but in taking over the theory, Marx applied it more rigorously and consistently than his predecessor. If one assumed a capitalist economy in equilibrium, he argued, all commodities exchanged at their labour-input values – there was no value created by the process of exchange – and this was true of that commodity the worker sold on the labour market, his or her own labour-power. Its value was determined by the labour-time necessary to produce it. How then were surplus value and the capitalist's profit created? The answer, Marx thought, lay in the prolongation of the working day beyond the time necessary to recompense the worker for the value of his or her labour. It was as if in a twelve hour day, the worker worked six hours in exchange for the means of subsistence, and six hours *gratis* for the employer.

Marx was not unaware of the enormous problems with this theory of value (such as the heterogeneity of labour which makes it virtually impossible to define a common measure of input). The theory cannot be put to use to predict prices and is generally regarded as invalid by modern economists. It has a central ideological place in Marx's thought because it demonstrated that, in its wealth-creation and economic dynamism, capitalism *systemically* exploited labour. Intervening in the pattern of distribution (as J. S. Mill had suggested) would not alter the exploitative character of the system.

The classical tradition provided a second theory which was central to Marx's analysis of the future of capitalism; this was that there was an inexorable tendency for the rate of profit to fall. His predecessors, who had been chiefly concerned with agrarian production, argued that the combined effect of population growth and depletion of natural resources was to slow down economic development, with stagnation as the ultimate outcome. Demographic pressure, they argued, led to the demand for more food, and the use of lower quality land; hence higher prices, higher wages and lower profits. Marx believed that the same tendency would arise simply within industry itself from the technical innovations capitalists made in order to meet competition.

To understand his argument we need to know that in Marx's view only 'living labour' (which he called the 'variable capital') could produce surplus value. The machines – or what he called the 'constant capital' – used in production could not add any value to the 'past labour' embedded in them. The rate of profit, therefore, was determined by the ratio of constant capital to labour. To put the matter more precisely, Marx formulated that

$$p = \frac{S}{(C + V)}$$

where p = the rate of profit, S the rate at which surplus value is extracted, C = constant capital and V = variable capital (or labour). Marx argued that the rate at which workers were exploited or surplus value extracted from them would remain constant. But as technical changes were implemented by capitalists, the ratio of constant to variable capital would alter because machines are normally labour-saving (that is the rationale for their introduction). It followed from his fundamental equation that in a technically dynamic system the rate of profit had an inherent tendency to decline, although Marx acknowledged a number of countervailing factors.

The law of the falling tendency of the rate of profit had a considerable significance for Marx because it demonstrated that capitalist production had certain internal barriers to its own indefinite expansion. He viewed the process in a characteristically Hegelian light: by introducing machines, capitalists were raising the productivity of labour and the general level of productive forces up to a point where they would sustain the new mode of production, socialism. But because the falling rate of profit induced bankruptcies and business crises, it showed the way capitalism would 'negate itself'.

> The development of the productive forces of social labour is the historical task and privilege of capital. It is precisely in this way that it unconsciously creates the material requirements of a higher mode of production . . . [But the demonstration of the falling rate of profit shows that capitalist production] has a barrier, that it is relative, that it is not an absolute but only a historical mode of production corresponding to a definite and limited epoch in the development of the material conditions of production. (*Capital 3*, 1933 edition, p.304)

This 'law of tendency' identified by Marx has proved no more robust than the labour theory of value. There is no empirical evidence for a secular fall in the rate of profit, and there are conceptual flaws in the theory. (For example, Marx did not think through the labour-saving consequences of technical innovation for the capital goods industries which would tend to keep the ratio of C to V constant.)

Despite its weaknesses, the law had a long subsequent history in Marxian economics, for it was linked with the theory of capitalist crises and became part of the explanation for the imperialist expansion which took place at the end of the nineteenth century. Marx observed a ten-year 'business cycle' (to use the modern term) of boom and depression and regarded the fall in the rate of profit as the mechanism which chokes off economic expansion, and precipitates business failures and mass unemployment. Marx offered no detailed account of the collapse of capitalism, but one would infer from his scattered writings that this recurrent cycle leads to the concentration of capital (as surviving capitalists buy up their bankrupt rivals) and increasing social polarization. In the final crisis, economic breakdown interlaces with the revolutionary action of the working class.

> Along with the constant decrease in the number of capitalist magnates . . . the mass of misery, oppression, slavery, degradation and exploitation

grows; but with this there also grows the revolt of the working class, a class constantly increasing in numbers, and trained, united and organised by the very mechanism of the capitalist process of production. The monopoly of capital becomes a fetter upon the mode of production which has flourished alongside and under it. The centralisation of the means of production and the socialisation of labour reach a point at which they become incompatible with the capitalist integument. This integument is burst asunder. The knell of the capitalist private property sounds. The expropriators are expropriated. (*Capital 1*, 1976 edition, p.929)

There then follows a paragraph which shows most vividly how Marx viewed the long process of capitalist development, and foresaw its demise, through the prism of Hegelian reasoning and rhetoric:

The capitalist mode of appropriation, which springs from the capitalist mode of production, produces capitalist private property. This is the first negation of individual private property, as founded on the labour of its proprietor. But capitalist production begets, with the inexorability of a natural process, its own negation. This is the negation of the negation. It does not re-establish private property, but it does indeed establish individual property on the basis of the achievements of the capitalist era: namely co-operation and possession in common of the land and the means of production produced by labour itself.

## Theory of class division and revolutionary transformation

We have come, finally, to Marx's theory of class division and the role of class conflict in revolutionary transformations. We can cite texts which would suggest that this is where we should have started. In his last years, when criticizing the Gotha programme of the newly formed German Social Democratic Party, Marx wrote that for almost forty years he had 'emphasized the class struggle as the primary motive force of history, and especially the class struggle between bourgeoisie and proletariat as the great lever of modern social change'. Best known of all his texts is *The Communist Manifesto* (1848) which tells us: 'The history of all hitherto existing society is the history of class struggles.' Rather than define a class struggle in the *Manifesto*, Marx gave successive historical instances: 'Free-man and slave, patrician and plebeian, lord and serf, guild master and journey-man', and argued that they carried on an uninterrupted fight which ended either in a revolutionary reconstitution of society or the common ruin of the contending classes. Marx argued that whereas these class divisions of earlier historical epochs had co-existed with complex social ranking, the tendency of modern bourgeois society was to simplify class antagonism. Society was, he thought, 'more and more splitting up into two great hostile camps, into two great classes directly facing each other: bourgeoisie and proletariat'.

Even the *Manifesto*, we should note, does not claim that this is the *only* class struggle: the bourgeoisie, Marx argued, found itself involved in a constant battle with the aristocracy, and even 'with those portions of the bourgeoisie itself whose interests have become antagonistic to the progress of industry'. And, additionally, there was a constant struggle with the bourgeoisie of foreign countries. Consequently, the bourgeoisie would try to ally itself with the prolet-ariat, 'to ask for its help, and thus to drag it into the political arena'. Furthermore, the advance of industry impoverished or threatened certain property owners who were 'precipitated into the proletariat' and supplied it 'with fresh elements of enlightenment and progress'. Indeed, in the decisive hour of the class struggle 'a small section of the ruling class cuts itself adrift and joins the revolutionary class, the class that holds the future in its hands'. So, while Marx regarded the division between capitalists and the working class as the fundamental immanent tendency of bourgeois society, he recognized (in what is, after all, a none too subtle party political tract) ways in which this dichotomy is overlaid by class alliances and class fragmentation.

These sophistications of his class analysis became more evident in his writings on British, French and German politics in the 1850s and 1860s, which show a shrewd awareness of conflicts between financiers and industrialists within the capitalist class, of ethnic divisions (between, for example, English and Irish) among workers, and of cross-class alliances.

Class was the key concept in Marx's sociological theory but it has presented quite a challenge to commentators who have sought to elucidate it and establish its place in his ideas as a whole. For a start, Marx nowhere defined the concept of class; the manuscript of *Capital* breaks off at the very point where Marx asks 'What constitutes a class?' From the classical economists he took the three-fold division of modern capitalist society into wage-labourers, capitalists and landowners ('the three great social classes') but he rejected the idea that the identity of revenues or sources of revenue were responsible for class formation. Even more of a problem is the place of class division and oppression in the theory of historical materialism outlined on pages 57–9. The term 'class' simply does not appear in the Preface to *The Critique of Political Economy* where Marx set out his theory of history; there, the dynamic of historical change appears as the conflict between the forces of production and the relations of production (or the economic structure) – not the class struggle.

We can suggest a two-fold place for class-division in Marx's theory of history: firstly, classes are an outcome of the division of labour which is necessary for the maximum development of the forces of production. There are economies of effort if the planning and administration of work are separated from its execution and undertaken by a different group; so classes are functional for economic efficiency. Secondly, productive labour is usually repellent, and a dominant class is needed to compel others to work and yield surplus value; so classes are required for social control. It seems plausible to attribute both notions to Marx when considering classes in relation to his theory of history. That theory does not, however, give us a very convincing reason for the development of revolutionary consciousness among workers in capitalist society: are we to believe that workers overthrow capitalism either because they see it as an 'integument' (*Capital 1*, p.929) on the forces of production or in order to bring a further expansion of the forces under socialism? Neither seems very likely, and the actual history of socialist revolutions has been quite different. They have occurred in economically under-developed, predominantly peasant societies (Russia, China, Vietnam, Cuba) where industrial capitalism was a relatively novel phenomenon at the time of the revolutionary outbreak.

It is clear from Marx's writings that classes were not to be defined by income levels and that they were different in character from the juridically recognized estates of post-feudal society. In bourgeois societies, the possession by some private individuals of property in production (capital) and dispossession of many others of all means of production save their own labour are basic complementary criteria for class definition. They result in two groups who need each other (capital 'presupposes' labour and it cannot accumulate without the surplus value extracted from labour) but whose relationship is antagonistic. Marx supplemented these criteria by pointing to the subjective and cultural conditions necessary for class formation when he wrote: 'In so far as millions of families live under economic conditions which separate their way of life, their interests, and their education from those of other classes and oppose them to these, they constitute a class' (*The 18th Brumaire of Louis Bonaparte*, 1852).

Marx insisted that institutions such as private property and even the concept of the private individual were historical; they cannot, therefore, enter into a definition of class applicable to pre-capitalist societies. A more generally applicable criterion for defining classes to be found in his writings revolves around the 'pumping out' of unpaid surplus labour from immediate producers. The specific economic forms in which this has occurred varied according to the successive modes of production and Marx regarded this relation between those who control the conditions of production and the immediate producers as determining the wider authority structure of any given society. It is 'the hidden basis of the whole construction of society, including the political patterns of sovereignty and dependence, in short, of a specific form of government' (*Capital 3*).

This notion of 'pumping out' surplus labour enables one to define the proletariat in modern capitalist societies as those workers whose manual labour contributes to surplus value. This provides a rigorous criterion for setting a boundary between the working and other classes, and some Marxists have advocated it because rigour is, after all, a good thing. (I can think of no scholarly endeavour in which sloppiness is a virtue.)

Unfortunately, the criterion has absurd consequences: in modern capitalist societies, the number of manual workers whose labour contributes to surplus value has been inexorably diminishing for several decades and by this definition the working class is now of pygmy proportions. If we do not insist on manual labour as part of our criterion and include within the proletariat all wage workers who contribute to surplus, then we find that highly-paid executives are working class, but dustmen are not.

There are a number of ways out of definitional dilemmas such as these, and though I am principally concerned with Marx's ideas it would, I think, be useful to indicate them:

1   Use the term class as shorthand for the stratification of society according to such objective variables as income, property, educational qualifications, and more subjective factors such as social prestige. Stratification analysis on these lines differs from class analysis as Marxists understand it because it is undertaken for a different purpose. The purpose of stratification theory is to correlate the behaviour and attitudes of *individuals* with these variables (which we can call 'class' or 'status' indicators). The purpose of class analysis, on the other hand, is to explain *collective* action in terms of the class position of the individuals engaging in it.

2   Untie the concept of class from the possession or non-possession of property in production (and by extension the creation of surplus value) and use it to refer to asymmetrical relationships between groups based on a more general criterion, such as authority. The attractions of this are that it allows us to identify class differences among the employees of one firm or corporation, and it also allows us to apply class analysis to states which have socialized the means of production.

The main problem with this revision of the class concept is that authority in modern societies is delegated throughout complex hierarchies and if we make it our class criterion we end up with an enormous number of classes.

3    Ally class analysis with non-Marxian social theory, notably that of Max Weber (1864–1920). So much of Weber's work was explicitly directed against Marxism as espoused by the German Social Democratic Party that it is a real disservice to understanding to hyphenate Weberian-Marxism as if there is some single broad tradition of incomprehensible Germans. Weber's best-known study, *The Protestant Ethic and the Spirit of Capitalism* (first published in 1904–05) was an attempt to demonstrate the autonomous influence of religious belief on material, economic life. It is an explicit critique of what Weber calls 'the doctrine of naive historical materialism' according to which ideas such as those in Calvinist beliefs are regarded simply as 'reflections' of economic conditions. Equally explicit was Weber's criticism of the Marxian view (expressed in the quotation from *Capital* above) that economic class divisions determine in a monocausal way the political pattern within a society. Weber regarded economic class as only one dimension of social power; he identified two other dimensions with the political party and the status group whose members constitute a subcultural community, bound by a common sense of social honour and enjoying a common style of life. Furthermore, we should note that whereas Marx took the dichotomous division of society into two antagonistic classes to be the basic tendency of modern capitalist societies, Weber's viewpoint emphasized a pluralistic conception of classes.

For Weber, class was an objective economic fact primarily determined by the market situations of individual social actors, situations which create different social interests and 'life chances'. Among the wealthy, he argued, different types of property had the effect of differentiating the class situation of (to give a broad example) the rentier from the entrepreneur. Similarly, among the propertyless, sharp class differentiation occurred according to the marketable value of the skills and expertise of individuals. One of the attractions of this approach is that the class location of salaried professional and educated workers is far less of a problem than it is for a dichotomous theory of society. Symbolic skills and educational qualifications enabled certain workers to offer a distinct set of services on the market and put them in a class situation quite different from that of manual labour.

This 'educated salaried middle class' can be linked with Weber's vision of the future of capitalist society, a vision which was very different from Marx's. Weber believed that, in industrial societies (whether capitalist or socialist), there was an inexorable tendency for rationalization – or the application of calculative, scientific norms to human conduct – to penetrate all spheres of social life. The typical form of the 'rational' social institution for Weber was the modern bureaucracy, and the spread of bureaucratization encourages the growth in the proportion of non-manual workers in the labour market. Weber regarded the Marxist vision of a classless society as a utopian illusion: though a revolutionary political party might seize political power, it could not avoid the structures of domination implicit in bureaucracy. This pessimistic appraisal of the likely direction of revolution was reinforced by the fact that the revolutionary parties known to Weber regarded revolution as a route to modernization.

Weber argued that economic interests formed the core of the 'subjective' content of class, and that this content was strengthened by the strategies class collectivities could adopt to defend their interests and exclude others from certain material advantages. These strategies he designated 'social closure', and two examples would be the restrictive practices of skilled trade unions which limited the number of apprentices in certain trades and the monopoly of legal services by the legal professions. Weber did not deny the possibility of economic class becoming a status group, for these are not exclusive terms but refer to the different ways social collectivities can be oriented to social action. In the circumstances of Imperial Germany, where the exclusiveness of the rest of society, the denial of access to higher education, and the social zoning of the new cities created a community of experience among workers, then the working class took on many of the features of a status group.

This summary of Weber's views should have demonstrated their incompatibility with Marx's historical materialism and his concept of class; any conjunction of the two theorists is bound to jettison much of the thought of one or the other.

## References

Cohen, G. A. (1978) *Karl Marx's Theory of History*, Oxford University Press.

Marcuse, H. (1955) *Reason and Revolution*, Routledge and Kegan Paul (first published in 1941).

Marx, K. (1976) *Capital 1*, Penguin (first published in 1867).

Marx, K. (1933) *Capital 3*, Charles Kerr (first published in 1867).

# UNIT 2  EUROPEAN ARMIES, GOVERNMENTS AND SOCIETIES IN 1914

*Clive Emsley*

**Open University students of this unit will need to refer to:**

Set book: J. M. Roberts, *Europe 1880–1945*, Longman, 1989

*Documents 1: 1900–1929*, eds Arthur Marwick and Wendy Simpson, Open University Press, 1990

*Maps Booklet*

Video-cassette 1, items 1–4

# INTRODUCTION

This unit focuses on the armies and navies of the European states in 1914 and on the perceptions of what it meant to go to war. From this focus it moves on to give you a broad introduction to the economic, political and social structures of these states – issues that will be taken up and explored in greater detail in subsequent units.

When you have finished this unit you should have a detailed knowledge of:

the attitudes towards war in the different countries of Europe in 1914;

the composition and organization of the European armies and navies in 1914;

the different relationships obtaining in the different countries between the armies and the monarchs and/or civilian authorities which they served.

In addition you should have a preliminary knowledge of:

the structure of the different states in 1914;

some of the pressures for change to be found in these states.

The unit is divided into four sections:

1   Going to war in 1914
2   The armies and navies of the great powers
3   The armies in the Balkans
4   Summing up and looking ahead

# 1 GOING TO WAR IN 1914

For many people the events of 1914 mark a decisive turning point after which the world was never to appear the same again; thus, for example, many history books have 1914 as a terminal date, as do many history courses. Yet turning points in history can look very different from different national perspectives. For Balkan peoples, and it was in the Balkans that events occurred which sparked the war, the conflict which began in the summer of 1914 can appear as an extension and widening of a series of wars beginning in 1912. For the Italians participation in the war did not come until the early summer of 1915. In the USSR the decisive turning point is 1917 rather than 1914, and the experience of war was to continue for many Russians until 1920. Furthermore, after the end of the war against the central powers (Germany and Austria-Hungary) a few British and French troops found themselves deployed in Russia against the new Red Army. Besides the danger of perceiving 'key dates' or 'turning points' with a kind of national, tunnel vision, there is also the danger of perceiving such occasions with hindsight and assuming that the actors involved in events were aware of their significance and potential outcome. (Table 2.1 lists the combatants of World War I and their period of involvement.)

**Exercise**   Study Tables 2.2 and 2.3.

1   What does the information contained in these tables suggest to you about the expectation and understanding which the soldiers and sailors of 1914 had about the physical reality of modern war?

**Table 2.1**    *The Combatants of World War I*

| | 1914 | 1915 | 1916 | 1917 | 1918 |
|---|---|---|---|---|---|
| *The Central Powers* | | | | | |
| Austria-Hungary | July | | | | Nov |
| Bulgaria | | Oct | | | Sept |
| Germany | Aug | | | | Nov |
| Turkey | Nov | | | | Oct |
| | | | | | |
| *The Entente Powers and their Allies* | | | | | |
| France | Aug | | | | Nov |
| Belgium[1] | Aug | | | | Nov |
| Great Britain | Aug | | | | Nov |
| Greece | | | | June | Nov |
| Italy | | May | | | Nov |
| Portugal | | | March | | Nov |
| Japan | Aug | | | | Nov |
| Montenegro[2] | July | | | | Nov |
| Romania | | | Aug   Dec | | Nov |
| Russia | July | | | March | |
| Serbia[2] | July | | | | Nov |
| USA | | | | April | Nov |

[1] Virtually the whole of Belgium was under German occupation from the autumn of 1914.

[2] Montenegro and Serbia were destroyed as independent states in the winter of 1915-16, but guerrilla warfare continued and both states had governments in exile. Eventually, at the end of the war, they were amalgamated with other territories into the new state of Yugoslavia.

2    When war broke out in the summer of 1914 there was talk of it being 'over by Christmas'. How might looking back over wars in the preceding half century have contributed to this? ■

**Specimen answers**    1    It should be clear from Tables 2.2 and 2.3 that very few of the soldiers from the major European powers (Austria-Hungary, France, Germany, Great Britain and Russia) who embarked on war in 1914 had any experience of the reality of modern warfare against well-armed, well-trained adversaries.

2    None of the wars fought in Europe since the 1850s had lasted for more than ten months; the conflicts outside Europe had impinged little on the everyday lives of Europeans, and thus it was natural to suppose that the conflict which began in 1914 would not take much longer than its immediate, European predecessors.

**Discussion**    Of course, some troops had experience in colonial wars outside Europe; in addition the British had fought against the Boers in South Africa and the Russians had fought the Japanese in Manchuria. Some lessons had been learned from the American Civil War about the devastating nature of modern firepower: the Prussians developed loose formation and the use of cover in response to this danger during 1870; the Russians were slower, and consequently suffered 35 per cent casualties in their initial assault on Turkish positions at Plevna in 1877. Yet the experience of battle was wanting for most troops in 1914, and the experience of moving large numbers of men in the heat and confusion of battle was wanting for most senior officers. Some generals, particularly in France, still tended to emphasize the *élan* of large-scale assaults with fixed bayonets; and certainly this was the image which inspired some popular artists and writers (and indeed which continued to inspire them when war actually came). □

*Table 2.2*   *European wars and their duration 1853–1913*[1]

| War | Principal states involved | First hostilities | Armistice | Duration in months |
|---|---|---|---|---|
| Crimean | Great Britain / France / Turkey } vs Russia | 23 Sept 1853 | 1 Feb 1856 | 27 |
| Franco-Austrian | France vs Austrian Empire | 29 April 1859 | 8 July 1859 | 3 |
| Schleswig-Holstein | Prussia / Austrian Empire } vs Denmark | 1 Feb 1864 | 1 Aug 1864 | 4[2] |
| Seven Weeks[3] | Prussia / Italy } vs Austrian Empire | 14 June 1866 | 26 July 1866 | 2 |
| Franco-Prussian[3] | Prussia vs France | 19 July 1870 | 1 March 1871 | 9 |
| Russo-Turkish | Russia vs Turkey | 24 April 1877 | 31 Jan 1878 | 10 |
| First Balkan | Bulgaria / Serbia / Greece / Montenegro } vs Turkey | 8 Oct 1912 | 22 April 1913 | 2 |
| Second Balkan | Serbia / Greece / Montenegro / Romania / Turkey } vs Bulgaria | 30 June 1913 | 21 Aug 1913 | 2 |

[1] Excluding the smaller Balkan conflicts between Bulgaria and Serbia (1885) and Greece and Turkey (1897)
[2] Truce in May and June
[3] Smaller German states were also involved in these conflicts, notably Saxony and, indirectly, Bavaria on the side of Austria in 1866; significant numbers from the German states fought alongside Prussia in 1870–71

*Table 2.3*   *Other wars involving 'modern' armies 1861–1905*[1]

| War | Principal states involved | First hostilities | Armistice | Duration in months |
|---|---|---|---|---|
| American Civil | United States of America vs Confederate States | 12 April 1861 | 9 April 1865 | 48 |
| Spanish-American | United States vs Spain | 21 April 1898 | 12 Aug 1898 | 5 |
| Boer | Great Britain vs Boer Republic | 9 Oct 1899 | 31 May 1902 | 32 |
| Russo-Japanese | Russia vs Japan | 8 Feb 1904 | 6 Sept 1905 | 22 |

[1] That is involving troops on both sides equipped with modern weapons and excluding conflicts between 'western' armies and tribal forces.

**Exercise**    Look again at Table 2.2. Do you detect a shift in the combatants and the regions of Europe where wars were fought between 1853 and 1913? ■

**Specimen answer**    From the late 1850s to the early 1870s the wars in Europe were between major powers and were fought in the centre and west of the continent. From then on there was no open conflict between major powers (except for the Russo-Turkish war if Turkey is considered still to have been a major power) and the wars were confined to the Balkans.

**Discussion**    The wars of the mid-1850s through to the early 1870s have a broad claim to the description of wars of liberation: out of them emerged a united Italy, under the house of Savoy, and a united Germany, under the dominance of Prussia. Note here that although Germany was united and that the king of Prussia was Kaiser (emperor) of the Reich, there were still technically twenty-five federal states in Germany (four kingdoms, six grand duchies, five duchies, seven principalities and three free cities) with varying degrees of independence and local government. Bavaria, the largest kingdom after Prussia, jealously maintained its own army, and while Bavarian regiments were increasingly integrated into the German Army, a Bavarian military plenipotentiary was resident at the Kaiser's court in Berlin maintaining the Bavarian army's separate rights and privileges and acting as the direct representative of the Bavarian minister of war who, under the Reich's constitution, considered himself the equal of his Prussian counterpart. Austria – generally referred to after 1867 as Austria-Hungary when the *Ausgleich* (compromise) acknowledged a dual monarchy in which the emperor of Austria was also the king of Hungary – had vied with Prussia for hegemony over the smaller German states; she lost significantly by the wars of the 1850s and 1860s – in prestige, to Prussia, as well as lands, to Italy. The struggles in the Balkans were the result of the various Slav peoples of south-east Europe seeking to break away and carve their own nation states from the last vestiges of Turkey's European empire. These conflicts had involved the great powers, obviously Russia in 1877–78. But the First and Second Balkan Wars also witnessed considerable diplomatic man-oeuvring by the great powers to ensure peace and what they considered to be a proper balance in the region; this diplomacy was occasionally backed up by the threat of force, most notably in May 1913 when Austro-Hungarian troops were mobilized on the frontiers of Montenegro.

You should follow up the basic detail of great power diplomacy in the Balkans in Roberts, pages 266–9. It would be a good idea to do this now. □

The Balkans, then, were recognized as an international trouble spot when, on 28 June 1914, the heir to the Austrian and Hungarian thrones was assassinated, together with his wife, by a Bosnian Serb in Sarajevo, a town in the imperial province of Bosnia. Historians have written at length about 'the July crisis'; the term has been used as the title for books as well as chapters within books. Essentially the July crisis concerned the upper echelons of governments and their diplomats; the general publics of the great powers were largely unaware of the notes passing between monarchs, ministers and diplomats. For one thing, the assassination of royal personages was in no sense an unheard-of event in this period: the Empress of Austria had been murdered in 1898; followed by the King of Italy (1900), the King and Queen of Serbia (1903), the King of Portugal with his heir (1908) and the King of Greece (1913); several leading politicians had met a similar fate, most recently Count Stolypin in Russia in 1911. Nor had previous

Balkan wars involved the powers of Europe in war against each other. Besides, in Britain and France the newspapers – and remember that people relied upon the newspaper press for their national and international news – found plenty of good copy much closer to home. For much of July 1914 French newspapers were full of the trial of Madame Caillaux; she was the wife of a former finance minister who, incensed by the campaign which *Le Figaro* had orchestrated against her husband, had shot dead that paper's editor. British newspapers were preoccupied with a worsening crisis over Ireland where Ulster Protestants were arming to oppose their inclusion in an Ireland with a Home Rule parliament in Dublin. The newspapers began to devote more and more space to the diplomatic events of the July crisis only after Austria-Hungary presented an ultimatum to Serbia on 23 July. Just over a week after the ultimatum the armies had mobilized.

There seems to be an overwhelming impression, especially in popular history books and in media representation of the beginning of World War I, of nations and populations united, and of men going cheerfully and eagerly to war throughout Europe. There is evidence of politicians declaring a new kind of national unity: for example, the president of the French Chamber of Deputies proclaimed, 'There are no more adversaries here, there are only Frenchmen'; and Kaiser Wilhelm declared, 'Henceforth I know no parties, I know only Germans'. It is understandable that internal differences would be forgotten in time of crisis, but whether populations were quite as jingoistic and as eager for war as is sometimes implied, is a moot point and one that I want us to explore now.

**Exercise**    First of all I should like you to consider some film evidence. Look now at video-cassette 1, items 1–4. These are all sequences from 1914 newsreels showing recruitment or men leaving for war. As you watch the film note down what you think is useful to the historian in these sequences, and what they tell us about the popular attitude to war in Britain, France and Turkey in 1914. ■

**Specimen answer**
**and discussion**    These sequences give a good idea of uniforms and equipment and, put together in this way I think that they emphasize some of the contrasts between combatants and the societies from which they came. But, unfortunately, I do not think that there is much here that we can use to establish popular attitudes to the war: if people are waving at the troops in London and Paris, don't people often wave and cheer military parades? If troops wave cheerfully at the camera, is it because they are cheerful about leaving for war, or simply because people often smile and wave when they see a camera? A more telling image of eagerness and enthusiasm might have been put across with the use of sound-material – music and a commentator; but, of course, film in 1914 was silent and had such commentary existed, would you have *seen* eagerness and enthusiasm any more than you do now, or would you have *accepted* that it was there because martial music *implied* it and the commentary *asserted* it. The French historian Marc Ferro, who has made a detailed study of film as well as writing one of the best single-volume histories of World War I, wrote of the images of the soldiers of 1914: 'They marched off to war, their faces a picture of delight. Film is of course deceptive and a more searching examination would show other images – the anguish of a father, a fiancé, or a husband' (*The Great War 1914–1918*, 1973, p.xi). Unfortunately, in the examples that I and my BBC colleagues were able to find of film shot in the summer of 1914 of men going to war, these 'other images' were also difficult to pinpoint. None of this is to say that the soldiers of 1914 were not eager and enthusiastic: war probably did seem like a great adventure, especially since so few had any personal

experience of it. Perhaps, too, there was a degree of exhilaration since, after all the talk and the arms race, the event had finally arrived. But the visual images, sadly, are not especially helpful to the historian on this matter.  □

I want to turn now to the recollections of men who enlisted in 1914. The examples which follow are all taken from the British experience but, as will be discussed later, Britain was the only country which did not have a conscript army and which did not, therefore, have a large reserve of trained manpower to call upon in 1914. If the eagerness for war was manifested by volunteering then, presumably, this should be revealed in men's recollections of why they volunteered.

**Exercise**     Read the following extracts and note:

1    the reasons given for volunteering;

2    how these examples support the popular image of jingoism and eagerness for war.

*Extract (a)*
Several of us said good-bye to Marlborough at the end of July 1914, fully expecting to be back again in September . . . My age then was not quite seventeen and a quarter . . . Like multitudes of other young men, I became filled with a passionate desire to take part in [the war]. I drank in everything that was said or written by statesmen, ministers of the Church and newspapers about the nobility of our ideals and the righteousness of our Cause. It wasn't a matter of 'our Country, right or wrong'. Our country was 100 per cent right and Germany 100 per cent wrong. We were fighting for King and Country and Empire, and 'gallant little Belgium'. We were fighting to uphold the principles of justice and freedom, and international morality and to smash Kaiserism and German militarism . . . We had been taught to worship God one day a week but to worship Country and Empire seven days a week. The British Empire was the greatest empire the world had ever known, and its greatness was due to the superior qualities of the British. Foreigners weren't cast in the same mould. (H. V. S. Nisbet, 'Diaries and memories of the Great War', Imperial War Museum, 78/3/1)

*Extract (b)*
Why did I join the army in 1914? How many give a concise honest answer to that question twenty years afterwards, and say that they enlisted for any one reason. Probably a glance through their old letters sent home at that time may give an impression of patriotic fervour, but was it fervour or fever?

On the day when England declared war on Germany, we (the family) had gone to Lancaster from Morecambe and saw the Territorials mobilised there. I remember marching alongside them, stirred like most of the onlookers by the noise of the bugles, and the electric atmosphere of that August day. Possibly I got bit with the fever germ then. Our folks always said so, and although I knew there were strong reasons why I should not leave business, I was pretty restless for the next few weeks.

During this time I was subjected to a continual bombardment of skilled propaganda from the War Office, newspapers, friends who had joined up, recruiting meetings, and even pulpits. The occupants of the latter would have served their cause much better by remaining silent. The accusing finger of Kitchener stabbed me at every bill-posting, and tales of German atrocities and stricken Belgium dinned into my ears daily. I suppose it was a combination of these many urgings which sent me to the local drill hall on November 15th. My age then was seventeen and a half. My parents made no objection to my going, beyond advising me to wait till I was old enough. I forget how I got over the age difficulty on enlisting, and presume I must have appeared big enough. (Papers of F. L. Goldthorpe, c.1934, Imperial War Museum, P113)

The following six extracts, (c) to (h), are taken from letters to the producers of the BBC television series *The Great War*. They were written in July 1963 in response to a request for help and information in the preparation of the series. The correspondence is now in the Imperial War Museum, IWM BBC/GW.

*Extract (c)*
I was born on March 5th 1896 leaving school at age 14. I had a very happy school life but my family were very poor. So my only prospects on leaving school was to find work as soon as possible. I did, starting at a flour factory where they made assorted cake mixtures, bun flour etc.

Working hours 6 a.m. until 6 p.m. Saturdays 6 a.m. until 2 p.m. half hour for breakfast break and one hour for dinner.

The factory being within walking distance I had my meals at home. If I wanted to go footballing, it was direct from work.

I stayed there until after breakfast on the morning of September 7th 1914. Incidentally my wages [were] about twelve shillings per week. Returning to work on said morning I met a neighbour's son and we decided to enlist which we did at Camberwell [in south-east London] Town Hall. We joined the 6th Battalion Dorset Regiment and the same morning marched away with a few hundred others . . . along with us marched wives, mothers and girl friends, not many fathers. They were working or serving. (James H. Ellis)

*Extract (d)*
With some of my pals I volunteered when eighteen years old, to join . . . our local infantry Regiment in Birkenhead, 4th Battalion the Cheshire Regiment.

The declaration of war, on 4.8.1914 seemed to us to be the only effective course to protect the trade interests of the nation and counteracting the unemployment caused by the dumping of cheap German manufactured goods. (G. W. Evans)

*Extract (e)*
It was Saturday 1st August 1914. I, along with some friends had returned to Aberdeen after a cycling holiday, to be greeted by newsboy shouts of 'Great European War Clouds. War imminent'.

Of course, we had previously heard of the assassination of Crown Prince Ferdinand in Bosnia, but never, for a moment, dreamt that this foul deed was the go-ahead signal for the greatest and most bloody war of all times . . .

There was little excitement among the general public during the first days of the war. It took some time for the gravity of the situation to sink in. The recruiting authorities, however, became increasingly active, so that within a month of the declaration of war every youth in the country was made aware of his importance as a serviceable unit for the cause of King and Country. Thus on the 4th of September 1914 I, along with my chum, joined the 2nd Highland Field Co. Royal Engineers at Aberdeen . . .

I had no real patriotic ideals, but I liked the life, the open air and the exercise, in contrast to the hum-drum, closed in atmosphere of the factory, besides, the prospect of adventure was alluring. (William M. Fraser)

*Extract (f)*

On the 19th September about a dozen clerks downed pens and walked out of a large City business firm to enlist in a City of London Regt. in Farringdon Road. This movement was very much resented by the office manager who could foresee nothing but chaos that would follow by such a depletion of his staff. Incidentally this action was immediately followed by quite a number of warehousemen. (Bertram C. Glover)

*Extract (g)*

I joined the Army as a volunteer in Kitchener's Army at the age of nineteen and eleven months – after having fought hard against the stubbornness of a government department to let six of their staff – (Welshmen from Cardiff) – to join to 'fight for freedom'. This was not a sentimental whim; we were genuinely moved by the raping of Belgium by the Hun. The big menacing finger of Kitchener from our hoardings had not yet been devised. It is possible his finger did later move those who could not make up their minds.

After three weeks of wrangling with the government department, which should in all conscience have been the first to allow their men to join, we were given permission. Certain regiments, such as the Welsh regiments, were not yet open for recruits. Queues outside recruiting offices in the city were tediously lengthy and men were in a hurry. And as we could not wait we decided to go to Penarth (in 1914 a small seaside town 5 miles from Cardiff), the home of one of the six, and who, because of his seniority and wisdom (he was 29) also became our spokesman. He was also a fluent English speaker.

I wore pince-nez: this worried the other five who were anxious we should keep together. On the train journey from Cardiff to Penarth (there were no buses then) they advised me to take off my pince-nez to get accustomed to the air and the general atmosphere. All the way they became my mentors by asking me how many cows and how many sheep I could see in the surrounding fields (since built over).

And we strode into the recruiting office, having put away my glasses. We were received by two stern sergeants in a tiny, untidy office on the first floor of a building no longer identifiable. We had already decided we should like to join the 21st Lancers. It sounded grandiloquent and presented to us a picture of well-upholstered recruits in the resplendent uniform of a Lancer charging, in due course, like the German Uhlans of whom we had read and cursed for their inhumanity. (W. R. Owen)

*Extract (h)*

On the 5th August 1914, when I was a raw lad of 18, times were hard in my home town of Bradford, and I, in common with many others, was working only three days a week and having three days dole money.

Idling the time away one day, my friends and I were discussing the dreariness of unemployment when someone suggested we should enlist and the Hussars was mentioned. This sounded to me like a glorious adventure . . . (Thomas E. Peers)

*Extract (i)*
I returned to my old farm at Akenfield for 11s. a week, but I was unsettled. When the farmer stopped my pay because it was raining and we couldn't thrash, I said to my seventeen-year-old mate, 'Bugger him. We'll go and join the army'. (Leonard Thompson to Ronald Blythe, quoted in Peter Vansittart (ed.) *Voices from the Great War*, 1981) ∎

**Specimen answers**    1    These extracts give a variety of reasons for volunteering: patriotism is there, but so too is the desire for adventure, and the belief that the army offered an escape from unemployment or a humdrum existence. I think it is also significant to note how young men often appear to have goaded each other on; they enlisted as groups of friends intending to share the adventure together. There also appears to have been an element of pressure from newspapers, pulpits, and then from displays on hoardings, especially that showing the famous Alfred Leese poster of Field-Marshal Lord Kitchener urging young men to join the army.

2    The extracts qualify the popular image of why men enlisted; the motives of the volunteers were complex and cannot be explained away simply with the label jingoistic. It is also interesting to note the reluctance of employers to let their men go; this reluctance is understandable, but not something which immediately springs to mind given the popular image of the beginning of the war.

**Discussion**    Of course I have only given you a few brief extracts here, and there were thousands of volunteers. Moreover these extracts are, in the main, taken from men looking back from a distance of fifty years. Recollections, of course, have to be treated with the same kinds of rigour as any other evidence. But what is interesting about the British volunteers of 1914, and about the soldiers of the other powers, was an innocence about modern industrial warfare. War, and the threat of war, were still largely accepted as extensions of diplomacy and war in the popular imagination was still colourful and heroic; W. E. Henley's *Lyra Heroica*, a popular anthology of verse for boys first published in 1892, was designed, for example, 'To set forth, as only art can, the beauty and joy of living, the beauty and blessedness of death, the glory of battle and adventure, the nobility of devotion – to a cause, an ideal, a passion even – the dignity of resistance, the sacred quality of patriotism . . .' (quoted in Peter Parker, *The Old Lie*, 1987, p.139). This attitude to war was not something purely English or British. Ernst Jünger enlisted in the Hanoverian Fusiliers at the end of 1914 aged only nineteen; he went on to win the Iron Cross, First Class and the Pour le Mérite, and to become a lieutenant of the crack stormtroopers. In his autobiography of the war years he recalled:

We had left the lecture-room, class-room, and bench behind us . . . We had grown up in a material age, and in each one of us there was the yearning for great experience, such as we had never known. We had set out in a rain of flowers to seek the death of heroes. The war was our dream of greatness, power and glory. It was a man's work, a duel in the fields whose flowers would be stained with blood. There is no lovelier death in the world . . . anything rather than stay at home . . . (Ernst Jünger, *The Storm of Steel*, 1929)

For Jünger the glamour of war lingered, but for others – probably for the majority – the trenches were to be a rude awakening. The horror of the war from the soldier's point of view paradoxically may have contributed to an overemphasis on the patriotic eagerness and enthusiasm of July and August 1914. It also contributed to the more sombre reactions which greeted the outbreak of war in 1939, and again perhaps, this has distorted the sentiments and attitudes present at the beginning of World War I. □

**Exercise** Turn now to *Documents 1* and read documents I.1, I.2 and I.3. To what extent does the content of these documents also call into question the universality of an eagerness for war in 1914? ∎

**Specimen answer** The documents show that at least two groups were either lukewarm or downright hostile to the war: socialists and some British intellectuals who were reluctant to see their country going to war against 'civilized' Germany and on the side of the Slavs.

**Discussion** In the decade or so immediately before 1914 some socialists, as well as Liberals like Norman Angell, had continually preached against war; a few socialists had even adopted it as policy that a declaration of war would be taken as a signal for a general strike, the herald of socialist revolution. European governments' fears of the socialists, and of the effects of socialist and of anti-war propaganda were probably greater than the reality. At the same time it suited many of these governments to play up the extent of the perceived 'threat' to their own advantage. □

In 1914 the largest party in the German *Reichstag* was the *Sozialdemokratische Partei Deutschlands* (SPD). An avowedly Marxist party, it had, in the elections of 1912, secured 4.25 million votes, or 34.7 per cent of the total. The party's newspaper *Vorwärts* was critical of 'the frivolous provocation' of the Austro-Hungarian ultimatum to Serbia, and it urged the government of the Reich to avoid 'war-like interference'. The SPD executive directed party members to demonstrate for peace and against Austria-Hungary; in consequence there were violent clashes between the police and demonstrators. Wilhelm II contemplated arresting the SPD leadership while some of his generals contemplated more extreme measures. However, the party's leadership was not as radical as its rhetoric, and as the diplomatic crisis deepened the SPD leaders assured the Reich government that they were loyal Germans with no plans for a general strike, for sabotage or any similar action in the event of war. On 4 August 1914 the SPD deputies voted unanimously for war credits and the *Burgfriede* (a domestic political truce). This unanimity marked a division within the party since, at a caucus meeting on 3 August, fourteen members had stood out against such a vote and only sided with their seventy-eight colleagues because of the tradition of voting as a single body; the division became public, and serious, as the war continued.

French socialism was split among several factions; the largest party, the *Section Française de l'Internationale Ouvrière* (SFIO) was much smaller than the German SPD with about 90,000 members as opposed to a million. The founder and leader of the SFIO was Jean Jaurès. He was a former university teacher and a man of exceptional ability; a reformist rather than a revolutionary, a brilliant orator, and a passionate opponent of militarism. On 29 July Jaurès was in Brussels meeting with other leading European socialists; that evening he appeared to address a mass, open-air meeting with his arm around a German comrade. The meeting dispersed with crowds singing the 'Internationale' and carrying banners with the slogan *Guerre à la guerre* (War against war). Jaurès returned to Paris, only to be assassinated there on 31 July by a demented, ultra-French nationalist. In spite of

Jaurès's efforts, most notably in the SFIO newspaper *L'Humanité*, and those of others (*La Bataille Syndicaliste*, for example, the organ of the French trades unions was among those demanding that the declaration of war be met with a declaration of a revolutionary general strike), less than 2 per cent of the men called to the colours in 1914 failed to respond to the call. The French government had feared that as many as 13 per cent would fail to turn up and, as a result of the actual response, it felt able to dispense with the plans for the mass arrest of militants named on the notorious blacklist, the *Carnet B*. Following President Poincaré's declaration on 4 August of *l'union sacrée* (the sacred union of all Frenchmen for the duration of the war) socialist deputies supported the war budget; and on 26 August two of them entered the government.

The issues of nationalism and the internationalism of socialism will be taken up again in Unit 3, but I think it fair to conclude here that, while the different European governments found their call to arms met in 1914, and while many men went to war enthusiastically, there were others with considerable reservations. Given the sudden surge of the July crisis as far as the general mass of the European populations was concerned, together with the urgings, particularly from socialist parties, to oppose war up until the eleventh hour, and the personal family 'anguish' noted by Ferro, the emotions of the men going to war were far more mixed than the popular picture would imply.

# 2 THE ARMIES AND NAVIES OF THE GREAT POWERS

I want to turn now to look in some detail at the armed forces of the great powers in 1914. In particular I want to explore how far the armies of 1914 were microcosms of the states which they served, and how far they reflected social structures and internal problems.

**Exercise**  Study Table 2.4 on pages 80–1 and note down:

1  the major differences and similarities between the recruitment of the armies of the great powers;

2  the major sea power. ■

**Specimen answers**  1  All of the continental powers had conscript armies, though they did not necessarily call on every young man to serve in the regular army. After their period with the colours the men generally passed into a reserve and then into some form of militia. The exception was Britain, the only power with a volunteer regular army which was, in consequence, much smaller than the armies of the major continental states.

2  But if Britain's army was smaller, her navy was much larger. Even excluding the three dreadnoughts requisitioned at the outset of the war, Britain outnumbered her nearest rival in this class of shipping (Germany) by three to two. □

During the nineteenth century the British navy had been the largest in the world by a wide margin, and a successful naval lobby had convinced government after government of the need to maintain this superiority, not the least to ensure the

**Table 2.4**  Military strengths of the great powers in 1914

| State | Population (in millions) (c.1910) | Armies | | | Navies | | |
|---|---|---|---|---|---|---|---|
| | | Peacetime | Mobilization | Recruitment | Dreadnoughts | Battle cruisers | Pre-dreadnoughts |
| Austria-Hungary | 51.4 | 450,000 | 3,000,000 | 2 year conscripts divided between (a) the 'Joint Army' (which took the bulk of the conscripts); and (b) the Austrian *Landwehr* and the Hungarian *Honvéd* which divided the remainder between them for a total of 20 weeks training. Men remained reservists until aged 32, and then passed into the *Landsturm* (militia) until aged 42. | 3 | 12 | 3 |
| France | 41.5 | 736,000 | 3,500,000 | 3 year conscripts (raised from 2 year conscripts in 1913). Followed by period as reservist, up to the age of 33. There were also territorials recruited from men aged 34–47. | 14 | — | 9 |
| Great Britain | 42.1 | 234,000 | 380,000 (plus 313,000 men of the Territorial Army). | 7 year volunteers. Followed by 5 years as reservist. Also a volunteer Territorial Army. | 24 (includes 1 built for Chile and 2 for Turkey requisitioned in August and September 1914) | 10 | 33 |

*Table 2.4*  Military strengths of the great powers in 1914

| State | Armies | | | | Navies | | |
| | Population (in millions) (c.1910) | Peacetime | Mobilization | Recruitment | Dreadnoughts | Battle cruisers | Pre-dreadnoughts |
|---|---|---|---|---|---|---|---|
| Germany | 58.5 | 856,000 | 3 year enrolment (with a maximum emergency strength of 8,500,000 involving the mobilization of the *Ersatz* Reserve and *Landwehr*). | 13 in *Landsturm* Class I at the age of 17, of which (a) about half served 2 years in regular army then going into the reserve for 5 years (the periods of service were respectively 3 years and 4 years if the conscript joined the cavalry or artillery); and (b) the remainder were enrolled in the *Ersatz* reserve for very limited training. All men served in the *Landwehr* (militia) from age 27 to 39, then in the *Landsturm* Class II from 39–45. | 6 | 30 | — |
| Italy | 36.2 | 306,300 | 700,000 | 2 year conscripts followed by 4 years in the mobile militia. | 1 | — | 17 |
| Russia | 153.8 | 1,423,000 | 4,423,000 (with an additional 3,500,000). | 3 year conscripts drawn from about half of the men aged 20. Followed by 15 years in the reserves and then 5 years in the territorials. | 3 | 1 | 7 |

safety of British trade and of the empire in India. Towards the end of the century, as British naval dominance was eroded (see Table 2.5), the Admiralty was concerned to be able to take on the combined fleets of France and Russia. However, by the beginning of the twentieth century British attention was switching to the fast-growing German navy.

**Table 2.5**    *Battleships of the great powers 1883 and 1897*[1]

| State | 1883 | 1897 (plus those being built) |
|---|---|---|
| Britain | 38 | 62 |
| France | 19 | 36 |
| Germany | 11 | 12 |
| Russia | 3 | 18 |
| Italy | 7 | 12 |
| USA | 0 | 11 |
| Japan | 0 | 7 |

[1] 'The figures come from *"Die Seeinteressen des Deutschen Reiches"*, a memorandum laid before the *Reichstag* on 30 December 1897 in an effort to convince the deputies that the German navy needed to be increased. Although it was simply stated that these totals were all of battleships over 5,000 tons, the Imperial Navy Office had a habit of allotting to Britain's number many vessels which the Admiralty in London held to be unseaworthy. According to *Brassey's Naval Annual* (1898), eighteen of these British ships would be third-class battleships, and the battleship totals for her rivals were considerably higher' (Paul M. Kennedy, *The Rise and Fall of British Naval Mastery*, 1983, p.368; figure on p.209).

Admiral Alfred von Tirpitz, the State Secretary of the Reich Navy Office from 1897, had proposed a massive expansion of the German navy since he believed:

1   that without a global foreign policy Germany would slip into being a second-rate power – only a navy could guarantee the success of such a foreign policy;

2   that a glamorous naval programme could advance social integration by mobilizing patriotic sentiment behind the conservative, autocratic monarchy; and,

3   that the naval programme could be used to assert the rights of the crown over the elected *Reichstag* – here he planned to follow a policy already successfully pursued with regard to the army. The size of the peacetime army was fixed at 1 per cent of the population and the *Reichstag* could only review the budgetary demands of the army every five years; moreover the Kaiser was free to use the army externally and internally as he wished. Tirpitz's plan was for a fixed number of warships and for their automatic replacement after a certain period; the *Reichstag* was to have limited financial supervision as with the army. Two navy bills were introduced in 1898 and 1900 with these ends in view.

Tirpitz's plans had obvious attractions for the Kaiser and his entourage; the prospect of steady navy contracts was equally attractive to the big industrialists who owned iron, steel and munition works. But Tirpitz's naval plan also drew on, and fed back into, contemporary theories of naval power. In 1890 Alfred T. Mahan, an American naval officer, published *The Influence of Sea Power upon History*, which asserted that sea power was vital to national growth, to national prosperity and security. The book was both successful and influential. In it, and its immediate successors, Mahan concentrated on the period from the mid-seventeenth to the early nineteenth centuries, during which British sea power had reached its zenith. But Mahan doubted whether Britain could maintain her supremacy: 'whether a democratic government will have the foresight, the keen sensitiveness to national position and credit, the willingness to insure its prosperity by adequate outpouring of money in times of peace, all of which are necessary for military preparation, is yet an open question' (quoted by M. T. Sprout, 'Mahan: evangelist of sea power', 1971, p.422).

Tirpitz and the German Naval Command may have been encouraged by such conclusions, but they also embarked upon some complex calculations regarding the British and German fleets. It was accepted thinking among naval strategists then, that in an all out battle, a navy *on the defensive* only two-thirds the size of an *attacking* opponent had a chance of victory. Tirpitz reckoned that if he could build three ships a year for twenty years, after which date he planned to have ships replaced automatically, then Britain would need to build and/or replace ninety ships over the same period, not to mention the large number of ships that had to protect Britain's enormous overseas interests in addition to facing the German fleet. Tirpitz and his staff calculated that Britain probably could just manage such a building programme but, given that the Royal Navy, like the British army, was recruited entirely from volunteers in contrast to the German navy which could call on conscripts, then manning this fleet would create a major problem. None of this proves that Tirpitz and other elements of the German High Command were planning a war against Britain – remember that naval strategy suggested that the smaller force stood a chance of victory when it was on the defensive. The new German navy was not necessarily being designed to attack the British fleet, merely to challenge its supremacy. What completely upset Tirpitz's calculations was the launching of HMS *Dreadnought* in October 1906; this warship was qualitatively superior to everything else afloat in terms of firepower, speed and strength. When the German government agreed to follow suit with their own dreadnought programme the naval race became qualitative as well as quantitative, and infinitely more dangerous and expensive.

If Britain set the pace as Europe's greatest naval power, Germany provided the model for continental armies. Debates over mass armies, conscription and citizen soldiers went back into the eighteenth century. During the 1790s the French governments had introduced conscription to preserve the Revolution; the idea of the nation in arms initially had democratic associations, but it was taken over and developed to new levels of efficiency by Napoleon Bonaparte. Conscript armies had increasingly become the norm in nineteenth-century continental Europe, and the democratic notion of a nation of citizen soldiers took second place to the incipient militarism of many of Europe's rulers. With some justification autocratic rulers did not believe that they could rely on patriotism to discipline their armies; for one thing not every monarch ruled a state which was nationally homogeneous, and while the heady inspiration of 'liberty, equality and fraternity' may once have encouraged citizen soldiers to fight, these were not political notions which many of Europe's monarchs wished too much to encourage. A ten-year struggle was waged in Prussia from 1857 to 1867 between the king, Wilhelm I, who wanted what he understood as a professional, albeit conscript, army directly under his control, and the liberals, who feared that the result of the king's aspirations would be a militarized society rather than a nationalized, civilian army. The king won, and his army went on to trounce the French, convincing the major rulers of continental Europe that the way to military victory was through a system of universal service in a regular standing army rather than in citizen militias. A few, particularly on the Left, kept the democratic idea of the 'nation in arms' alive in the years immediately before 1914. Notable among these was Jaurès who, in 1911, published *L'armée nouvelle*. Jaurès proposed an army of just 4,000 professionals with all other men compelled to serve for just six months, followed by training periods in the reserve. The professionals were to be recruited from the sons of the working class and trained in universities rather than in élitist military academies. The latter proposal reflected another concern of the Left about professional soldiers: they appeared as reactionaries who destroyed republics and revolutions and who repressed workers.

The subject of conscript armies also generated other debates about the relationship between the military and society, particularly in the event of war. The elder Helmuth von Moltke, chief of the Prussian General Staff between 1857 and 1888, believed that bringing educated men into the army as conscripts, or as reservists in time of war, would be one way of moderating the violence of war. The short period of conscription, with a subsequent period in the reserves, was proclaimed as common sense by its supporters since it appeared to provide ample men in the event of war, but it also meant that the developing economies of the European states would be largely unimpeded in peacetime by military necessity. The idea that wars would be short was subsumed in this; few people pondered on what might happen to a state's economy if a war was long, and one man who did, a Polish banker, J. G. Bloch, who published a six-volume military treatise in 1898, concluded that this prospect coalesced with other problems to make war impossible:

> . . . universal military service for short periods presents conditions in which lie concealed the germs of the impossibility of war itself. This impossibility lies mainly in the difficulty of providing for immense masses, as a consequence of the diminution in productiveness, the possibility of economic crises, and popular commotions, and, finally, in the extreme difficulty of directing armies consisting of millions of men. (Quoted by Hew Strachan, *European Armies and the Conduct of War*, 1983, p.110)

The requirement that all young men present themselves for military service led some individuals to focus on what was happening to the 'national stock': were the young men of a nation physically fit and able to serve as soldiers? In France these concerns were linked with worry about the country's static population. (See table 1 in Roberts, Appendix, p.581, for comparative population rates between the states of Europe.) One reason for increasing the period of conscription from two to three years in 1913 was because the pool of young Frenchmen available for the army was declining in comparison with the pool available to the German army; thus the only way for the French to field an army capable of matching that of the Germans was to increase the period of service. We will return to questions of national fitness in Unit 3.

Of course conscript armies were not commanded by conscripts. Officers were generally recruited from the middle and upper classes, usually they were professionals, but their training and prestige varied greatly. The German officer corps provided a model: it was the best trained; it had an arrogant, aristocratic ethos – even the officers of the autonomous Bavarian army increasingly assumed 'Prussian' officer characteristics. The proportion of aristocrats in the German officer corps had actually fallen in the years before 1914, from 65 per cent in 1860 to a mere 30 per cent. Exclusive cavalry and guards regiments remained the preserve of aristocrats notably, in the Prussian regiments, of the Junkers – the noble landowners of East Prussia. Furthermore, the General Staff was gradually becoming more aristocratic. Two-fifths of the Russian officer corps up to, and including the rank of colonel, originated in the peasantry or in the lower middle class. As in Germany, the élite regiments and the most senior ranks of the army were utterly dominated by the nobility; but unlike Germany, training and ability for these senior ranks were scarcely considered. The Austro-Hungarian officer corps lay between these two extremes. It was drawn from a wide range of social backgrounds, from the minor nobility to the lower middle class. Two-thirds of the officers originated from the German half of the empire (generally known as Cisleithania), the others from the Hungarian (Transleithania), but neither Cisleithania nor Transleithania were themselves nationally homogeneous. Each half of the empire contained a variety of ethnic groups (see map 2 in the *Maps Booklet*). The officers were discouraged from excessive loyalty to their own national groups and were encouraged to learn the languages of the men under their command. The British officer corps was rooted in the landed aristocracy, though this aristocracy was a relatively fluid group by the end of the nineteenth century, with old established families losing their fortunes or simply vacating estates to be replaced by those who had made money in commerce, in industry, or by speculating in land. It was rare for men to be promoted from the ranks and as late as 1910 members of the Army Council were declaring, categorically, that the ranks preferred to be led by their social superiors and that they disliked those who showed ambition above their station. Elite regiments of cavalry and guards remained the preserve of those from the wealthier families of some pedigree. In France the radicals and the Left labelled the officer corps as aristocratic, staunchly Catholic and supporters of the monarchy (France having been a republic since 1870–71). Such conservative elements did appear dominant during the Dreyfus affair which spluttered on from 1894 to 1906, but a closer analysis reveals that French officers were mainly drawn from the middle classes and that their attitude to politics was essentially neutral. Military reforms introduced in the wake of the Dreyfus affair led to a decline in the number of able men offering themselves. The prestige of the officer corps was deliberately undermined by the government to ensure that it did not become a caste apart. Changes in the military schools designed to democratize the officer corps tended rather to lower the standard of entrants. Low pay and slow promotion exacerbated the problem.

During the Dreyfus affair the political Right in France had equated attacks on the army's honour with attacks on the nation itself. When the facts of the affair came out in detail the prestige of the officer corps was seriously undermined; a reactionary officer corps had, it seemed, been more intent on covering up for itself than in assessing the evidence against Dreyfus fairly. By contrast in Germany, and especially in Prussia, the army officer remained a man of unrivalled prestige. The amazing escapade of Wilhelm Voigt, 'the Captain of Köpenich', demonstrated the power of the Prussian officer's uniform. Voigt was a Berlin shoemaker who, in October 1906, dressed himself as an army captain, recruited a squad of soldiers and policemen (who had never seen him before) and travelled to the small town of Köpenich just outside Berlin. In Köpenich 'the Captain' demanded, and got, money from the town hall, arrested the local mayor, and sent him under guard to Berlin. Voigt himself was arrested and imprisoned; on his release, as something of an international celebrity, he toured Europe in his captain's uniform.

Few of the other stories were as humorous. Above all the Zabern affair of 1913 demonstrated the determination of the Reich's government to uphold the honour of the army. A lieutenant stationed at Zabern in Alsace referred, abusively, to Alsatians as *wackes*. The remark, reported in the local newspaper, caused indignation and this was exacerbated by the local commanding officer's refusal to give an apology. When the offending lieutenant was jeered at in the street, the local army commander appears to have lost his grip on reality and assumed that revolt was imminent. The army threatened the local authorities with the imposition of a state of siege; the local newspaper's offices were searched, quite illegally, on army orders; some soldiers and about thirty civilians were arrested – the former accused of giving information to the press, the latter charged with ridiculing the military. The climax came when the commanding officer ordered his men to clear a square at bayonet point even though no demonstration was occurring. The civilian authorities protested, but Wilhelm II backed his army. Admittedly the offending commander at Zabern was given a new posting but this was not made public; what was made public, however, was the Kaiser's subsequent instruction making the army responsible for law and order in Zabern. The chancellor, Theobald von Bethmann Hollweg, was concerned about the direction which events had taken; nevertheless he regarded it as his duty to defend the army in the *Reichstag*. Deputies from the Centre united with the Left and passed a motion of no confidence in Bethmann Hollweg, demanding his resignation; but such was the constitutional structure of Wilhelmine Germany that the Kaiser and his government could, and did, ignore it.

Non-commissioned officers (NCOs) throughout Europe were drawn from the same social classes as the conscripts of the respective armies. In some armies the NCOs were largely professional, long-service soldiers, who had re-enlisted after their period of conscription; such was the case in the German army. In France, however, many of the best men who wanted to make the army a career sought promotion to commissioned ranks. In consequence there was a shortage of able sergeants and corporals; conscripts had to be appointed to these ranks, but these did not re-enlist in significant numbers after their period of compulsory service. The lack of experienced and dedicated NCOs weakened discipline in the ranks, and discipline was especially poor among the reservists when they were recalled for training. Indicative of this weakness were two large, but isolated, mutinies in the south of France during 1907, when troops were called out to police trouble provoked by a crisis in viticulture. A contributing element to the mutinies was the fact that conscripts (and reservists when recalled for training) generally served in their region of origin. Men of the 17th Infantry Regiment who mutinied in June 1907 were concerned that they were to be moved from their native south to the Alps or the Vosges; when they resolved to march home to Béziers (Hérault) they spoke of going to defend their families. The pull of their *pays natal* (literally the 'country of their birth') remained strong with French peasants, particularly those from the south and the west; but it is also true that a series of elements was acting as solvents to this regionalism, and military service in the French army could itself be one such solvent.

**Exercise**   Given the issues raised in the preceding pages, what would seem to have been the principal tasks of these armies before the European war of 1914? ∎

**Specimen answer**     I would list four things here:

1   preparation and planning for war;

2   imperial defence and/or conquest;

3   internal order;

4   education.

**Discussion**     I hope that you noted (1), (2) and (3). Congratulations if you suggested (4) as well since this is not, I think, so apparent, but remember my comment that the French army was seen as something of a 'solvent' for regionalism. I want now to explore each of these tasks in turn. □

Of course all armies can be expected to prepare for the next war; however, there is some justification for arguing that the military preparations for mobilization and war in 1914 actually contributed to the events. Moving troops to the potential fronts on mobilization required an efficient use of railway networks; the plans of the German generals allowed for no pauses or reassessments because of changed diplomatic circumstances once mobilization and the movement of men had begun. Also, the German Schlieffen plan required that France be knocked out of the war before Russia, her ally; the attack on France was planned to go through Belgium and, while Britain and France had only an understanding (the *Entente*) rather than a formal alliance, Britain did have treaty obligations to Belgium. Russian mobilization was far more lumbering than that of Germany, but like that of Germany, it was rigid. Russian generals had only planned to mobilize against *both* Austria-Hungary and Germany; when it was suggested that they mobilize partially against Austria-Hungary alone there was consternation and doubt as to whether this was possible. The generals on all sides might be blamed for this, but then military plans as the generals understood and intended to operate them (and after all military plans are conceived by and for generals) were concerned with military rather than diplomatic considerations. Admittedly the series of alliances in existence in 1914 suggested that war against one opponent would mean, in the event, war against that opponent's allies too, but the problem was that the General Staffs of several European states were under no restraint from, and had little or no regard for, civilian politicians.

The German General Staff was the most efficient and practised in 1914. It was divided into three sections: movement, railway and supply, and intelligence. Staff officers sharpened their skills with war games and exercises; they were given wide discretionary powers when acting with troops in the field – they knew the intention of headquarters and were expected to use their initiative to achieve this intention according to changing situations on the ground. Since 1866 the Chief of the General Staff had authority to communicate directly with his commanders without having to go through the war ministry; since 1883 he had direct access to the Kaiser. Boosted by the successful campaigns of the 1860s and 1870–71 the German General Staff was able to develop largely free from civilian political supervision and, consequently, without any real need to consider political or diplomatic constraints. Austria-Hungary began to follow the German model in the 1870s and it was during the following decade that General von Beck, the Chief of the General Staff, secured his independence from the minister of war. The shock of their showing in the war against Japan led to a reorganization of the Russian General Staff in 1905–06. Significantly, a German was appointed to head it, and Tsar Nicholas was happy to see a direct link established between himself and his army since this bypassed the war ministry which was answerable to the *Duma*.

Politically Britain and France were very different from the three empires to the east of Europe. The political structures of these two countries militated against General Staffs with direct links to the chief of the state and largely independent of civilian politicians. In Britain, for a variety of reasons, no General Staff was established until 1906, and then there was a determination to keep it under ministerial control. However, since Germany was increasingly perceived as the enemy, the British General Staff did begin planning for joint deployment with its French equivalent in 1910. As noted above, the politicians of the Third Republic were determined to keep the military under civilian control after the Dreyfus affair. Promotions and postings became more dependent on political influence than on military ability. The overall decline in military prestige, together with the lowering of the quality of officer recruits, tended to produce officers who took refuge in the red-tape of military administration rather than men who thought about what tactical developments might be necessary in the wake of new technology and the example of recent conflicts. The French General Staff has been much criticized for pursuing naive and simplistic tactics at the beginning of the war – the offensive at all costs. In reality the reliance on attack and *élan* in the notorious Plan XVII seems to have been less the result of considered military thinking and more the result of the problems which beset the army. The mass armies of the French Revolution appeared to have been successful because of attack and *élan*, and this made such tactics popular with the politicians; a weak high command, whose personnel owed much to political connections, was not inclined to challenge these ideas, and nor were any ambitious young officers appointed to the General Staff.

Most of the men who had seen action in the major armies of 1914 had done so in colonial conflicts. French troops had campaigned in Africa, Madagascar and Indo-China. Italian troops had been involved in the conquest of Tripolitania in 1912, and were still engaged in 'pacifications'. British troops had fought in South Africa and some had participated in policing actions on the north-west frontier of India or in other parts of the empire. Russia's disastrous war with Japan had been fought over disputed territory and influence in Manchuria and Korea. Men who wanted action and glory volunteered for colonial service. French colonial officers offer a particularly interesting case. For a variety of reasons they enjoyed much greater independence from local colonial administrators than the officer corps at home had from the politicians. During the decade before 1914 several of the campaign-hardened officers of the colonial armies who had held and extended France's overseas empire began to see themselves as saviours of the motherland. They urged the deployment of the colonial army in France; its experience and undisputed courage would, they argued, add fibre to the army at home with its officers obsessed with red-tape and its poorly trained, poorly disciplined conscripts and reservists. Some went further and suggested large-scale recruitment in the empire; notable among these was Colonel Charles Mangin who published *La force noire* in 1910. But the government in Paris was wary; there were fears that conscription in the colonies might provoke insurrection, while concessions to the indigenous populations which sweetened conscription could provoke white colonists. Furthermore the General Staff cast doubts on the capability and dependability of black or yellow troops.

Britain had a vast empire on which she could, and did, call for military support. Australian infantry and artillery had voyaged to Egypt in 1885 to fight alongside

British troops, and the White Dominions all sent troops to assist in the 'imperial' effort against the Boers. Although in 1914 it was not considered as available for service in a European war, the British Indian Army had 164,000 trained black troops.

Some Russian troops had seen action in suppressing revolution at home in 1905–06. This was the most dramatic incidence of internal disorder affecting the great powers in the decade before 1914, but the use of troops to maintain internal order and to support police forces became commonplace. Coal, dock and rail strikes led to the deployment of thousands of troops in Britain in 1910 and 1911. The movement of troops during the 1911 rail strike brought ferocious criticism particularly because the government did not, as was customary (and some would say as was legal under Common Law), wait for requests for military assistance from local magistrates. Moreover, a joint Home Office/War Office body was set up to supervise matters, dominated by senior army officers, and the troubled districts were divided into seven strike areas each one run by a senior officer who reported directly to the War Office. Four people were shot dead by troops – two in Liverpool, two in Llanelli. Yet disorder in Britain paled into insignificance beside some of the continental troubles. In June 1914, for example, Italy seemed to contemporaries to be on the brink of revolution as a General Strike called simultaneously by the Socialists, Syndicalists and Republicans developed into 'the Red Week', and tens of thousands of soldiers and paramilitary police were deployed to suppress it.

Such military deployment was not always because of industrial action by workers or the threat of revolution. Following legislation in 1905 which separated church and state in France, troops often found themselves required to break into churches so that government inspectors might make inventories of church property. Some officers had sudden, diplomatic illnesses when receiving such orders, a few simply refused to obey and, when courts martial refused to convict them, the minister of war had to discipline them. The soldiers' distaste for these anti-clerical policing tasks was, very often, less a result of staunch Catholicism and more the result of dislike and embarrassment at having to chase women and children from church premises.

Some British army officers were concerned about being ordered into a policing action against the Protestant Ulstermen who opposed the Irish Home Rule Bill. In March 1914 fifty-eight officers of the 3rd cavalry brigade stationed at the Curragh informed the commander-in-chief that they would 'prefer to accept dismissal if ordered north'. Whatever contemporary socialists may have thought, it is clear that in Britain and France at least many army officers intensely disliked having to police strikes, and it was not unknown for some to have sympathy with the strikers.

In contrast few, if any, German officers appear to have voiced regrets about their role in the maintenance of internal order. Some toyed with the idea of *Staatsstreich*, by which the repressive power available to the crown would be used to forestall any real or imagined threat from the SPD; universal suffrage and the few trappings of parliamentary constitutionalism would be dismantled and an older form of autocratic government re-established. The drawback was that *Staatsstreich* would almost certainly be followed by civil war and, while the military would probably win, there was no guarantee that the regime would actually be strengthened. Nevertheless the idea was dusted down periodically, and not only by the generals. In 1913, for example, Bethmann Hollweg expressed concern that the Kaiser was continually talking about abolishing or at least chastising the *Reichstag* and using one of his adjutant generals for the task.

German generals were suspicious of SPD conscripts. During the 1890s there had been official attempts to exclude them and those who did become soldiers and maintained loyalty to their party were persecuted. This official policy was given up at the turn of the century. However it appears that the army continued to exclude socialists. The figures from the recruitment bureaux are not particularly helpful, but correspondence and statements by senior officers and members of the war ministry suggest that many SPD men were rejected on the grounds of being physically unfit for service. Proposals to expand the army in 1913 brought concerns about socialist conscripts to the surface once again. It was far better, argued generals and conservatives both then and in earlier debates, to rely on simple, honest peasants for soldiers. In support of the argument it was asserted that rural dwellers were fitter and tougher than the youth which had been born and bred in urban squalor, and the organization of conservative landowners, the *Bund der Landwirte*, took the argument a stage further to demand state subsidies for agriculture: not only did they produce food for Germany, they also produced the best soldiers.

Yet however worried they were about the SPD, German generals also recognized that the period of conscription could be used to endeavour to educate young men into accepting the military's image of the nation and how it should be governed. Similar notions of the opportunity for instructing young men undergoing military service were to be found, in varying degrees, among the military and governing élites of the major powers of Europe; of course in Britain, with a volunteer army, the opportunity was strictly limited. In Russia, army service was seen as a way of educating the peasantry and improving literacy. In Austria-Hungary the army was the most obvious symbol of unity in an empire of many different ethnic groups. The two militias – the Austrian *Landwehr*, recruited in Cisleithania, and the Hungarian *Honvéd*, recruited in Transleithania – similarly provided foci of unity for the different ethnic groups who were enlisted. It had been policy to keep regiments from developing too close an association with recruiting districts, but by the twentieth century this had been relaxed to the extent that three-quarters of a regiment was usually stationed in its home district. Generally speaking the Austro-Hungarian army resisted the disintegrative effects of ethnicity, and the various nationalisms. In Italy there were problems stemming from the very recent unification of the country, the marked differences between the primitive south and the industrializing north, the variety of dialects and languages spoken. It was decreed that a regiment must always consist of men recruited from two regions and that it must be stationed in a third. The army was thus a way of making men aware of the new nation, of 'their nationality', and of introducing some of them to 'their language' – Italian. Though a nation state for centuries, France had experienced similar problems during the nineteenth century. A military report on Brittany dated October 1880 reported:

> The young Bretons who don't know how to read, write, or speak French when they get to their units are promptly civilized . . . lose the prejudices of their *pays*, abandon native suspicions and backward opinions; and when they return to the village, they are sufficiently Frenchified to Frenchify their friends by their influence. (Quoted by Eugen Weber, *Peasants into Frenchmen*, 1976, p.299)

By the 1890s it seems that the army was increasingly accepted by French peasants as 'ours' rather than 'theirs', but regionalism could still create problems as the mutinies of 1907 proved, and a few of the men mobilized in 1914 still used French as their second language.

Military service also educated conscripts in ways that were not deliberately intended by the authorities. Many peasant conscripts had their horizons considerably broadened by their period of military service. This was especially the case for those men drawn from the more remote and backward districts such as, for example, the south and west of France and the east of Prussia. The army provided some of these men with a degree of social mobility in that they could become NCOs and, in a few instances, even officers. Similarly, while many men may have resented their period of conscription, the peacetime military standards of accommodation, diet, dress, health and hygiene were well above those of some sections of the working class, both rural and urban. 'The army is good, it cannot be better. And the soup is good, it cannot be better,' goes one French conscript song (sung in Flemish):

> Everyday, meat and soup,
> Without working, without working.
> Everyday, meat and soup,
> Without working in the army.
> (Quoted in Weber, *Peasants into Frenchmen*, 1976, p.300)

Finally, if conscripts were required, as part of their civic duty, to serve 'their nation', there was a potential problem for any autocratic regime seeking to limit or reduce any representative elements in the constitution; conscripts might then be urged to ask what was 'theirs' about the nation state. Conscripting men into the armed forces had thus given the General Staffs the opportunity for fielding massive armies as well as for civilizing peasants and educating young men about their nation; but it might also produce some men who were dissatisfied with the lot offered them in civilian life, and some of this dissatisfaction could assume a political complexion.

## 3 *THE ARMIES IN THE BALKANS*

**Exercise**   Study Table 2.6 and answer the following questions.

1    What is noticeable about the Balkan armies compared with those of the great powers shown in Table 2.4 on pages 80–1?

2    Does anything strike you about the origins of the monarchs? ∎

**Specimen answers**   1    The most obvious difference is how much smaller the Balkan armies were than those of the great powers – understandable given their much smaller populations. However, if you compare these armies proportionately with their populations you will see that, Montenegro excepted, they drew on the same kind of percentage of the population as continental powers. Recruitment was by conscription, as with the continental great powers.

2    Two of the five monarchs in the Balkans on the outbreak of World War I were born German princes (Tsar Ferdinand of Bulgaria and King Charles of Romania); a

*Table 2.6*    *The Balkan states and their armies in 1914*

| State | Date of origin | Monarch | Population (in millions c.1910) | Peacetime | Armies war effectives | Recruitment |
|---|---|---|---|---|---|---|
| Bulgaria | Principality (1878) Independent kingdom (1908) | Ferdinand (of Saxe-Coburg Gotha) | 4.3 | 66,000 | 340,000 | Conscription for 2 years (3 years if in the cavalry) followed by 18 years in the reserve and then 6 years in the territorial reserve. Muslims were exempt. |
| Greece | Independent kingdom (1829–33) | Constantine (son of 'George I of the Hellenes' who had been born a Danish prince and christened William) | 2.8 | 29,000 | 120,000 | Conscription for 2 years followed by 21 years in the first reserve and then 8 years in the second reserve. |
| Montenegro | Independent state since the middle ages generally ruled by bishops until 1850s. Kingdom in 1911 | Nicholas I (nephew of Danilo who was responsible for secularizing the state during the 1850s) | 0.2 | — | — | Montenegro had a long tradition of mountain guerrilla warfare against the Turks. All men were required to serve for two periods of sixty days and then remained as reservists until the age of 62. |
| Romania | Principality (1878–79) Independent kingdom (1881) | Charles (of Hohenzollern-Sigmaringen; since Charles was childless Ferdinand of Hohenzollern had been named as his heir) | 7.2 | 99,000 | 250,000 | Some conscripts were required to serve 3 years in the regular army followed by 7 years in the reserves; the others had to serve periodically in semi-permanent regiments for 5 years followed by 5 years in the reserves. All were then required to do 6 years in the militia, then 10 years in the territorial reserve. |
| Serbia | Autonomous state (1830) Independent kingdom (1882) | Peter Karageorevic (son of the first ruler of the autonomous state) | 2.9 | 31,000 | 195,000 | Conscription for 2 years (reduced to 18 months in 1914) followed by 8 years in the reserve and then 10 years in the militia. |

third, King Constantine of Greece, was admittedly the son of a previous king of Greece – but this king had been born a prince of Denmark.

**Discussion**   The armies and the monarchs of the Balkans were both examples of the western and northern European structures imposed on the largely peasant peoples when independence from the Turkish Empire was achieved. There was often little in the way of nobility and gentry in these states, at least as the terms were understood elsewhere in Europe; there was even less of a middle class. □

**Exercise**   What do you suppose was the effect of this shortage of nobility, gentry and a middle class on the officer corps of the Balkans? ∎

**Specimen answer**   It was often difficult to find adequate officer recruits.

**Discussion**   In spite of these difficulties the Balkan officer corps looked to the larger continental powers for their organizational and behavioural models. Furthermore these officer corps often saw themselves as both modernizing influences and the spearhead of nationalism. Such attitudes led them to dabble in politics. The end of the Obrenovic regime with the assassination of King Alexander of Serbia together with his Queen, Draga, her brothers, the Serbian premier and minister of war, was organized by army officers, notably Colonel Dragutin Dimitrievic-Apis. In 1911 the Colonel founded a secret society, mainly among his fellow officers, called Union or Death (but commonly known as 'the Black Hand') which aimed at uniting the South Slavs. Dimitrievic became chief of intelligence on the Serbian General Staff in 1913, and in the spring of the following year he was suspected of organizing a new coup against the civilian government. He was also known to have had connections with the Bosnian terrorists who assassinated Franz Ferdinand at Sarajevo. Less conspiratorial and less violent, but by no means uninfluential, were the military leagues organized in Greece in 1909 and in Bulgaria in 1913 to pressurize their respective monarchs into following particular policies.

The Greek Military League drew some inspiration from the Young Turk movement. The latter was essentially a movement of army officers combining with liberal, civilian opposition to the Sultan. The officers were particularly worried about the gradual dismemberment of the Turkish Empire. In 1908 they began an uprising which had as its ultimate aims secularization, modernization and the creation of a centralized and efficient state. Increasingly in the years before the war the government of Turkey was taken over by a triumvirate of army officers and steps were taken towards the realization of these aims. In particular there were developments and improvements in municipal government and military organization: German expertise was enlisted to improve the Turkish army, British expertise to improve the navy. But problems and difficulties beset the Young Turk regime. Internally they were confronted by devout Muslims, who objected to what they regarded as alien Western ideals and models, as well as by the largely Christian Slavs still within the Turkish Empire who looked to the new Balkan kingdoms for aid. Externally the government in Constantinople found the fringes of the empire continually menaced by these kingdoms and others – some provinces were lost without bloodshed (such as the annexation of Bosnia-Herzegovina by Austria-Hungary in 1908), others were lost in war (such as Tripolitania seized by Italy in 1911, and those lands lost during the First Balkan War). □

# 4  SUMMING UP AND LOOKING AHEAD

This unit has concentrated on armies and attitudes to war, yet this is not a course about military history. Our interest and focus is the societies from which the soldiers and sailors came and in which these attitudes to war were held. More to the point, our interest is in what happened to these societies in both the short term and the long term as a result of participation in the total wars of the twentieth century.

**Exercise**   I noted earlier that in 1914 most people believed that the war would be short, and that few considered what impact a long war would have on the economy; however in the recollection of some of the British volunteers there were references to employers' concern about the loss of men to the army. Given the *month* that war did break out in 1914, can you think of an immediate economic problem for the societies which we are discussing? ■

**Specimen answer**   The obvious problem was getting in the harvest when a high proportion of the young men in the countryside were recalled to the colours as reservists. □

**Exercise**   How could this problem be resolved? ■

**Specimen answer**   By calling on the labour of those men too old to fight, of boys who were too young and on women.

**Discussion**   The schoolmaster of Lalley (Isère) in south-east France reported that in the late summer of 1914

> . . . the appearance of our village changed. Out of a population of less than 400 inhabitants, 53 men, the young, the strong, those who shouldered the weight of the work in the fields, had gone. A grim calm, a sense of the void descended. Haymaking had not yet been finished; the harvest beckoned imperiously, with a south wind drying the corn and turning the oats yellow. And so, people came to each other's aid. There were signs of remarkable dedication: young lads aged 15 to 20, young girls taking off their aprons and putting aside the needlework they had begun, resolutely took up their sickles and lent a hand to the women left alone with their young children. (Quoted by Jean-Jacques Becker, *The Great War and the French People*, 1985, pp.15–16)

The employment of women in jobs traditionally done by men was to become a feature of the societies engaged in World War I. The extent to which this acquisition of men's economic roles and tasks contributed to change in the economic, social and political role of women is an issue which was touched on in the introduction to the course, and which will be discussed subsequently with reference to both wars.

   The mutual assistance and dedication which struck the schoolmaster of Lalley was not something apparent to every commentator. The shortage of labour brought about by the war gave new economic muscle to those who remained at home, and within days of the outbreak of war there were complaints of French farm labourers demanding double or triple the usual daily wage. Similar complaints were received from industrial employers throughout Europe as the war wore on. Again the potential boost given to labour activists by wartime demands is an issue to be analysed at length in subsequent units. □

But the states of Europe were differently organized and differently ruled: responses and results could therefore be different. From this narrowly focused introduction you will probably already have noted differences in political and constitutional structures, hierarchical social structures and economies. You may also have noted implicit references to pressures for change working on these societies – industrialization, nationalism and socialism for example. The next units will move from the narrow military focus here to explore in detail the structures of the states which went to war in 1914 and the pressures within them for change.

## References

Becker, J.-J. (1985) *The Great War and the French People*, Berg.

Ferro, M. (1973) *The Great War 1914–1918*, Routledge and Kegan Paul.

Jünger, E. (1929) *The Storm of Steel (In Stahlgewittern)*, Chatto and Windus.

Kennedy, P. M. (1983) *The Rise and Fall of British Naval Mastery*, Macmillan (first published in 1976).

Parker, P. (1987) *The Old Lie: The Great War and the Public School Ethos*, Constable.

Sprout, M. T. (1971) 'Mahan: evangelist of sea power' in Earle, E. M. (ed.) *Makers of Modern Strategy*, Princeton University Press (first published in 1943).

Strachan, H. (1983) *European Armies and the Conduct of War*, Allen and Unwin.

Vansittart, P. (ed.) (1981) *Voices from the Great War*, Cape.

Weber, E. (1976) *Peasants into Frenchmen: The Modernization of Rural France 1870–1914*, Stanford University Press.

# UNIT 3 INDUSTRIALIZED AND 'ANCIEN RÉGIME' SOCIETIES

*Clive Emsley*

**Open University students of this unit will need to refer to:**

Set book: J. M. Roberts, *Europe 1880–1945*, Longman, 1989

*Documents 1: 1900–1929*, eds Arthur Marwick and Wendy Simpson, Open University Press, 1990

*Maps Booklet*

# INTRODUCTION

In this unit you will begin the detailed comparisons and contrasts of the principal European countries on the eve of World War I by examining those areas traditionally seen as most obviously dividing one state from another: the constitutional structures; the scale of economic development and performance; how far each nation and state was coterminous and how far the claims of different nationalities were serious issues. The overall purpose is to prepare you for the task of assessing the impact and significance of the war.

When you have completed the unit you should have a knowledge of:

the different constitutional systems of Europe in 1914, the similarities and the differences between assemblies, governments and bureaucracies;

the scale of economic development in the different countries which will enable you later to explore questions about
- economic rivalry as a cause of war, and
- the economic impact of war;

the perceptions of the 'nation' and the different kinds of 'nationalism' which will enable you later to explore questions about
- nationalism as an element in the war, and
- the development of the concept of national self-determination during and immediately after the war.

The unit is divided into three sections:

1   Constitutional systems

2   Economy

3   Nationalism

The set book for this course, J. M. Roberts, *Europe 1880–1945*, contains important background information for each of these sections and consequently each section begins with a statement of preliminary reading from Roberts. In addition to Roberts you will also need to refer to *Documents 1: 1900–1929*.

# 1   CONSTITUTIONAL SYSTEMS

In order to help you to understand the developing constitutional systems in Europe on the eve of World War I, I want you to start by reading Roberts, chapters 5 and 6, concentrating particularly on pages 130–3, 152–4, 176–81, 189–201, 206–11 and 215–20. You should read these pages now.

## 1.1   Governments and 'parliaments'

In Unit 2 we identified, very broadly, two different kinds of states existing among the great powers of Europe in 1914: 'liberal' states in the West, autocracies in the East. Each of the major states had experience of some kind of legislative body chosen by some kind of elective process involving a percentage of the adult, male population; each legislature contained a variety of political parties.

The oldest of Europe's parliaments was that which met at Westminster. The

British parliament was a bicameral legislature: the House of Lords was made up of peers of the realm and bishops; the House of Commons was elected on a limited franchise of adult males occupying land or lodgings worth at least £10 a year – this occupier franchise, together with problems of registration, meant that only about 60 per cent of men were actually qualified to vote at elections. There were four parties represented in the parliament: Conservative and Liberal (the two largest), and Labour and Irish Nationalist. Following a general election the leader of the party with the largest number of seats was invited, by the monarch, to form a government.

The French Republic also had a bicameral legislature in its National Assembly. The members of the Senate, the upper house, were elected by local representatives organized in such a way as to ensure the dominance of rural France; the Chamber of Deputies, on the other hand, was elected by universal manhood suffrage. The two chambers elected the president of the republic who served for a term of seven years and who possessed many of the attributes of a constitutional monarch: it was he, for example, who invited one of the parliamentary leaders to form a government. The parties in the National Assembly were not as tightly organized as those in Britain; indeed there was an influential school of thought in France which maintained that strong party machines would only reduce the electors' links with their deputies, this, in turn, would enhance the power of government – and all governments, if unchecked, could become tyrannies. In the decade before 1914 the SFIO, the Socialist Party, was the first to impose strict discipline and organization on its deputies. Most governments were formed by coalitions of factions, and these factions were drawn largely from the *Parti-Radical et Radical-Socialiste*, once the extreme republican Left but by the beginning of the twentieth century more liberal and moderate than socialist and radical.

A similar constitutional structure was to be found in Italy, but presided over by a constitutional monarch rather than a president. Apart from the royal princes, members of the Senate were appointed for life by the king; most of these appointments were high ranking officials drawn from the state bureaucracy, the judiciary or the army. Before 1912, when the vote was granted to all men aged thirty and above, the franchise for electing members to the lower house depended upon both a property qualification and literacy. These qualifications had exacerbated the differences between north and south; parts of the north were experiencing massive economic development, but the south was agricultural, and its agriculture was primitive – the peasants owned no land, they often did not speak Italian, let alone read and write it, and the area became notorious for politicians manipulating constituencies in their own interest. The Liberals were the dominant party in the assembly, but they had little formal organization and discipline; the haggling between the different Liberal factions in the assembly in Rome, together with a succession of financial scandals involving politicians, did little to strengthen the legitimacy of the parliamentary system in the eyes of Italians.

Whatever their faults, the elected assemblies in the West could bring governments down thus requiring either an election or, at least, the head of state (monarch or president) to find a new chief minister. This was not the case in the East. Here the monarchs did not choose their chief ministers from elected representatives in the assemblies; rather they looked to men who were servants of the state – diplomats, administrators or soldiers. Again there were bicameral legislatures, but the upper houses drawn overwhelmingly from aristocracy and gentry were generally far more ready to side with the monarch and his ministers than with the elected lower houses.

The German *Reichstag* was elected by universal manhood suffrage (granted to all men over twenty-five), but it did not initiate legislation, rather it debated those laws put to it by the *Reichs Kanzler* (chancellor). The chancellor, not a member of the *Reichstag*, was usually also the prime minister of Prussia – the state which held the real power in the Reich. A restricted franchise in elections for the Prussian assembly ensured the dominance of the conservative interests there. In the *Reichstag* there were four main groupings: the Conservatives, largely representative of the agricultural interest; the Liberals; the Centre Party, which was increasingly representative of the Catholics in the empire and, as such, was particularly strong in the Rhineland and the south; and the SPD, a Marxist party which, as was noted in Unit 2, had emerged in the elections of 1912 as the largest single party in Germany with 110 seats. Increasingly during the years before 1914 the *Reichstag* extended its power and influence; on occasions it was able to moderate or shift government policy and, while it could not remove a chancellor (remember the Zabern affair from Unit 2), any chancellor who consistently failed to get its support became a liability to the Kaiser.

It was the Russian Revolution of 1905 which compelled Tsar Nicholas II to take a hesitant step towards some representation of his people in national government. The *Duma* was elected by representatives from electoral colleges which gave some recognition to the ethnic complexity of the Russian Empire but which were based on social divisions – landed proprietors, peasants, business and professional men and workers. However, the Tsar was so appalled by the reforms proposed, particularly by the second *Duma*, that he dismissed it and changed the electoral rules, drastically reducing the representation of national minorities, peasants and workers, and increasing that of landed proprietors and businessmen. Subsequent *Dumas* were more pliant to the imperial will, and while the acceptance of a constitution and parliamentary structure with the *Duma* system implied the possibility of some future liberalization, the Tsar continued to appoint his chief ministers without reference to the *Duma*, its proceedings or its wishes. It should be noted here that, reactionary though he was, Nicholas II did appoint some capable and far-sighted men to key ministerial posts, in particular Witte and Stolypin.

The 1905 revolution in Russia contributed to the bringing forward of proposals for universal manhood suffrage in Austria-Hungary. It was not that Franz Joseph and his advisers were converted to the idea of representative government, rather they hoped that the move would undermine middle-class nationalist parties. The dominant Magyar radicals in Transleithania were demanding greater independence; the threat of universal manhood suffrage and what this would do to Magyar dominance over the other nationalities in Hungary was sufficient to cow the radicals – universal manhood suffrage was not introduced and the limited franchise favouring the Magyars survived. In Cisleithania, however, the reform was introduced giving the vote to all men aged twenty-four and over. New electoral districts were drawn up which favoured the Germans in the empire, but the new assembly was the nearest thing yet seen to a truly representative body in the empire. Unfortunately with three dozen factions based largely on nationality the *Reichstat* became chaotic and incapable of any positive decision; early in 1914 the Emperor and his ministers suspended it and began to govern by decree.

In the same way that their armies aped those of the great powers, so the Balkan constitutional structures had a surface similarity to those elsewhere in Europe. There were elected legislatures, and in Bulgaria there was even universal manhood suffrage. There were parties in the legislatures, often taking titles much like those elsewhere in Europe. Yet the constitutional structures and party names were often only a façade. Parties continually fragmented and/or formed different alliances usually centring on a dominant personality or family. Wealthy landowners maintained an overwhelming influence in the political structures, and even the universal manhood suffrage of Bulgaria was emasculated by rigged elections and the machinations of Tsar Ferdinand, a shrewd political operator who increasingly extended his authority at the expense of politicians.

## 1.2    Government bureaucracy

The decades before World War I witnessed most European governments introducing, and legislatures passing, more and more legislation which increasingly involved the state in the everyday lives of the population. Governments felt the need to have more information about their populations and about the national economy; they took a greater hand in the management of the economy and provided much of the necessary infrastructure – railways, roads and communications (post and telecommunications). Public inspectorates were established to check abuses in the private sector, in factories for example. Educational provision was increased; state welfare began to be provided for the old, the sick and the infirm. In return the state required the individual's loyalty and, in most instances, it required all of its young men to serve in its armed forces.

This growth of state power did not go unchallenged. At one end of the social scale there were members of the working class who co-operated with employers against factory inspectors: new safety regulations could hamper production and reduce wages; new regulations on child labour could limit the amount which children contributed to the family budget. Peasants and members of the urban working class kept their children away from school for this last reason; also girls might be kept from school to look after younger brothers or sisters. The state responded here with more legislation, and more bureaucrats – inspectors and policemen. But the challenge to the growth of the state could also be intellectual. In Britain, for example, one strand of liberalism still clung to the notion of *laissez-faire* and it had found a champion in the popular philosopher Herbert Spencer who, in 1884, published a book with the self-explanatory title *Man versus the State*. Increasingly however it was another strand of liberalism that was becoming dominant.

From the middle of the nineteenth century the disciples of Jeremy Bentham had urged the growth of the state to alleviate injustice and squalor on the one hand, and working-class 'idleness' and irresponsibility on the other. In the last two decades this kind of liberalism was boosted further by the publication (largely posthumous) of the work of the Oxford philosopher T. H. Green. Green argued that society only existed for the proper development of individuals and that civic and political institutions were valuable only in so far as they aided this development. In France there was also debate over the power of the state *vis-à-vis* the individual. France had the largest state bureaucracy in Europe in the mid-nineteenth century; the prefectorial system dating back to the first Napoleon put a state official (the prefect) in an administrative and supervisory capacity at the head of each *département*, and thus ensured a degree of central government involvement in provincial life undreamed of in Britain. Yet in the closing years of the nineteenth century the Council of State, the supreme judicial courts of administrative law, succeeded in impeding the development of welfare services and actually forbade municipalities from developing publicly owned enterprises in competition with private firms.

The growth of the state meant the growth of state bureaucracies. For much of the nineteenth century 'bureaucracy' had meant literally 'rule from the bureau' and in consequence was often contrasted with rule by representative government. Such 'bureaucracies' appeared to be most prominent to the east of Europe and it is generally acknowledged that the most efficient of the pre-war bureaucracies, in the more general sense, was that of Prussia. It was in the period before World War I that the more general meaning of bureaucracy was fostered, partly through the growth of the state but also through the work of the German sociologist Max Weber. Briefly Weber defined bureaucracy as a system of administration conducted by trained professionals according to prescribed rules. Ideally his bureaucracy had four principal attributes:

1   It was hierarchical; there was a division of labour with the different officials responsible to a superior.

2   There was continuity; bureaucratic posts were full-time, salaried occupations with a career structure.

3   It was impersonal; strict rules prescribed the officials' actions; the officials acted without arbitrariness or favour, and kept written records of their proceedings.

4   It was marked by expertise; bureaucracies were staffed by trained professionals, selected according to merit.

The bureaucracies of early twentieth-century Europe varied from state to state and it is difficult to get overall comparative figures. Table 3.1, drawn from H. Finer, *The Theory and Practice of Modern Government* (1932, vol.2, p.1167) gives some idea of the growth of bureaucracies, and some idea of the problems of comparative assessment.

**Exercise**   As with any theoretical social model the four points drawn from Weber and noted above constitute an ideal type; such models provide a means for analysing institutions, they are not developed so that historical (or any other) data might be used to prove simply that the model is correct. Is there anything about the social structure of late nineteenth- and early twentieth-century Europe which you think must have impeded state bureaucracies from developing in this ideal form? ■

**Specimen answer**   It seems to me that the hierarchical structure of pre-World War I society (something which we discussed in Unit 2 with reference to the armed forces), together with the lack of equal educational opportunities (something which I think is implicit in much of what has been said in Unit 2 and above), were bound to militate against the selection and promotion of personnel according to merit.

**Discussion**   In parts of the bureaucratic structures of most states, generally those parts away from the centre or connected more directly with local administration, it was possible to rise through merit. A man born into the British working class could, for example, join the police as the lowest grade of constable and end his career as the head of a borough police force. A Russian peasant, as was noted in Unit 2, could rise to the rank of colonel in the Russian army. But while possible in theory, it was never the case that a British working man joining the police before World War I had risen to be the chief constable of a large county police force, or of one of the

**Table 3.1**   *The growth of civil services[1] (central and local[2]), 1800–1929*

| | Great Britain | | France | | Prussia | | Germany | |
|---|---|---|---|---|---|---|---|---|
| | Civil service[3] (000s) | Population (m.) | Civil service (000s) | Population (m.) | Civil service (000s) | Population (m.) | Civil service (000s) | Population (m.) |
| 1800 | — | — | — | — | 23 | — | — | — |
| 1821 | 27 | 14.1 | — | 30.4 | — | 11.6 | — | — |
| 1841 | 17 | 18.5 | 90 | 34.2 | — | 15.0 | — | — |
| 1850 | — | — | — | — | 25 | — | — | — |
| 1861 | 59 | 23.1 | 248 | 37.4 | — | 18.5 | — | — |
| 1881 | 81 | 29.7 | 379 | 37.6 | 152 | 27.5 | 452 | 45.4 |
| 1901 | 153 | 37.0 | 451 | 39.0 | 250 | 35.0 | 907 | 56.9 |
| 1911 | 644 | 40.8 | 699 | 39.6 | 342 | 41.0 | 1159 | 65.4 |
| 1921 | 958 | 42.8 | 1212 | 39.2 | 390 | 38.1 | 1753 | 63.2 |
| 1928 | 1024 | 44.7 | 1008 | 40.7 | 443 | 39.1 | 1187 | 64.4 |
| Occupied population | | | | | | | | |
| | — | 17.2 | — | 21.7 | — | 12.5 | — | 32.1 |

[1] *Caution.* In spite of the greatest care and use of the best sources, these figures are only approximate; it is highly dangerous to compare those for each country in different years (since census methods and scope have varied), and even more dangerous to compare the figures for different countries since here even the definition of civil service varies. We have attempted to include all paid, professional, full and part time servants of the central and local authorities, *excluding* military and naval services, judges and magistrates, police and teachers. We have *included* all other servants whether 'established' or 'unestablished', whether administrative, clerical, manipulative, or 'industrial' (postal and railway workers, for example), whether drawing salaries, fees or wages. The task has been exceedingly difficult, and there are errors and uncertainties. A fascinating history could, of course, be written, recounting *why* the growth we record took place.

[2] We attempted originally to include only the servants of the central authority, but France and Germany lump *all* officials together; their method was followed in order to get the major amount of comparison possible.

[3] No local government officials included until 1861. In earlier years there were none; later, not available, until 1861. The apparently astonishing leap after 1901 is due to the inclusion of large classes of 'additional' workers, that is, mainly industrial and manipulative. The census, before 1911, was unsatisfactory on this score.

principal city forces; such positions were reserved for 'gentlemen'. Similarly the Russian peasant colonel could not rise to command élite regiments or serve on the General Staff, where aristocratic birth and bearing remained crucial. Of course even at the centre of government tasks varied greatly. In some areas aristocrats clung on to their offices in the belief that their birth and education gave them special qualities. The diplomatic corps is the obvious example; even in republican France up until 1894 candidates for posts in the foreign service had to have a private income of 6,000 francs a year. Treasury departments, in contrast, were acknowledged as requiring rather different abilities and skills. □

**Exercise**   But what impact do you suppose the growth of state bureaucracies had on their 'openness'? ∎

**Specimen answer**   The bigger the bureaucracies became, so the necessity emerged of offering posts to a wider variety of people. It simply was not possible for a small élite to staff the expansion even at the centre of government.

**Discussion**   Thus the expansion of the state can be said to have had a diluting effect on the traditional élites. Of course the new men drawn into the upper echelons of state administration were drawn from the well-educated classes; generally they were the sons of successful business and professional men. To take another example from republican France: if a young man wanted a good post in the ministries of finance or foreign affairs, it was in his interest to attend the Ecole Libre des Sciences Politiques which had something of a monopoly in preparing candidates for these ministries; but the Ecole was a fee-paying institution. However, the key question in all this is: were these new men actually 'diluting' the élites and making them more open? Or were they simply scrambling to be part of the old élite and ultimately helping the preservation of its values? ☐

**Exercise**   A final question for you to ponder in this section: the ideal bureaucracy is meant to act impartially, without arbitrariness or favour, but can you see the possibility of a different relationship between the chief state ministers and the chief state bureaucrats in the East and the West of Europe? ■

**Specimen answer**   There surely is a difference in that ministers in the West had some claim to being the elected representatives of the people and there was thus some separation between government and the professionals of the state bureaucracy. In the East, however, the ministers were appointed by the monarchs with no reference to the elected legislatures and the ministers had invariably risen through the ranks of the state servants.

**Discussion**   Bureaucrats in both the East and West aspired to be apolitical, working in the national interest. But this division from 'politics' and perceptions of the 'national interest' varied considerably because of the constitutional systems. In the West state bureaucrats were responsible to politicians and, while they may have disapproved of certain politicians (and even been obstructive), it was these politicians who defined the current national interest. In the East, in contrast, governments claimed to be working in the 'national interest' and above the squabbles of elected party politicians in the assemblies. Arguably this state of affairs in the East helped to confirm the élites' views of elected assemblies (they feared what would happen if such irresponsible individuals ever acquired the reins of government) and confirmed the elected deputies' suspicions of governing élites as dismissive of the popular will. ☐

# 2   ECONOMY

First read Roberts, pages 22–53 on population, economy and world trade, and pages 105–18 on imperial expansion. Appendices 1 and 2 (pp.581–3) give you some useful statistical information on population and industrial development. Read these sections now.

## 2.1   Economic structure

**Exercise**   Study Tables 3.2 and 3.3 and answer the following questions.

1   What does Table 3.2 suggest about agriculture in contrast to industry in Germany before World War I?

2   What does Table 3.3 suggest about the pattern of landholding in pre-war Europe? ■

**Table 3.2**     *Agriculture and industry in Germany*

|  | Agriculture | Industry |
|---|---|---|
| *(a)   Contribution to Gross National Product in percent* | | |
| 1848–54 | 45.2 | 21.6 |
| 1870–74 | 37.0 | 31.7 |
| 1895–99 | 30.8 | 38.6 |
| 1910–13 | 23.4 | 44.6 |
| *(b)   Share of active employed force in percent* | | |
| 1849–58 | 54.6 | 25.2 |
| 1878–79 | 49.1 | 29.1 |
| 1895–99 | 40.0 | 35.7 |
| 1910–13 | 35.1 | 37.9 |
| *(c)   Absolute numbers employed (000s)* | | |
| 1849 | 8,298 | 3,491 |
| 1871 | 8,541 | 5,017 |
| 1900 | 9,754 | 9,525 |
| 1913 | 10,701 | 11,720 |

(From Robert G. Moeller, ed., *Peasants and Lords in Modern Germany*, 1986, p.4)

**Table 3.3**     *Landholdings before World War I*

|  |  | Less than 5 hectares[1] | | 5 to 100 hectares | | 100 hectares and over | |
|---|---|---|---|---|---|---|---|
|  |  | % of landholders | % of area | % of landholders | % of area | % of landholders | % of area |
| Austria | (1902) | 71.8 | — | 27.5 | — | 0.7 | 49.5 |
| France | (1892)[2] | 85.1 | 27.0 | 12.5 | 30.0 | 2.4 | 43.0 |
| Germany | (1907) | 74.2 | 15.3 | 25.4 | 61.5 | 0.4 | 23.2 |
| Hungary | (1895) | 72.6 | 16.1 | 26.9 | 42.1 | 0.5 | 41.8 |

[1] A hectare is roughly two and a half acres.
[2] The figures for France are for less than 10 hectares, 10–100 and 100 and over.
(From Jerome Blum, *The End of the Old Order in Europe*, 1978, p.437)

**Specimen answers**     1     Table 3.2 suggests three things:

(a)     agriculture's contribution to Germany's Gross National Product was declining, though it remained significant;

(b)     agriculture and industry had roughly changed places in their contributions in the half century before the war;

(c)     agriculture's share of the labour force was declining, though the numbers employed continued to rise.

2     Table 3.3 shows clearly the great discrepancies in landholding in pre-war Europe; a very large percentage of landowners held tiny parcels of land, while a very small percentage of landowners held vast estates. ☐

Analyses of economic development before World War I often used to ignore the importance of agriculture and the very large numbers engaged in agricultural work. Perhaps we are rather too inclined to generalize from perceptions of our own country's past, but Britain was, as in many other instances, quite exceptional in having, by the middle of the nineteenth century, a majority of its population living in urban areas and as few as one-fifth of its labour force engaged in agriculture. By the beginning of the twentieth century Germany was the only other major power with a higher percentage of its labour force engaged in industry rather than agriculture; as you can see from Table 3.2, this change had been very gradual and the preponderance of the industrial labour force was still only marginal.

There were great varieties in agricultural practice between different countries and between the different regions of different countries. Britain, as in so many other ways, was the exception in European agriculture: first, it had been geared overwhelmingly to cash cropping since the eighteenth century; second, it had no peasant proprietors, indeed it had no real peasantry. In the western and southern regions of European Russia private, capitalist farming was becoming dominant with thousands of peasants working as hired labourers; in central Russia, in contrast, peasants worked more or less permanently on allotments assigned to them by their commune. In Italy it was only the four northern provinces of Piedmont, Lombardy, Veneto and Emilia-Romagna which witnessed an agricultural revolution partly to meet the needs of the industrial triangle whose fixed points were Milan, Genoa and Turin. These cities, where industry boomed at the beginning of the twentieth century, helped to absorb the surplus peasant population of the northern provinces; the cities of the south offered no similar haven and peasants of the backward south migrated in their thousands to the USA and Argentina. Generally speaking it was only on the larger holdings geared to cash cropping where agricultural improvements and new techniques were liable to be found. Elsewhere in the Balkans agriculture was backward, regardless of whether the land was held principally in large estates, as in Romania, or by small peasant farmers, as in Bulgaria. It was only during the second half of the nineteenth century that the Balkan populations began moving from semi-nomadic, livestock breeding communities, to more settled communities practising arable, mainly grain farming. This change occurred with only a very gradual introduction of natural fertilizers and hardly any mechanization. Nor were all of the developments in agriculture at the end of the nineteenth and beginning of the twentieth centuries in what might be considered as 'progressive' directions. In France, for example, there were positive efforts to revive sharecropping between 1880 and 1914. Sharecropping involved a division between the sharecropper, who provided the labour, and the landowner, who provided the land and probably also the working capital, animals, machines and fertilizers. The resulting produce was divided, generally, on a fifty-fifty basis. The reason for this revival appears to have been less for economic and more for social benefits; sharecropping was seen as a way to keep the peasantry quiescent and to maintain the authority of the existing ruling classes.

Throughout Europe the larger agricultural enterprises were hit by the depression which lasted from the mid-1870s to the mid-1890s. The depression led to a decrease in the amount of cultivated land in Europe; the expanding population benefited from the ability of American farmers to produce food which, in spite of transportation costs, was cheaper than that grown in Europe. The depression also encouraged the exodus from the countryside to the towns where wage rates were generally higher. Farmers found themselves having to pay higher wages to keep workers on the land and having to rely more and more on seasonal migrant labour. There were enormous seasonal movements of agricultural labour during the period 1890 to 1914; German farmers recruited labourers, often female, from Poland and Galicia; French farmers attracted labour from Italy, Spain and Belgium. Sometimes these seasonal agricultural labourers could also be seasonal industrial workers: Frenchmen in the Limousin moved from porcelain factories to wood cutting according to season; many workers in the large textile enterprises of Moscow province shifted seasonally from factory to land and back.

In other ways the division between factory worker and rural worker was blurred. While more and more of the rural immigrants to cities were staying and becoming urbanized, it was possible to find immigrant ghettos where peasants continued to speak in their local dialect and had their eyes and thoughts firmly fixed on what the French call their *pays natal*. Many of the Italian peasants who migrated across the Atlantic sent money back to their relatives, or brought money back to buy land of their own. In the decades before World War I over 300 million *lire* came to Italy each year by this route enabling it to finance a large trade deficit and to import machinery and raw materials for its new industries. In Germany, while as a result of the depression the amount of land under cultivation declined, the number of very small landholdings actually increased. Often small parcels of land were purchased by men who lived in villages but travelled daily to work in the towns. Many of the smallholdings shown in Table 3.3 were such properties; 32.7 per cent of all landholdings in Germany in 1907 were less than half of a hectare, and such a holding could only be used to supplement a wage earned elsewhere. But rural dwellers did not have to travel into the towns to participate in small-scale industry; outwork, the system by which merchants from towns delivered raw materials to a peasant family and returned to collect finished goods and pay for them, could still be found in many parts of Europe.

In Russia in 1902 more than half of the industrial plant and more than half of the labour force were to be found outside the cities. The principal reason for this seems to have been that employers found labour to be much cheaper in the countryside, and they were prepared to invest in massive complexes which combined a variety of processes under one roof (metal working with mechanical construction, for example) as well as providing machine repair shops, workers' housing, hospitals, schools, abattoirs and bakeries. Moreover, until the reforms of 1906 the institutions of the commune tended to tie the peasant to his village. The Russian peasant had been freed by the Emancipation of 1861, but in most instances land had not been transferred to the individual peasant who worked it but to the commune in which he lived. Since from time to time the commune might decide on a redistribution of land among the villagers, peasants were reluctant to break their close links with their village in case they lost out in such a redistribution. Also the commune could be reluctant to let a peasant leave, and could prevent him from doing so, as this could mean the loss of one of those responsible for sharing its financial burdens. The reforms of 1906, introduced partly to reduce peasant discontent and disorder, weakened the hold of the commune and enabled the peasant to consolidate personal holdings; a government-financed bank was also established to help peasants purchase more land, and technical assistance was offered in farming. These reforms, together with the fostering of migration to Siberia, increased the amount of Russian land under the plough, improved agricultural yields, and helped in the formation of a class of well-to-do peasants. In 1914 about 80 per cent of the population continued to derive their livelihood from the land.

**Table 3.4**   *Industrial establishments in France*

|  | Percentage of total number | |
|---|---|---|
|  | 1896 | 1906 |
| Less than 10 employees | 62 | 59 |
| 11–100 employees | 17 | 16 |
| Over 100 employees | 21 | 25 |

(From Roger Price, *An Economic History of Modern France 1730–1914*, 1981, p.233)

**Table 3.5**   *Percentage of employees by trade and size of establishment in France 1906*

|  | Number of employees | | |
|---|---|---|---|
|  | 1–10 | 11–100 | Over 100 |
| Food | 62 | 25 | 13 |
| Wood | 58.5 | 32.0 | 9.9 |
| Building and public works | 47 | 40 | 13 |
| Quarries | 28 | 46 | 26 |
| Printing and allied trades | 18 | 45 | 37 |
| Metal processing | 27 | 27 | 47 |
| Glass | 14 | 30 | 56 |
| Chemicals | 11 | 36 | 53 |
| Paper | 7 | 34 | 59 |
| Textiles | 9 | 22 | 69 |

(Based on information in François Caron, *An Economic History of Modern France*, 1979, pp.164–5)

**Exercise**   What do Tables 3.4 and 3.5 suggest about industrialization in France before 1914? ■

**Specimen answer**   Table 3.4 points to a gradual increase in the number of large enterprises in France, though it also shows that a high percentage of small firms remained. The figures in Table 3.5 indicate, predictably perhaps, that different kinds of establishments had different sizes of workforce, and that what might be considered as the establishments benefiting from machine production and industrial development had larger numbers of people within the same plant.

**Discussion**   Developments of this sort were common throughout Europe though, of course, the actual figures for different countries vary considerably. Generally speaking the largest concerns involved heavy industry and combined the mining of coal and iron with steelmaking, processing and machine construction; several giant concerns of this kind were to be found dotted throughout Europe, notably the works of Krupp at Essen in the Ruhr and those of Skoda in Bohemia.

But it would be wrong to think of this stage of European industrialization simply witnessing more and more people working in bigger and bigger factories. Industry required services, which meant, for example, more transport work, more dock labour; the latter was generally casual work often with men from the poorer areas of seaports and cities hired by the day. Furthermore many industrial concerns required skilled labour and not simply machine minders. The new motor vehicle industry offers a good example. The motor car was initially seen literally as a 'horseless carriage', a luxury vehicle for the well-to-do crafted by skilled artisans. France had become Europe's premier car and lorry maker by 1914, yet there was no mechanized production line and each worker built, on average, a mere 1.6 cars a year. However car makers like Louis Renault in France and Giovanni Agnelli of Fiat in Italy were looking to Henry Ford's developing production system in the United States. While modern, mass car production remained a long way off, by 1914 Fiat in particular was on the point of producing cheaper cars in much greater numbers. ☐

## 2.2   The patterns of economic development

It is easy to make the assumption that because Britain experienced the first industrial revolution in the late eighteenth and early nineteenth centuries, it provided the model of industrialization which other countries had to follow. However, the more that economic historians probe the processes of industrialization, the clearer it becomes that there are a variety of routes which can be taken. You ought to be clear, from your reading of Roberts and from the previous section, that there were considerable variations in the extent of industrialization in the European states in 1914: some of these states can be termed 'advanced' while others were 'backward'; and even within the states there were major differences. Some German historians have written of the *Gefälle* or gradient in various aspects of Europe's economic and social life. Industrialization had begun, and by 1914 had its strongest grip in the north-west of Europe: Britain, the Ruhr, the north-east of France and Belgium; the further east and south that you travelled, the more sparse the pockets of industrialization became. In the Balkans industrialization could scarcely be found at all; here small-scale handicraft industry was the norm, but agriculture dominated the national economies.

In many respects the Austro-Hungarian Empire models the *Gefälle* in miniature. Cisleithania had been on a level with Germany as an industrial power until the latter's rapid spurt ahead in the last third of the nineteenth century. The Czech lands were the most industrialized area of Cisleithania; by 1900 they were more heavily industrialized than France, and in 1914 the area around Prague and Brno and along the northern frontier with Germany was one of the most advanced industrial regions of Europe. In contrast the Hungarian half of the empire, together with the northern and southern extremities, remained overwhelmingly agricultural. The two economies became interdependent: Hungary, like its Balkan neighbours, switched from stockbreeding to grain production, most of which went to Austria, and it imported a high percentage of its manufactured goods from Austria. Arguably this relationship gave Hungary a higher income than it would have enjoyed on its own but, at the same time, it checked its industrial development. Such industrialization as there was in Hungary in 1914 was primarily the result of Austrian investment seeking an area where labour was cheaper.

Investment is, of course, crucial to industrial development; but investment cannot generate industrialization on its own – entrepreneurs, competent managers, a pool of relatively mobile labour to work new processes in new centres, and markets for the new products, are all also required. In the early instances of industrialization from the late eighteenth to the early nineteenth centuries, these elements were, to some degree, all present within those few societies which began an industrialization process. Alexander Gerschenkron, a leading economic historian, has argued that economically 'backward' societies have had to find substitutes for these elements in their own processes of industrialization. Gerschenkron's work has concentrated principally, but by no means exclusively, on Russia which experienced a massive spurt in economic development during the 1890s. He argues that:

1   The state provided investment for industry 'substituting' for the lack of investment from private entrepreneurs and banks. The money for this investment was raised by foreign loans and by heavy taxes (to pay off the loans) imposed on the peasantry. This taxation was largely indirect on cloth, sugar, tallow, tea, vodka and yeast, but it had the additional, money-raising attribute of forcing the peasantry to sell more grain which could then be exported; the money raised from grain exports was used to pay for valuable imports.

2   The state imposed prohibitive tariffs on foreign manufactured goods and, where there was no internal market for Russian products the state itself 'substituted' as a buyer, particularly through its programme of railway building – hence the concentration of Russian industry on iron, steel and machinery.

3   The most modern manufacturing equipment was purchased (principally from Germany) and this 'substituted' for the shortage of skilled labour.

4   The very large industrial plants which were a prominent feature of Russian industrialization 'substituted' for the lack of managerial and entrepreneurial talent in the empire; massive plants enabled the small amount of such talent as was available to be spread to supervise industry.

**Exercise**   1   What growing national institution figures prominently in the substitution process as described above?

2   In the light of our discussion in section 2 of this unit, try to generalize about the role of this institution in the industrialization process, and particularly in the industrial catching-up processes of backward economies at the end of the nineteenth and beginning of the twentieth centuries. ■

**Specimen answers**   1   The state.

2   In Gerschenkron's model the state plays a significant role in the catching-up process, and a much larger role than in the first industrial nations. But in section 2 of this unit we noted the increasing power of the state in the decades before World War I and its greater involvement in the lives and behaviour of its people. Gerschenkron's insistence on the importance of the state in forcing backward economies to catch up is probably right, but even in advanced economies the state was expanding its involvement. □

During the early and middle years of the nineteenth century the dominant ideology of leading merchants and industrialists had been free trade. Since most of these merchants and industrialists were British, and since Britain's industrial superiority enabled them to undercut their competitors, it might be argued that free trade was in their own, and consequently in Britain's own, interest. But free trade was also the aspiration of many European liberals, particularly where, for example in early nineteenth-century Germany, they saw internal customs barriers inhibiting trade. However the industrialization of powers other than Britain meant competition and this, together with depression (notably that during the 1870s), brought strident demands for protection. The historian David Landes has described a kind of Darwinian perception emerging:

> The shift from monopoly to competition was probably the most important single factor in setting the mood for European industrial and commercial enterprise. Economic growth was now also economic struggle – struggle that served to separate the strong from the weak, to discourage some and toughen others, to favour the new, hungry nations at the expense of the old. Optimism about a future of indefinite progress gave way to uncertainty and a sense of agony, in the classical meaning of the word.
> (David S. Landes, *The Unbound Prometheus*, 1969, pp.240–1)

Within nations, and sometimes across national frontiers, industrialists organized cartels to protect prices and to control output. These were notable in the chemicals, coal and iron industries, and particularly successful in Germany where the cartels could enforce their contracts in the courts. The Rhenish-Westphalian Coal Syndicate, established in 1893, became the model for many; the German Steel Producers Association set up eleven years later involved eighty-nine firms and controlled virtually all of Germany's basic steel production. Yet even before the development of these cartels the states of Europe had begun taking action to protect and foster their native industries; most of the leading states made significant moves towards the rebuilding of high tariff walls during the 1870s.

I have said little about the British economy so far in this section. From being the 'workshop of the world' for much of the nineteenth century, Britain was, by the closing decades, lagging behind several of its economic competitors. It could no longer depend on industrial superiority to undercut and outsell competitors, and rivals were aware of Britain's vulnerability to their own, in many instances, technically superior industries. The mid-1890s witnessed a particularly pained outcry in Britain against 'unfair' German trading in markets like Australia, South America and China, which the British had tended to regard as a private preserve; even the United Kingdom itself was being infiltrated by a variety of cheap German goods – the government had actually purchased Bavarian pencils! Yet the British economy was continuing to expand and, while dropping behind competitors in some industries, Britain was strengthening its position as a service centre for the international economy. It enjoyed massive invisible earnings from insurance, from shipping – its merchant fleet was the largest in the world – and from banking. Britain had gone on the gold standard, by which the monetary unit of a country is kept at the value of a fixed weight of gold, in 1821. France, Germany and the United States had followed suit during the 1870s, and from the mid-1890s the gold standard was an international system involving most of the world's great trading nations and establishing an international medium of exchange and unit of account. The London money market, with its long experience of the gold standard, became the focal point of international finance and exchange.

## 2.3   Economic rivalry, investment and imperialism

David Landes has argued that the new perception of economic growth as struggle both contributed to, and was strengthened by, growing political tensions; in turn these helped to generate what has been called 'the New Imperialism'. The closing decades of the nineteenth century and the years up to 1914 witnessed an expansion in the European overseas empires most apparent in the 'grab for Africa'. From the beginning of the twentieth century, with the publication of J. A. Hobson's *Imperialism: A Study*, the economic origins of the New Imperialism have been hotly debated.

**Exercise**   Read the extracts from Hobson in *Documents 1* (I.4 and I.5) and answer the following questions.

1   According to Hobson which group of people was responsible for the New Imperialism?

2   What is his evidence for this conclusion?

3   What economic pressures, does he argue, have fostered imperial expansion?

4   What is Hobson's proposed remedy? ■

**Specimen answers**   1   Hobson accuses the sectional business interests, which were making substantial profits out of imperialism, of usurping control of the nation's resources to their own ends and being responsible for the policy. These interests have been able to draw support from military and Indian civil service personnel who perceive opportunities for themselves in imperial expansion.

2   In the passages reproduced in *Documents 1* Hobson gives no hard evidence of how these sectional interests have been responsible for the policy. What is presented here is almost the classic conspiracy theory: these individuals have benefited, the policy is in their interest, therefore they must be responsible for it. (Hobson's study is loaded with statistics about the colonies and about financial proceedings; in the case which he knew from personal experience as a correspondent of *The Manchester Guardian* – South Africa – there was an element of conspiracy by some capitalist investors. But at no stage does he demonstrate, with hard evidence, how business interests actually succeeded in hijacking the state to pursue a policy which, to his mind, was so obviously disastrous.)

3   For Hobson it was over-production and a surplus of capital which fostered the need for imperial expansion.

4   Hobson's remedy was to divert surplus capital to the home market either by paying higher wages or by taxation; this would boost consumption and thus improve the economic and social conditions of the majority. □

Hobson, a radical Liberal economist, developed this theory of under-consumption elsewhere in books and articles. He feared that the maldistribution of wealth, and particularly over-saving by the wealthy, presented a serious threat to capitalism. Economic assessments of imperialism, totally hostile to capitalism (in a way that Hobson was not) were also made by Marxist theorists, notably Rosa Luxemburg, Rudolf Hilferding, and Lenin. In *Imperialism: The Highest Stage of Capitalism* (1916), Lenin drew on Hobson's work and sought to explain the nature of World War I in terms of the logical development of capitalism and imperialism.

The principal feature of the latest stage of capitalism is the domination of monopolist associations of big employers. These monopolies are most firmly established when all the sources of raw materials are captured by the one group and we have seen with what zeal the international capitalist associations exert every effort to deprive their rivals of all opportunity of competing, to buy up, for example, ironfields, oilfields, etc. Colonial possession alone gives the monopolies complete guarantee against all contingencies in the struggle against competitors, including the case of the adversary wanting to be protected by means of a law establishing a state monopoly. The more capitalism is developed, the more strongly the shortage of raw materials is felt, the more intense the competition and the hunt for sources of raw materials throughout the whole world, the more desperate the struggle for the acquisition of colonies.

The characteristic feature of imperialism is precisely that it strives to annex *not only* agrarian territories, but even most highly industrialized regions (German appetite for Belgium; French appetite for Lorraine), because (1) the fact that the world is already partitioned obliges those contemplating a *redivision* to reach out for *every kind* of territory, and (2) because an essential feature of imperialism is the rivalry between several great powers in the striving for hegemony, i.e. for the conquest of territory, not so much directly for themselves as to weaken the adversary and undermine his hegemony. (Lenin, *Imperialism*, 1964 edn, vol.22, pp.260 and 268–9)

But there are problems with the economic theories about the causes of the New Imperialism.

*Table 3.6*     *Foreign investments 1913–14*

| Creditor | Billion | Debtor | Billion |
|---|---|---|---|
| Great Britain | 18.0 | Europe | 12.0 |
| France | 9.0 | USA & Canada | 10.5 |
| Germany | 5.8 | Latin America | 8.5 |
| USA | 3.5 | Asia | 6.0 |
| Belgium, Netherlands, | | | |
|     Switzerland | 5.5 | Africa | 4.7 |
| *Other countries* | 2.2 | *Australia* | 2.3 |
| | 44.0 | | 44.0 |

(From Gerd Hardach, *The First World War 1914–1918*, 1987, p.6)

**Exercise**     Look at Table 3.6 which shows the amount of investment which the creditor states of the world had in other countries together with the amount of investment in the debtor states; then answer the following questions.

1     Where were the principal investments of the European powers in 1913–14?

2     If capital travelled in the same direction as imperialism, where do you suppose the principal investments of these powers should have been found?

3     Are there any powers which engaged in foreign adventures which do not appear to have been investing capital overseas? ■

**Specimen answers**     1     The chief debtors were in Europe itself, the USA and Canada. Investment in these areas was more than twice that in other areas of the world.

2    If surplus capital and imperialism were as inextricably mixed as Hobson, and others, maintained, then it might have been expected that most investment (or at least more than 24 per cent) would have been in Asia and Africa.

3    I have not looked in detail at which powers were seizing overseas empires but, from your reading of Roberts, you will have noted that both Russia (in Asia) and Italy (in Africa) were engaged in foreign adventures; neither appears on the list of creditor nations. (In fact if Table 3.6 had given a very detailed breakdown of debtors you would have seen that both Russia and Italy were major *importers* of capital.) □

The figures in Table 3.6 do not tie in precisely with the period of the 'grab for Africa' and exact figures for investment in the late nineteenth century are difficult to construct. However the trend reflected in Table 3.6 appears to hold good for the period of the New Imperialism. British capital had been invested abroad from early in the nineteenth century. Moreover it seems that in general the growth of foreign investment was actually greater in the years 1820 to 1870 than in the period 1870 to 1914. It can be argued that trade, investment, and economic interdependence between the principal European powers was of greater economic importance than their economic rivalry in the decades before World War I. Three other points are worth making here:

●    Overseas investments followed a variety of different routes. While much British export capital was invested in infrastructure (railways, ports and harbours, and other public utilities), French investors generally favoured fixed interest government securities. The French had, for example, invested heavily in Russia; between 1899 and 1914 never less than one quarter of the total French overseas investment was held in Russian Bonds, and just over one quarter of the Tsarist government's debt was owed to French investors.

●    The demands of the domestic economy led the German government to discourage overseas investment for a time and when German capital did go abroad it was very often tied closely to German exports and native industry as, for example, in the case of the Siemens electrical and tramway companies in Austria, Italy and Latin America.

●    The cartels so prominent in Germany (and an obvious form of monopoly) were much less apparent, and much less successful in Britain and France. Furthermore it was Britain and France, with the least concentrated and least monopolized industrial structures, which were the largest exporters of capital.

It is stating the obvious to say that the New Imperialism had a variety of causes among which we can include:

●    Empire offering an alternative to a feeble and uninspiring foreign policy. German unification and victory over France in 1871 had resulted in Germany dominating western and central Europe; only war seemed likely to shift the territorial balance. The French Third Republic, the power which had reason to want to shift this balance, was in no position to wage war during its early years; imperial adventure offered the prospect of an exciting and perhaps profitable foreign policy. Significantly, given the situation in Europe, French imperialism was encouraged by Bismarck, who reasoned that if the French were concerned with adventures outside Europe they would be less inclined to worry about Germany and to concern themselves with defeat in 1870–71 and the loss of Alsace-Lorraine.

- National pride and 'nationalism' could be boosted by imperial adventure; and the acquisition of colonies was one way of affirming, or reaffirming, a state's claim to great power status.

- A focus on overseas issues through imperial expansion was also a way for some politicians to seek to deflect criticism of their internal policies.

But none of this is to suggest that economic causes should be ignored. Joseph Schumpeter, who taught economics in Austria and Germany, and who served as Austrian Finance Minister in 1919–20, published *Imperialism and Social Classes* in 1919 insisting that capitalism was basically pacific and that the New Imperialism was principally the result of 'an atavism in the social structure', namely the survival of pre-capitalist institutions especially autocracy and militarism. The problem with such an argument is resolving the question: why did Britain, with a long tradition of pacific, free-trade capitalism, indulge in the New Imperialism with as much vigour, and considerably more success, than states where capitalism was more recent and 'atavism' more apparent? For Germany, and the Hohenzollern monarchy and the Junker class were the obvious targets of Schumpeter's charge, the case is more plausible. It might be possible to argue that German capitalists and industrialists were tainted by interests essentially antipathetic to their own (though this is assuming that the historian can state objectively what the interests of one class were). The research of Fritz Fischer into German *Weltpolitik* and war aims (which you will explore in some depth in Unit 6), shows that powerful German industrialists were deeply involved in attempts to acquire a Central African Empire, as well as in the creation of a German-dominated *Mitteleuropa*. The latter became an increasingly popular idea in the two years before 1914 when aspirations for an African Empire seemed to have been thwarted. There was no single perception of what *Mitteleuropa* might involve, but even many of the moderates saw a customs union in central Europe, protected by high tariff walls, as only a preliminary step. *Mitteleuropa*, one enthusiast proclaimed, would enable the Germans to survive the threat from 'Greater Russia, World Britannia, [and] Pan America'. For most enthusiasts the ideal would have included the Balkans, and some had visions of *Mitteleuropa* stretching to Baghdad and the Middle East – in which case they believed they would have to get there before the British.

# 3   NATIONALISM

First read Roberts, pages 18–22, on the complexity of nationality, and pages 69–72 on nationalism and racialism.

## 3.1   Contemporary beliefs

Nationalism, the nation and the nation state were all concepts current in Europe in 1914, and concepts of considerable weight in political perceptions and discourse. Nationalism had been a liberal aspiration during the first half of the nineteenth century in Europe as many young, intellectual romantics, loosely allied with business and professional men, sought the unification of their countries under progressive governments and with assemblies elected, generally, on a property-based franchise. The high point of this romantic nationalism had been the revolutions of 1848, often referred to as the 'springtime of peoples'; ultimately reaction triumphed over the revolution, yet the nationalist aspirations of 'forty-eighters' in Germany and Italy were, at least to some extent, achieved by unification later in the century. Towards the end of the nineteenth century much of the liberalism in nationalist ideals was giving way to notions drawing on Darwin's theory of natural selection: nation states were engaged in a struggle for national survival and the weakest would go to the wall. In the previous section I quoted David Landes on how economic growth was being perceived, increasingly, in terms of struggle with the weakest going under. In 1898 Lord Salisbury, the British Prime Minister, could tell a meeting of the Primrose League:

> You may roughly divide the nations of all the world as the living and the dying . . . the weak states are becoming weaker and the strong states are becoming stronger . . . the living nations will gradually encroach on the territory of the dying and the seeds and causes of conflict among civilized nations will gradually appear. (Quoted in Zara S. Steiner, *Britain and the Origins of the First World War*, 1977, p.16)

For General Friedrich von Bernhardi such causes were well apparent when he published *Deutschland und der nächste Krieg* in 1912 declaring: 'Strong, healthy, and flourishing nations increase in numbers. From a given moment they require a continual *expansion* of their frontiers, they require new territory for the accommodation of their surplus population.' Furthermore when a state renounced the extension of its power and recoiled from a war necessary for expansion, then it was doomed. In Russia, General A. A. Kireyev argued similarly: 'Of course we, like any powerful nation, strive to expand our territory, our "legitimate" moral, economic and political influence. This is the order of things.'

If successful nations were to fight in order to expand and survive, then much depended on the manhood of the nation. Again Darwin's ideas were of significance in the way that contemporaries thought about the issue. Some believed that they could pinpoint the perfect race; the poet, philosopher and musician Houston Stewart Chamberlain, for example, published two volumes of mumbo-jumbo in 1899 called *Foundations of the Nineteenth Century* in which he pointed to the Teutons as the master race. Other work was more serious if, to modern eyes, equally wrong-headed. Many contemporary observers, notably in Britain, France and Germany, were concerned about preserving their nation/race (and the two were often intertwined) from an apparent, and alarming, degeneration. In France such observers looked anxiously at the declining birth rate; the disaster of 1870 seemed to have been the herald of an overall national decline. Adopting medical metaphors, and drawing on contemporary medical research and theories, they feared that their nation was grievously ill; alcohol, pornography and prostitution were both symptoms of, and contributory elements to, the disease. The remedy was seen, at least partly, to lie in the promotion of health and vigour through sporting organizations, many of which were established in the years immediately before 1914. Similar British fears about the decline of the national stock had originated in the concern over the squalor of the urban slums and the 'residuum' which inhabited them. The poor level of fitness among recruits during the Boer War aggravated these concerns. Proposals were made to segregate the residuum who were accused of benefiting unduly from welfare provision; 'the survival of the most fertile' was, according to one eugenicist, in danger of replacing 'the survival of the fittest'. The decade before 1914 saw a campaign organized by some concerned gentlemen, politicians and military officers for the regeneration of British 'national efficiency'. In Germany too there was concern about a gradual decline in the birth rate, though it was less marked than in Britain and far less marked than in France. The concern was stimulated by Germany's rapid industrialization and urbanization; and, as elsewhere, pornography, prostitution and abnormal sexuality were seen as both contributing to, and as manifestations of, national degeneracy. The issue exploded in a series of homosexual scandals involving a number of the Kaiser's entourage in the first decade of the twentieth century. Concerns about degeneracy led the state to clamp down on the traffic in erotic materials and to co-operate with purity crusaders. German feminist leaders dropped their support for abortion and added to their list of reasons for women having the vote the fact that they bore and bred the nation's soldiers. Arguably the homosexual scandals led the Kaiser, his entourage, and many military officers to adopt aggressive public postures of military manliness.

Neues preußisches Wappen
(Liebenberger Entwurf)

A. Weisgerber (München)

(a)

(b)

*Two cartoons from the period of the Eulenburg scandal: (a) from Jugend (published in Munich, 28 October 1907) portrays Philipp, Prince zu Eulenburg-Hertenfeld (the central figure in the affair) on the left, and General Kuno, Count von Moltke, the military commander of Berlin, on the right. The caption is 'New Prussian coat-of-arms (Liebenberg design)' and the banner reads 'My soul, my little old man, my one and only cuddly-bear' (Photo: Bildarchiv Preussischer Kulturbesitz);*
*(b) from Der wahre Jacob (published in Stuttgart, 26 November 1907) portrays the commander of the élite Garde du Corps, Lieutenant General Wilhelm, Count von Hohenau, about to inspect his regiment. Von Hohenau, a relative of the Kaiser, had recently been charged with homosexual behaviour. The title of the cartoon is 'Military innovations', and the caption reads:*
*'Since when is an about-turn order given for inspections?'*
*'At your service, Captain. Beg to report that the division is being inspected today by Count Hohenau.'*
*(Photo: Professor J. D. Steakley, University of Wisconsin-Madison)*

## 3.2   Nationalism and the European states

When discussing nationalism and the state in Europe before 1914 it is possible to differentiate broadly between three different kinds of state:

● those, like Britain and France, which were long established and had long recognized an identity between nation and state;

● those, like Germany and Italy, which were newly created on the basis of such an identity; and

● the multinational empires, Austria-Hungary, Russia and, on the south-eastern fringe of Europe, Turkey.

As ever, of course, this division requires qualification and, furthermore, it must be remembered that as well as minority nations existing within these nation states and empires, there were also the Pan-German and Pan-Slav movements which claimed to speak respectively for two racial types and transcended the boundaries of the states.

The unity of the nation and the state theoretically went back hundreds of years in Britain and France. Welsh independence had disappeared at the close of the middle ages. The Scottish crown had been united with that of England in 1603; the parliaments were united in 1707. English occupation and plantation had a long history in Ireland; the parliaments were united in 1801. Both Scotland and Wales had relatively homogeneous cultures akin to that of England, but while Scottish authors (writing in English) found a ready market within their own country (as well as England), and while the use of the Welsh language was both vigorous and expanding, Scots and Welsh nationalists made little headway during the nineteenth century. Furthermore the pluralistic 'British' political culture had strong roots in Scotland and Wales as well as in the dominant England. Ireland, however, was another matter. Here there were two cultures: that of the Ascendancy, and that of the native Irish. Throughout the nineteenth century Irish nationalists had created problems for governments at Westminster; and proposals for Home Rule created problems with both Ulstermen and English members of parliament. As noted earlier in Unit 2, the Home Rule proposal of 1914 created a situation in which civil war threatened in Ireland, with British army officers threatening mutiny, and the Conservative Party, in opposition, publicly sympathizing with recalcitrant Ulstermen and mutinous soldiers.

In a book published at Quimper in Brittany in 1914, Camille Le Mercier d'Erm made a comparison of vanquished nations: alongside Bohemians, Irish, Finns and Poles he placed the central 'nation' of his book – the Bretons. The gradual moulding of Auvergnats, Bretons, Gascons and others into Frenchmen between 1870 and 1914 is the theme of Eugen Weber's influential *Peasants into Frenchmen*. Weber argues that this transformation was effected through new roads and railways, which aided migration and the spread of 'national' news, through schooling, and through conscription. Critics have challenged the extent of peasant separateness and urged that Weber puts too much emphasis on the south and west of France, where primitive peasant farming had remained strong and where French was often the second, rarely spoken, language. Yet Weber marshals considerable evidence to support his case. One issue which he does not raise, yet which adds weight to his conclusions about a general lack of French sentiment among peasants in 1870, is the relatively small number of natives of Alsace and Lorraine who opted to move to France when their provinces became part of the German Empire following the Franco-Prussian war – but then again, it could be argued that moving is scarcely an option for peasants. These provinces became the focus for the aggressive rhetoric of French nationalists, yet only 12.5 per cent of the population decided to keep their French nationality when the provinces were transferred to German control, and these were overwhelmingly from the urbanized middle class, probably the most 'French' of the population. About one and a half million people remained under German control.

Of course, as far as the rulers of Germany were concerned the provinces won in 1870–71 were German anyway; the peasant population spoke a variant of German, and the German Empire was a federation of twenty-five other 'states'. The united, Prussian-dominated Germany emerged out of customs unions and war; it was not the result of a mass, nationalist movement, but essentially of Prussian power. Italy, the other 'new nation', was similarly not brought into being by a mass, national movement; the military intervention of the state of Piedmont had been crucial. It was only after unification that Kaiser Wilhelm I and Bismarck, and Victor Emmanuele I and Cavour became, respectively, German and Italian national heroes.

The problem of transforming peasants into Italians was even greater than that portrayed by Weber for France. The difficulty was especially great in the south, or *mezzogiorno*, where farming was primitive, landholding was often semi-feudal, and banditry was rife. A strong military presence had to be maintained in the south to 'civilize' as well as contribute to the Italianization of the peasantry.

In the years before the outbreak of World War I both Italy and Germany had their share of politicians and publicists who argued that expansion and colonial possessions were imperative to demonstrate their status as great powers. Both participated in the scramble for Africa, and this brought them into conflict with other powers. The Italian seizure of Tripolitania (part of present-day Libya) involved war against Turkey and confrontation with Austria-Hungary. Wilhelm II's adventures in Morocco brought confrontation with Britain and France. The question is, of course, whether it was something about the 'newness' of the two new nation states which, in itself, prompted a heightened or more aggressive nationalism, or whether this 'newness' simply gave politicians the opportunity of playing to the gallery (possibly to divert popular attention from internal difficulties), and to urge that their nation had as much right to empire as any of their longer established rivals. In Germany such political arguments interacted with an intellectual tradition extolling the superiority of the state as, in the words of the philosopher Hegel, 'the realized ethical idea', and, in the words of the historian Treitschke, 'the highest conception in the wider community of man'.

The identification of state and nation was rather more difficult in the empires to the east and south of Europe. (Given that the bulk of its remaining imperial possessions were outside Europe I shall not look at Turkey in any detail. However it is important to remember that the distintegration of Turkey's empire in Europe had resulted in the formation of the Balkan states and of different Habsburg protectorates.)

**Exercise**    Study Tables 3.7, 3.8 and 3.9 and look at map 2 in the *Maps Booklet*. Then answer the following questions.

1   Which, statistically, were the identifiable national majorities within the two empires?

2   Comparing the ethnic compositions in the two empires, which 'nationality' do you find listed as existing in Russia but, curiously, not in Austria-Hungary? ■

**Table 3.7**    *National composition of the Romanov Empire*

*'Russia' (1897)*

| Nationality | Population (in millions) | % of total |
|---|---|---|
| Russia | 55.7 | 44.3 |
| Ukrainian | 22.4 | 17.8 |
| Polish | 7.9 | 6.3 |
| Belorussian | 5.9 | 4.7 |
| Jewish | 5.1 | 4.0 |
| German | 1.8 | 1.4 |
| Lithuanian | 1.7 | 1.3 |
| Latvian | 1.4 | 1.2 |
| Mordvin | 1.0 | 0.9 |
| Estonian | 1.0 | 0.9 |
| Other Finno-Ugrian | 1.5 | 1.5 |
| Others (mostly Asiatic) | 16.4 | 15.9 |
| Total | 122.7 | 99.9 |

*The Grand Duchy of Finland (1890)*

| Nationality | Population | % of total |
|---|---|---|
| Finnish | 2,048,500 | 86.1 |
| Swedish | 322,500 | 13.5 |
| Russian & Germans | 9,000 | 0.4 |
| Total | 2,380,000 | 100.0 |

(From Raymond Pearson, *National Minorities in Eastern Europe, 1848–1945*, 1983, p.69)

**Table 3.8**    *National composition of Austria-Hungary in 1910*

| Nationality | Population (in millions) | % of total |
|---|---|---|
| Germans | 12.0 | 23.9 |
| Magyars | 10.0 | 20.2 |
| Czechs | 6.5 | 12.6 |
| Poles | 5.0 | 10.0 |
| Ruthenes | 4.0 | 7.9 |
| Rumanians | 3.25 | 6.4 |
| Croats | 2.5 | 5.3 |
| Slovaks | 2.0 | 3.8 |
| Serbs | 2.0 | 3.8 |
| Slovenes | 1.25 | 2.6 |
| Others | 2.9 | 3.5 |
| Total | 51.4 | 100.0 |

(From Pearson, *National Minorities*, 1983, p.46)

**Table 3.9**   *Religious affiliation in Austria-Hungary in 1910*

| Religion | Population (in millions) | % of total |
|---|---|---|
| Roman Catholic (including Uniate i.e. those employing Orthodox liturgy under Papal Licence) | 39.0 | 77.2 |
| Protestant | 4.5 | 8.9 |
| Orthodox | 4.5 | 8.9 |
| Jewish | 2.1 | 3.9 |
| Muslim | 0.5 | 1.1 |
| Total | 50.6 | 99.8 |

(From Pearson, *National Minorities*, 1983, p.46)

**Specimen answers**   1   In the Russian part of the Romanov Empire there was a distinct majority of Russians; there was also an overwhelming majority of Finns in the Grand Duchy of Finland. In Austria-Hungary the two largest national groups, Germans and Magyars, almost made up the same percentage as Russians in Russia, but taking the empire as a whole there was no single dominant nationality.

2   Jews appeared as a nationality in the Romanov Empire; they appeared as a religious group in the Habsburg Empire.

**Discussion**   Eastern European censuses taken at the end of the nineteenth and beginning of the twentieth centuries, need to be treated with caution. Given the ethnic complexities of these empires the census was fraught with political problems. It is probable that local bureaucrats in the Romanov Empire falsified their returns to curry favour with their political superiors; they knew what the government wanted to see. Moreover this problem was exacerbated by the fact that the criterion employed by the census was language, not 'nationality' as such. Russian was the language of the empire and it was spoken by many educated non-Russians. It is possible that the number of Russians was, in the end, over-estimated by as much as 5 per cent. In Hungary, where the dominant Magyars were eager to boost their numbers, there was official pressure to this end and here Jews, not unwillingly, were often registered as Magyars. Religious affiliation was often central to national identity: the Poles clung to their Catholicism, and the Catholic hierarchy saw in this the opportunity of extending its influence among the Polish people; the Finns clung to their Lutheran Church as another way of maintaining their separate identity from Orthodox Russians; in Bohemia the Czechs focused on their national Hussite Church to maintain their distance from the Catholic Germans; the Slovaks remained loyally Catholic to distance themselves from Protestant Magyars. Bosnian nationalists increasingly looked to Islam.

The rulers of Russia did not perceive their state as a multinational empire and the census of 1897 appears to have given them something of a shock. The result of the census was to boost the policy of 'Russification'. This policy was not an all-out attack on every national minority, nor was it conducted with the same degree of intensity against every ethnic group. The worst sufferers were the Jews, who were generally confined to particular geographical areas in the west (in what had once been Poland) by legislation. They were commonly made scapegoats for local or national problems; some pogroms were spontaneous, but the Tsarist government also sought to cash in on popular antisemitism. Yet in spite of the violence directed against them, and the financial incentives to convert, the Jewish communities within the Russian Empire clung steadfastly to their religion and their cultural heritage; and while thousands emigrated, notably to the United States, many more remained.

The Finns, who had enjoyed a considerable degree of autonomy, were subjected to a vigorous Russification policy and to tighter control by the Tsarist government in St Petersburg. Moves among Finnish activists for a Greater Finland comprising Estonians and other Baltic peoples were the root cause of this action; the Tsarist government feared such moves could lead to a call for independence. The Polish lands of the empire had been cowed, militarily, following the abortive rising of 1863. Russification was not enforced with any great rigour in the years before 1914 and the campaigns for a modicum of Polish autonomy were very low key.

The groups that were most consistently 'Russified' were the Russians' fellow Slavs – the Belorussians and the Ukrainians. By 1914 the former were almost entirely integrated. The Russification of the Ukrainians was rather less successful; the Ukrainian language was kept alive by the peasantry and, in intellectual circles, almost single-handedly, by the nationalist poet Taras Shevchenko. In 1914 political nationalism was non-existent in the Ukraine itself, but it could be found among the Ruthenes, a Ukrainian sub-group, in the Galician province of the Habsburgs.

The *Ausgleich* had divided power between the two largest national groups in the Austro-Hungarian Empire. The Magyars dominated governmental, administrative and teaching posts in Transleithania. While they had been liberal in the early years of the division of power, they became more and more oppressive towards their subject nationalities: the Slovaks had their centre of cultural nationalism closed in 1875 for 'promoting Pan-Slavism'; the Croats had their degree of autonomy revoked in the 1880s. Yet the Magyars had the more difficult national elements in Transleithania, and their problems were aggravated by the progressive disintegration of the Turkish Empire in the Balkans with the consequent creation of independent states whose respective majority ethnic groups were minorities under Magyar rule.

After the Germans the largest ethnic group in Cisleithania were the Czechs. They enjoyed a strong cultural revival in the second half of the nineteenth century; the performance of Smetana's *Ma Vlast* (My Country) in Prague in 1882 became a great patriotic rally. But it can be argued that Czech nationalism was disarmed politically by prosperity; the Czechs' economic development outstripped the rest of the empire and few could see much point in agitating for autonomy, let alone independence, with the possibility of losing the considerable benefits that they were enjoying. Similarly the Polish gentry in Galicia, while always conscious of their nationality, were quiescent and content with a degree of autonomy and economic prosperity. Yet all was by no means peaceful in Cisleithania. In parts of Bohemia ethnic antagonism gave rise to two independent workers' parties, one Czech, one German, and both calling themselves 'national socialist'.

Minorities in the east and south-east of Europe engendered suspicion and fear; they also gave governments the opportunity to foster difficulties for their neighbours. There was friction between Italy and Austria-Hungary over the petty persecution of the Italian minority remaining within the empire; German and Italian students came to blows at the University of Innsbruck in 1902. The government in Vienna supported anti-Italian Slavs on the Adriatic littoral. The government in Rome encouraged outposts of Italian culture and influence in Trieste and the Southern Tyrol (or the Alto-Adige as the Italians called it). The government in Vienna allowed Ukrainian nationalists to organize in Galicia; at the same time it was alarmed by Pan-Slavism which appeared to be a Russian conspiracy to threaten the internal security of the empire – Slavs, after all, constituted over 40 per cent of the Habsburg's ethnic groups. □

In all of the states of Europe before 1914 there were political parties which played the nationalist card. Some of these parties were explicitly nationalist in their names; though none of these so-called 'nationalist' parties was ever significant enough to dominate the government of any particular state. Probably the most extreme of these parties was the Union of Russian People, established in 1905 and determined to preserve all things Russian – notably the God-given autocracy of the Tsar – from the encroachments of liberalism, capitalist industry and other such 'selfish' interests which had originated in the West. Initially the URP drew support from all classes, though its increasingly populist stance lost it support from many of the more well-to-do. It became involved in street violence, economic boycotts, strike breaking and political assassination; paramilitary gangs were organized. Historians in both the USA and USSR have referred to it as Europe's first 'fascist' party.

Besides the nationalist parties there were also nationalist pressure groups like the German Navy League (*Flottenverein*) and Colonial Association (*Kolonialgesellschaft*) and the British Navy League and its more extreme offshoot, the Imperial Maritime League. Like the nationalist parties, such organizations were small but exceedingly vocal. In the same kind of category were the Pan-Germans and the Pan-Slavs. The *Alldeutscher Verband* (Pan-German League) never had more than 18,000 members and its monthly magazine, at its peak, had a circulation of only 5,000. Its members had high, and varied, hopes: the unification of all members of the German race, a German-dominated Europe, the expansion of the German people into living-space (*Lebensraum*). Such ideas slotted in conveniently with the dream of the German-dominated *Mitteleuropa*. The League encompassed the aspirations of many German liberals in 1848, but the aggressive, expansionist aims of many of its members spread in a more sinister direction. Pan-Slavs had similar aspirations; their focal point was Russia which was seen as becoming the liberator and protector of southern Slavs from Muslim Turkey, and the guardian of all Slavs against contamination and/or domination by the peoples of the west. The Pan-Slavs looked forward eagerly to what they perceived as the imminent, and permanent, disintegration of the Turkish and the Habsburg empires. By 1914, however, Pan-Slavism was losing out to the nationalism of the new Balkan states, and the Bulgarians certainly did not perceive Russia as a protector. At the same time many of the south Slavs of the Austro-Hungarian monarchy were inspired by the idea of a large, united Slav state – Yugoslavia.

But if these pressure groups and nationalist parties remained small, nationalist ideas permeated much of the press and many popular books. In Britain the emerging popular press was influential in the 'We want eight and we won't wait' campaign for dreadnoughts; the proprietor of the *Daily Mail*, Alfred Harmsworth, allegedly claimed that the average Briton liked 'a good hate', and his paper offered the opportunity. Children's books carried patriotic messages (see the title page of *Jeanne d'Arc*) and so, very often, did lessons in school. Such books and lessons were not necessarily directed against other nations or people; more commonly authors and teachers appear to have been eager to inculcate a love of the motherland. Two questions arise here:

1   To what extent was this inculcation of patriotic and nationalist sentiment deliberate policy on the part of governments to undermine internationalism (particularly socialist internationalism) and to ensure loyal soldiers in the event of war?

2   To what extent was this inculcation (whether deliberate or not) successful?

Both of these questions are enormous and all I can do here is to offer a few fundamental observations. Certainly, in all the powers of Europe before World War I there were men in positions of power and influence who were worried about the internal stability of their country. The idea of thwarting socialist parties, which threatened revolution, by inculcating a love of country appealed to such men. There were also fears of external threats and war between nations, which underlined the different governments' needs for large, loyal armies. But it is a considerable jump to argue that because some men in positions of power perceived such needs, that they were able to mount successful campaigns of nationalist indoctrination to satisfy them. In those countries where teachers were civil servants, teachers could be instructed to teach love of the motherland. In France, for example, teachers were expected to teach 'not just for the love of art or science . . . but for the love of France'. History and geography were central here; Ernest Lavisse's *La Première Année d'Histoire de France* was published in 1884 as a school textbook, and the children reading it were told that through it 'you will learn what you owe your Fathers, and why your first duty is to love above all else your homeland (*la patrie*) – that is the land of your Fathers'. In Germany, the army, dissatisfied with the products of schools and concerned about socialist propaganda, set about educating conscripts with lectures designed 'to create and reinforce a sense of national identity'. The question, of course, is how many men were converted by such education? Clearly some young Germans went into the army from SPD families, experienced this indoctrination while with the colours, returned to their SPD homes, voted SPD in elections and supported their 'country' (like the bulk of the SPD) when war came. It is naive to believe that nationalist or patriotic propaganda in schools, in the army and through the media, had nothing upon which to build. I have already noted the 'national socialist' workers' parties in Bohemia. When national frontiers have divided men, the image that one group of workers has had of their counterparts in another country has not often been noted for its generosity. Nationalism (and nineteenth-century imperialism) received multi-class support, and it has therefore been tempting for some of those who believe that the working class should have combined and acted in its own interest, rather than in the so-called 'national' interest, to argue that the working class was misled and/or manipulated. This was the line taken by Lenin in his study of imperialism.

> The receipt of high monopoly profits by the capitalists in one of the numerous branches of industry, in one of the numerous countries, etc., makes it economically possible for them to bribe certain sections of the

*Title page of M. Boutet de Monvel's Jeanne d'Arc (1893) (Pierpoint Morgan Library, New York)*

JEANNE D'ARC

PAR

M. BOUTET DE MONVEL

E. PLON, NOURRIT & Cⁱᵉ, IMPRIMEURS-ÉDITEURS, 10, RUE GARANCIÈRE, PARIS

GRAVURE DF DUCOURTIOUX ET HUILLARD                    ENCRES DE LA MAISON CH. LORILLEUX ET Cⁱᵉ

workers, and for a time a fairly considerable minority of them, and win them to the side of the bourgeoisie of a given industry or given nation against all the others. The intensification of antagonisms between imperialist nations for the division of the world increases this urge. (Lenin, *Imperialism*, 1964 edn, p.301)

The difficulty with such an argument is that by identifying the problem (why didn't the working class oppose imperialism and/or war-mongering and the outbreak of World War I? And why didn't it act in its own interest?), it is suggesting that there is such a thing as objective class interest; it also provides an answer to the initial problem (manipulation) which absolves the unfortunate, misguided working class and blames the unscrupulous ruling class.

This leads to a final problem: of course governments, the leaders of certain pressure groups and parties, and some press barons, hoped that the masses would respond to particular issues in particular ways. Yet it would be very difficult to show a conspiracy among these disparate groups within one nation to manipulate the majority of that nation. In some countries, and Germany seems the obvious example, the ruling élite commonly adopted an aggressive nationalist stance, yet their policies did not follow wholeheartedly the demands of the different nationalist pressure groups or the aspirations of the Pan-Germans. Politicians were much more commonly pragmatists, who would play the nationalist card when it suited them but who might also be wary of extremist nationalist groupings. Politicians could also be sharply divided among themselves on issues regarding the 'nation', and this was not always simply a division between socialist parties and others as is revealed by the division over Irish Home Rule in the British Parliament in 1914.

## References

Blum, J. (1978) *The End of the Old Order in Europe*, Princeton University Press.

Caron, F. (1979) *An Economic History of Modern France*, Methuen.

Finer, H. (1932) *The Theory and Practice of Modern Government*, Methuen.

Hardach, G. (1987) *The First World War 1914–1918*, Penguin.

Landes, D. S. (1969) *The Unbound Prometheus: Technological Change and Industrial Development in Western Europe from 1750 to the Present*, Cambridge University Press.

Lenin, V. I. (1964) *Imperialism: The Highest Stage of Capitalism*, in V. I. Lenin, *Collected Works*, Lawrence and Wishart (first published in 1916).

Moeller, R. G. (ed.) (1986) *Peasants and Lords in Modern Germany*, Allen and Unwin.

Pearson, R. (1983) *National Minorities in Eastern Europe, 1848–1945*, Macmillan.

Price, R. (1981) *An Economic History of Modern France 1730–1914*, Macmillan.

Steiner, Z. S. (1977) *Britain and the Origins of the First World War*, Macmillan.

# UNIT 4 SOCIAL STRUCTURE AND HIGH AND POPULAR CULTURE

*Arthur Marwick*

**Open University students of this unit will need to refer to:**

Set book: J. M. Roberts, *Europe 1880–1945*, Longman, 1989

*Documents 1: 1900–1929*, eds Arthur Marwick and Wendy Simpson, Open University Press, 1990

Course Reader: *War, Peace and Social Change in Twentieth-Century Europe*, eds Clive Emsley, Arthur Marwick and Wendy Simpson, Open University Press, 1990

# 1 SOCIAL STRUCTURE AND SOCIAL GROUPS

The aims of this unit are: to help you towards an understanding of the way in which the words 'class' and 'culture' are used, and to lead you towards an appreciation that the very way in which these words are used can affect the answers given to questions about the nature of social and cultural change and the relationship of war to it; and to develop further the comparison and contrast between the different European countries on the eve of war by examining two phenomena which are intrinsically international in character, that is to say, social structure (or 'class') and culture ('high' and 'popular') with the overall purpose of further clearing the ground for our discussion of how far, if at all, World War I brought social and cultural change.

## 1.1   The language of class

Students, we know from experience, are not particularly keen on discussions of the different possible meanings of such words as 'class'. Why can't we just settle for one set of simple definitions and get on with it? There are a number of reasons which I shall list here.

1   Historians, whose books and articles you will be reading, do in fact use the word 'class' in different ways, and it is important that you should look out for this and be aware of the implications of the different usages.

2   Some writers slide from one meaning to another without seeming to notice: it is impossible to develop a logical argument if the words one uses keep changing in meaning.

3   Each country, and we are studying several in this course, has its own language of class: we have to be very careful that in using an English translation we don't in fact distort the original meaning. For example, in Germany people sometimes speak of the *Mittelstand*, which literally means 'middle estate', where in ordinary English usage we would probably say middle class, or perhaps lower-middle class (we'd have to go back to the eighteenth or early nineteenth century to find such a phrase as 'middling estate'). Does this matter? Well, I think we do have to look at the issue quite closely before deciding that it does or that it doesn't. In France, ordinary people quite readily use the term 'bourgeoisie', though in a variety of ways and with a variety of qualifying adjectives; in Germany there is the analogous word *Bürgertum*, a more general word than *Mittelstand*, and one which is sometimes rendered in English as 'middle class' and sometimes as 'bourgeoisie'. The British – academic sociologists and historians and political propagandists apart – do not normally use the word 'bourgeoisie'. When discussing France and Britain, should we use 'middle class' throughout, or 'bourgeoisie' throughout, or should we conclude that while we have a middle class, France has a bourgeoisie? But if so, what is the difference? These are all matters which have to be looked at, particularly if we are going to make comparative evaluations as to whether World War I had a greater or lesser effect on the class structure of France or Germany than it had on that of Britain.

4   The particular language used will usually relate to a specific theory about the nature of class. How one thinks about class may affect the answers one gives to

particular historical questions relating to class. In this course, we have a special concern with establishing how, if at all, European societies were changed by World War I. Very important questions to answer are: Were class structures changed? Did the working class become more powerful or, say, more unified? What happened to the upper class? What happened to the middle class? As you can see immediately, how we define these terms, or whether we accept their legitimacy in the first place, will shape our answers to such questions.

As I don't want to continue to deal in abstractions, I am going now to give you a very striking concrete example. The major work by a German historian, Jürgen Kocka, concerning the effects of World War I on Germany is (to give the title of the English translation) *Facing Total War*. In discussing 'the situation in 1914' Kocka spends a good deal of time establishing the position, status and outlook of the white-collar workers, craftsmen and small shopkeepers, all regarded in the Germany of the time as belonging to the 'new *Mittelstand*'. Kocka concludes his long discussion thus:

> . . . their objective class position was not the defining condition for the life-styles, expectations, organisation and political behaviour of either white-collar employees or of *Handwerker* [craftsmen] and *Kleinhändler* [small shopkeepers]. Both groups organised themselves predominantly against those whose class position they shared. Together they formed a significant factor by which Wilhelmine society was distinguished from a clearly marked, dichotomous class society. (Jürgen Kocka, *Facing Total War*, 1984, p.84)

He then continues with a sentence which in effect sums up one of his major points about the effects of the war on German society:

> Encouraged by the State, they acted as a sort of padding, which somewhat muffled the growing class conflict. During the War, this padding was ripped apart. (p.84)

Now I hope that you, without necessarily at this moment grasping the full implications of what Kocka is saying, can see how the manner in which he chooses to discuss class sets the framework for the answers he is going to give about the effects of the war, thus colouring, if not determining, the nature of these answers.

**Exercise**     What approach to class is Kocka taking? If possible, single out at least one phrase (I think there are certainly three, and perhaps four) that clearly indicates the approach being followed by Kocka. ■

**Specimen answer and discussion**     Well, I imagine that if you answered that one at all, you said 'Marxist'. If you are at all puzzled you should refer back to Unit 1. (Kocka is also strongly influenced by Weber; in Unit 1 I suggested that Marx and Weber shared a common 'conflict model' of society.) But the main point for now is that you should see that being aware of the different usages of class *does* matter. The key phrase, I think, is 'their objective class position'. The 'objective class positions' Kocka refers to are those of, on the one hand, the owners of capital who employ others, and, on the other, those who are employed and have no possession but their labour, the working class.

The same point is involved in the phrase 'those whose class position they shared'. 'Dichotomous class society' means society divided into two classes –

again the capitalist class on one side, the working class on the other. Kocka seems to be suggesting that Germany was rather peculiar in departing from this model, but that the war helped to bring matters back to the true Marxist state of affairs. 'Class conflict' is, of course, central to the Marxist notion of how historical change takes place. □

The quotation I gave you from Kocka was rather brief and, standing on its own, perhaps not too easy to grasp. What he is saying is that the white-collar employees really ought to occupy one 'objective class position', and the craftsmen and small shopkeepers ought to occupy another 'objective class position', whereas, in fact, both find themselves organizing against the other occupants of their own 'objective class positions'. To enable you to take this a little further, and also to help you to learn something useful about German society before World War I, I am going to give you a rather fuller discussion from Kocka. While reading it I want you to bear certain questions in mind, and then when you have finished write down answers to them.

**Exercise**   Read the passage from Kocka that follows (from which references have been deleted) and then answer these questions:

1   Which 'objective class' did the white-collar workers belong to?

2   Which 'objective class' did the craftsmen and small shopkeepers belong to?

3   Why did these two different elements in the *Mittelstand* in fact organize against their own 'objective class'?

4   (This is the difficult one!) Would it be possible, do you think, while retaining the important information conveyed by Kocka, to present this information in a slightly different way totally abandoning any notion of 'objective class position' and 'dichotomous class society'?

> There was little which bound this heterogeneous group [that is, the white-collar workers] together in terms of activity, function, education, income, legal status or other objective criteria, apart from their class position. They belonged to the category of the employed, the dependent workers, and not with the owners of the means of production. This was not, of course, specific to them; they shared their class position, as well as an increasing degree of division of labour and of collective behaviour with the manual workers. However they were distinguished from the latter by at least one, although more often several of the following characteristics: white-collar workers earned more, on average, than manual workers, even if there were many overlaps; their income was almost exclusively in the form of a salary rather than a wage; many of them still worked in closer proximity to and had more actual contact with their 'principal' (the entrepreneur), particularly in the commercial sector; they did no manual work, or at least not exclusively; as a rule they enjoyed greater security of employment as well as other privileges within the firm; and they differentiated themselves from manual workers in life style, patterns of consumption and career expectations. They did not consider themselves in general as employees, let alone proletarians, but as business people, technicians or 'private civil servants', and were accepted as such by most people. The concepts *'Privatbeamter'* [literally 'private civil servant', that is, white-collar worker in the private sector] and *'angestellter'* [refers to white-collar workers in general, whether in the public or private sector] denote much more emphatically and clearly than the Anglo-Saxon concept

of 'white-collar employee' or the French *'employé salarié'*, a distinct social stratum with a specific status and rights which embraced a large variety of occupations, but which was clearly separate from the manual workers on the one hand and on the other from those of independent standing such as employers.

The organisational and political behaviour of white-collar employees was generally very different from that of manual workers. Although in 1907 about one in three of white-collar employees belonged to an Employees' Association, most of the quite numerous associations (53 in 1913) were open to the self-employed as well, thereby demonstrating that they were not orientated towards pure unionism . . .

The gap between manual and white-collar workers was more of a social reality in Germany than in other comparable industrialised countries. The bureaucratic traditions of Prusso-German society served the quickly growing middle strata of employees, the *Privatbeamter*, as a model for collective self-identification and thereby as the basis for the claiming of privileges and a separation from manual workers. Confronted with a radical socialist protest movement, with a proletariat which appeared to be revolutionary and which was incompletely integrated into society, most white-collar employees stressed that they belonged to the middle class, to the non-proletarian and to the anti-Socialist camp. The more the working conditions and the economic situation of most white-collar and manual workers came to look alike, with continuing industrialisation, the more actively and determinedly white-collar workers defended their traditional privileges, their increasingly out-moded status advantages, and their consciousness of being 'different' from manual workers . . . Their efforts to distance themselves from the proletariat chimed in well with the anti-Socialist integration policies of both the middle-class parties and the Reich government, which wished to prevent the further growth of the Socialist camp through social legislation. From 1911 a series of Reich laws, at first concerned with social insurance, but soon with other areas as well, separated white-collar from manual workers by awarding privileges to the former and, unlike England and the USA, by cementing a socio-economic differentiation whose functional basis was increasingly being eroded by the advance of economic modernisation . . .

As a rule the middle and lower strata of the civil service were also included in the 'new *Mittelstand*', whose number before 1914 was reckoned to be between 1.5 and 2 million . . .

In Germany the distinction between *'Handwerk'* (skilled craftsmen, often self-employed) and *'Industrie'* (manufacturing firms of medium to large scale) has played a much larger role than in English-speaking countries, both as a semantic and as a social reality.

These two million *Handwerker* and *Kleinhändler* found themselves – seen in terms of their class position as independent owners of the means of production and, frequently, as small employers – in the same category as industrialists and other large entrepreneurs. However, they differed from these not only in their life-style, but also in their socio-economic and political orientation. (Jürgen Kocka, *Facing Total War*, 1984, pp.78–81) ■

**Specimen answers and discussion**

1    The working class.

2    The industrialists, large entrepreneurs, or capitalist class.

3    The reasons for white-collar workers organizing differently from the manual workers are very lucidly set out by Kocka in the latter half of the first paragraph, beginning 'several of the following characteristics', with further reasons set out in

the third paragraph, and don't need to be repeated here.

Kocka goes into much less detail over why the craftsmen and small shop-keepers did not line themselves up with the capitalists. He says that the distinction between craftworkers and large industry was a social reality, and then goes on to mention differences of lifestyle, and of socio-economic and political orientation. Kocka seems to be recognizing that it's jolly obvious that these *Mittelstand* groups are in fact very different from large capitalists.

4    And that leads me into the answer I was looking for here. To me, the evidence that these various groups in what was actually termed the *Mittelstand* were very different from both the capitalist class and the working class is so overwhelming that I would have thought there was a good case for abandoning any idea of a dichotomous class structure being objective or normal, and instead recognizing that at least three distinctive classes existed in Germany before World War I. And this takes us to the heart of what I am trying to get at. □

There is one main view of class which starts from a theoretical position (for very good reasons, I may say – I am not arguing that this approach should be abandoned); and there is another approach which looks at the complexities that actually exist and draws its picture of class structure to conform as closely as is possible with these complexities without necessarily postulating class conflict between objective classes. I would add a couple of further points. I believe that Kocka exaggerates the distinction between the German *Mittelstand* and analogous groups in Britain, France and America. I believe that in all three countries something which can legitimately be called a new middle class or a lower middle class had come into being. However, do note again that the Germans themselves do not speak of a class here but, to repeat, of a middle estate. They speak of a working *class* because they perceive the workers as organizing themselves in support of their own interests in accordance with the Marxist model, whereas they see the *Mittelstand* as too heterogeneous and disunited to be called a class in the Marxist sense. Personally, belonging to the non-Marxist persuasion, I think the word 'class' is perfectly appropriate in the sense of designating a broad group which is distinguished by its particular position in the social hierarchy. But I leave you to decide where you stand. The important thing is to understand the nature of the different approaches.

The other phrase of Kocka's I wanted to draw your attention to was the one in the middle of the third paragraph where he refers to how 'the more actively and determinedly white-collar workers defended their traditional privileges, their increasingly out-moded status advantages . . .' The phrase 'out-moded' is again very Marxist in implying that there is a definite direction in which 'history' must be going. Marxism postulates that such workers must be pushed down into the proletariat; actually all historical experience in recent times, and Kocka must be aware of this, suggests that white-collar workers have gone up in status rather than down, and that the advantages they enjoy today are far from 'out-moded'. Let me repeat: it is not for me to say that having a Marxist framework for the study of history is wrong; all I ask is that you look out for it when it manifests itself, and decide for yourself whether you find it helpful or not. I want to make it clear that what is being talked about here is a difference between two approaches to academic study, one more theoretical, the other less theoretical. It is not essentially a matter of politics, though, of course, Marxists do tend to be left-wing in their political outlook, and extreme anti-Marxists (of which I am not one) right-wing: political opinions do sometimes obtrude upon historical writing.

## 1.2    Social structure in 1914: did the aristocracy still govern?

In the previous section I was concerned mainly with illuminating the distinction between Marxist and non-Marxist approaches to class, but I wanted you also to learn a little about the nature of the *Mittelstand*. In this section I shall mainly be concerned with discussing the major question of who dominated Europe in the pre-war years, particularly with reference to Arno J. Mayer's contention that the old aristocracy still governed, a clarifying of this whole issue being essential if we are subsequently to be able to decide if, and how, World War I changed the distribution of power and wealth within societies. But it will be necessary to continue to be very self-conscious about the terms in which social structure is described and the meaning that is given to class.

If you are not already sufficiently familiar with them, I want you to read the opening pages of Arno Mayer's *The Persistence of the Old Regime* reprinted in the Course Reader. But then, for the purposes of this next exercise, I want you to concentrate on, and read very carefully, the part of the Introduction beginning on the middle of page 51, 'In any case . . .', and ending '. . . this towering hegemonic edifice' (p.53).

**Exercise**    Before reading carefully the passage from Mayer just identified, read the following questions, and then write down your answers once you have finished your reading.

1    What explanations, in this passage, does Mayer give for what he sees as the continuing predominance of the old aristocracy?

2    What phrases indicate that Mayer shares with Kocka Marxist views about 'history' and about 'classes'?

3    (This is the difficult one again.) Taking it that the information communicated by Mayer, like that communicated by Kocka, is broadly accurate, can you see a different way, using the same information, of pinning down who formed the dominant class or classes in the Europe of 1914? ■

**Specimen answers and discussion**    1    The explanations Mayer gives are that:

●    Helped by the central position still maintained by the monarchy (except in France) the aristocratic, landed class continued to control the main organs of government, profiting from the money made by the bourgeoisie, but keeping the latter firmly in their place.

●    It adapted and renewed itself by recruiting from below.

●    Without abandoning their aristocratic ways, they adopted capitalist money-making methods.

●    The bourgeoisie contributed substantially by itself accepting a subordinate place and seeking obsequiously to gain aristocratic honours and titles.

●    The bourgeoisie 'denied themselves' and instead bolstered the existing aristocratic cultural and educational system.

2    The phrases I noted were:

(page 52) 'the *grands bourgeois* kept denying themselves by imitating and appropriating the ways of the nobility in the hope of climbing into it'. This implies that the bourgeoisie *ought* to have done something else, that is to say, to fulfil their 'historical mission' of actually overthrowing the aristocracy.

(page 53) 'by disavowing themselves in order to court membership in the old establishment, the aristocratizing bourgeois impaired their own class formation and class consciousness and accepted and prolonged their subordinate place'. Again we have this implication that the bourgeoisie *ought* to act class consciously on behalf of their own bourgeois class, that they are somehow 'wrong' to aristocratize themselves, disavow their bourgeois nature, and impair the development of their class consciousness which *ought*, of course, to be directed to *overthrowing* the aristocracy.

(further down page 53) 'The bourgeois allowed themselves to be ensnared . . . the self-abnegating bourgeois'. Again there is this implication of the bourgeoisie failing to do what they *ought* to do.

3   Mayer's formulation is that, partly because the aristocracy exploited its own assets and cunning, and partly because the bourgeoisie deferred to it, the aristocracy continued to be the dominant class.

There are at least two other formulations one could give entirely consistent with the information Mayer presents:

•   The more successful members of the bourgeoisie saw absolutely no point in trying to overthrow the aristocracy. It was much pleasanter, and much more fun, to actually join the aristocracy and enjoy all the delights of aristocratic life. Thus the dominant class in 1914 was in effect an amalgam of the older aristocracy and the most successful bourgeois elements. This would be my own preferred explanation – though of course we will have to recognize that the exact situation (the exact extent to which successful bourgeois families had penetrated the aristocracy) differed from country to country.

•   Alternatively, one could argue that, *while remaining a separate class*, the bourgeoisie were *sharing* power with the aristocracy. Some historians (including Roberts) would feel that Mayer exaggerates the power of the aristocracy, and underestimates that of the bourgeoisie. □

However, I want you to consider very seriously Mayer's main contention that an older aristocracy, linked in most cases with the monarchy, continued to be of predominating importance in the Europe of 1914. It should be said that the argument is not nearly as novel as Mayer claims. As early as 1963, Michael Thompson, whom Open University Arts students encountered in an Arts Foundation course television programme, pointed out that the landed aristocracy in Britain preserved their dominant position throughout the nineteenth century. So let us look at the writings of some other top historians, to see how far they confirm and how far they conflict with Mayer's basic contention.

I'll start with Norman Stone on Russia.

**Exercise**   Bearing the following two questions in mind, read the passage which follows from Norman Stone's *The Eastern Front*, and then write down answers.

1   Summarize briefly what Stone is saying and decide whether that conforms or not to Mayer's thesis of continuing aristocratic domination, or to one or other of the two alternative formulations given above.

2   Norman Stone is very definitely a non-Marxist historian and might well be described as a 'conservative' historian (though, as I have already remarked, I do not necessarily think that a historian's political views need affect his writing of

history). Norman Stone is also renowned for his cutting wit. Can you spot an example of this as well as examples of his non-Marxist, 'conservative' outlook?

3    Does 'gentry' mean the same thing as 'aristocracy?'

> Tsarist Russia was not so uncomplicatedly a 'gentry-bourgeois State' as has sometimes been suggested. On the contrary, gentry figures provided much of the active opposition. Their economic basis had been weakened by emancipation of the serfs, and loss of two-thirds of their lands. Some found a way forward in the bureaucracy, or the *zemstva*; some stayed on their lands, and tried without much success, to make a go of them; some went into active opposition to the State now, seemingly, leaving them little place. A large number of liberals and revolutionaries came from their ranks – a tradition promoted by the Decembrists in 1825, and continued, in one form or another into the ranks of the Bolsheviks, of whose leaders at least Lenin and Chicherin could lay some claim to patrician status. It was useful to the State, in the circumstances, to recruit peasants whom it could then release against their masters; and such ex-peasants were frequently encountered in the army and the police, as Count Tolstoy discovered when the police raided his house, on suspicion that literacy was practised there. (Norman Stone, *The Eastern Front, 1914–17*, 1975, p.21) ∎

**Specimen answers and discussion**

1    Stone is denying that the landed gentry in co-operation with the bourgeoisie dominated the Russian state. The gentry had been economically weakened; many of them were leaders of the opposition to the state. For its part the state made use of peasants.

This view would certainly be in conflict with Mayer's view about the continuing dominance of the landed class and, though there is no detail on the bourgeoisie in this passage, also seems to be opposing the notion of the landed class and the bourgeoisie coming together to form one dominant class. There is not really enough to go on here, but Stone's views could be compatible with the notion that the landed class and the bourgeoisie both, separately, were important classes. It might be noted that if the gentry still do have a considerable influence on the running of the state (Stone does not really go into this here), *and* they provide the leadership for the opposition, this would tend to suggest that they are pretty important.

2    The wit is in the last phrase, 'on suspicion that literacy was practised there'. Stone resists the Marxist notion of one dominant class controlling the state; in fact, he says, members of the gentry were leaders of the opposition to the state. He is clearly not overly sympathetic towards the peasants who were recruited into the service of the state and, indeed, his joke is in some measure directed against them.

3    Stone seems to be using 'gentry' as a synonym for 'landed class'. However, it is very important to bear in mind that in most countries the landed class divided into rich and powerful landowners who were strongly placed to exploit the challenge of industrialization, and lesser men, who may well have been 'aristocrats' rather than mere 'gentry' but who were much more likely to suffer from industrialization. □

Let us note that just because some members of the landed class lead the opposition that does not mean that, as a class, they are not powerful – indeed it suggests their importance in different aspects of Russian life. Likewise the fact that *some* peasants serve the state by no means implies that as a class the peasants have power; the true nature of their condition we shall see shortly through the words of another Russian expert, Hans Rogger.

But for the moment I want to continue our exploration of what class, or classes, dominated the different European societies on the eve of war. I am now going to give you a series of extracts from standard secondary authorities on each of the countries we are concerned with. I want you to keep in mind Mayer's contention about the continued dominance of the traditional landed class, together with the two alternative formulations which I have offered.

**Exercise**   Read each of the following extracts, (a) to (d), and at the end of each extract note down what is being said about the nature of the dominant class, and how this relates to Mayer's version. You will find that one of the extracts presents a view of a merging of the aristocracy and bourgeoisie similar to the one I favoured in my alternative formulation, and also offers some elements similar to Stone's analysis; try to spot which extract this is. Finally, I hope you will note that the account given of Italy in extract (d) differs in one significant aspect from all of the others; see if you can also spot what this is.

*Extract (a)* (Germany)

For the shrewd and dynamic merchant or entrepreneur there was a great deal of money to be made. Despite repeated fluctuations, there was a general upward trend in income from investments. In the commercial centres like Frankfurt, Hamburg or Cologne, wealth had been accumulated over a longer period and was, perhaps, also less conspicuous. But new wealth was being generated very fast in places like Berlin, the capital of the German Empire and a major industrial and commercial centre. It was also acquired in the Rhineland in heavy industry, in Saxony and Silesia, or in Mannheim and Stuttgart with their growing engineering industries. Munich and Leipzig are other examples of cities which saw a good deal of affluence. In 1896, the Prussian Inland Revenue counted 9,265 taxpayers with an income of 30,500–100,000 marks and 1,699 with an income of over 100,000 marks per annum. By 1912 these figures had risen to 20,999 and 4,456, an increase of 126 per cent and 162 per cent respectively. And the *nouveaux riches* of the Industrial Revolution enjoyed showing off this wealth. In the late 1870s, the Krupps built their famous Villa Hügel in French chateau style on the southern fringes of Essen, overlooking the Ruhr valley and surrounded by quasi-royal splendour. Gerson Bleichröder, Bismarck's banker, was also doing quite well, as Benjamin Disraeli, a visitor from a not exactly underdeveloped country, had occasion to witness: 'The banqueting hall, very vast and very lofty, and indeed the whole mansion, is built of every species of rare marble, and where it is not marble it is gold. There was a gallery for the musicians who played Wagner, and Wagner only, which I was very glad of, as I have rarely had an opportunity of hearing that master. After dinner we were promenaded through the splendid salons – and picture galleries, and a ballroom fit for a fairy-tale, and sitting alone on a sofa was a very mean-looking little woman, covered with pearls and diamonds, who was Madame Bleichröder and whom he had married very early in life when he was penniless. She was unlike her husband, and by no means equal to her wondrous fortune.'

Indeed Bleichröder's was a very different story from that of the Prussian *Junker* who saw their economic position disintegrate while trying to maintain the life-style to which they were accustomed. As one of them, Elard von Oldenburg-Januschau exclaimed in 1904: 'Being poor is no misfortune, but lapsing into poverty is one!' Meanwhile, in 1895, Udo Count Stolbert-Wernigerode, son of an old Prussian landowning family, was forced to sell his town-house in Berlin because he was unable to afford the rates. This social humiliation provides a telling contrast with Bleichröder's affluence and illustrates what the Industrial Revolution was doing to the agrarian upper class on the one hand and the well-to-do bourgeoisie on the other . . .

The point to bear in mind . . . is that pre-war Germany was a clearly stratified society in which upward mobility beyond the class boundary was difficult. With the process of rapid industrialisation and urbanisation creating so much disruption at the grass-roots of society, the upper strata reacted all the more strongly against what they perceived as dangerous 'levelling' tendencies. The reaction was to maintain social barriers and to deny social recognition to those who had succeeded in acquiring the material pre-requisites of entry into the higher class. Thus a Berlin businessman who had amassed enough wealth to buy himself an estate north-east of the capital would more often than not fail to gain social recognition by the local Prussian nobility and squirearchy. (Volker Berghahn, *Modern Germany*, 1982, pp.7 and 12)

*Extract (b)* (Austria-Hungary)
As these economic developments occurred, the pattern of Austria's social and political forces had, up to a point, adapted itself to them, although the effects had inevitably lagged behind the causes which produced them. The most immediate and obvious of them were those deriving from the growth in numbers, wealth, and in the influence which it was able to exert through such channels as the Press, of the upper strata of the German-Austrian bourgeoisie of the German and Bohemian lands. This class, as we have seen, supplied the Ministers and their supporters from 1861 to 1878, and the legislation enacted by the Reichsrats [Imperial councils] of those years was, in the main, dictated by their interests and their *Weltanschauung* [general view of the world]. Even after the government slipped from their hands as from 1878, their wishes and interests remained something which no government was able to, or tried to ignore.

The advance of the bourgeoisie was naturally accompanied by retreats on the part of its chief opponents, the aristocracy and the Catholic Church. By 1890 the direct power of the aristocracy was a shadow of what it had been in 1848, not to speak of 1748 . . .

One must, however, be careful not to exaggerate the extent to which the bourgeoisie had triumphed over its rivals. The losses of those two factors were not mortal, and those of the Church, hardly even crippling . . .

Nor were the great landowners at all a negligible force, even in 1890 . . . Aristocrats still filled a large proportion of the highest administrative posts: in 1905–7 twenty-one of the thirty-four officials in the Ministry of the Interior of the grade of Ministerialat [ministerial adviser] and upwards were Counts or Barons, eight out of nineteen in the Ministry of Agriculture, and nine out of twenty-four Heads of Departments in that of the Railways. Only aristocrats were heads of *Stathaltereien* [provinces]: one Prince, seven Counts, five Barons, and one Ritter [knight]. And this position, too, was still backed by great wealth. The landed magnates had had their share of the difficulties that had overtaken all Austrian agriculture after 1849, when it had had to face the full competition of Hungarian wheat, livestock and wine, to which, after the mid-1870s, had been added the competition (which threatened Hungary also) of overseas wheat and cattle. But . . . most of the big men had survived this. With the compensation which they had received under the land reform, and the credit which they had been able to obtain after it, relatively easily and cheaply . . . they had been able to modernize and rationalize their production, cutting their labour costs by mechanization and extensive employment of seasonal labour, and to go over largely to the production of industrial crops, among which an enormous part was played by the production of sugar beet. The cultivation of this crop, after its small beginnings in the 1830s, had made extraordinary progress after 1850: in 1892, 175,800 hectares were under it in Bohemia and 73,500 in Moravia (it was almost confined to these two Lands). Most of this was grown on the big estates, and where it was grown by peasants, they took it to the local magnate's refinery. Thus in 1886, eighty out of the hundred and twenty refineries in Bohemia belonged to magnates, as did five hundred of the nine hundred breweries and three hundred of the four hundred distilleries. Another source of wealth was timber and its products. Many of the forests had, indeed, been bought by the big new industrial companies, but the magnates still had a share in the ownership of the forests and the exploitation of their products, including paper. In Bohemia, in 1886, they had in their service 72,000 workers, 300,000 day labourers, 15,500 foresters and gamekeepers and 40,000 carters.

It is true that appearance was often rosier than the reality, for many of the great estates were heavily mortgaged, and when Prince X figured as owner of a sawmill or a refinery, he might well be only a very minor participant in its profits. Nevertheless, the big landowners had been able not only to retain the nominal ownership of most of their estates, but to extend them . . . (C. A. Macartney, *The Habsburg Empire 1790–1918*, 1969, pp.620–3)

*Extract (c)* (France)
By the early years of the Third Republic, one can speak of a single 'traditional governing class' fighting to preserve its power. The term 'notables' is perhaps the commonest among historians today, and is certainly more satisfactory than 'bourgeoisie', for the challengers too were bourgeois, and the line between conservatives and liberals ran through the middle class. In his book *La Grande Bourgeoisie au pouvoir* (1960), Jean Lhomme argues that it was the 'grande bourgeoisie' who held economic, social and political power between 1830, when the aristocracy finally bowed out, and 1880, when it yielded power in its turn to the 'classes moyennes'. This perhaps underestimates the extent to which the aristocracy retained its social influence and remained part of the 'notables'. In the 1870s, the distinction between Legitimism and Orleanism still existed, and was based on the traditional class loyalties of the families concerned, but as the years passed it faded, and the conservative upper class came to think alike.

One element in it which was prominent at the time of the National Assembly was the provincial landed gentry, a class still thick on the ground in certain regions, which maintained a very distinctive set of values well into the twentieth century. They were Catholic, had a strong sense of patriotism and public service (generally frustrated by their reluctance to serve the Republic), and were inclined to see themselves as the last upholders of decency and tradition in a vulgar, materialist society. The romantic hopelessness of the Legitimist cause, especially after 1883, well expressed their social alienation. Some of them were small squires (*hobereaux*), but others were rich, and all retained some influence through their position as landlords. Land-ownership carried with it influence over tenants and other dependants, and a traditional position in the local community, at least in the many areas where there survived 'a conception of daily life and social organization founded on respect for the principle of property and for the hierarchy of ownership'.

The richer Legitimist nobles, however, were absentee landlords who lived in the larger provincial towns or in Paris (traditionally in the Faubourg Saint-Germain) and visited their estates only during the shooting season. At this level, it is difficult to see much difference between the older families and the Orleanist ones, whose wealth came originally from banking or industry but who had also become great landed proprietors. Conversely the nobility did not shun business activities. The agricultural depression beginning in the 1870s stimulated their movement into the boardrooms of industrial and commercial companies (and their willingness to marry bourgeois heiresses), but the phenomenon was not a new one: nobles had pioneered the development of coalmines, glassworks and ironworks on their estates since the eighteenth century, and in the nineteenth their local influence helped them become railway directors (30 per cent of whom were noble in 1902). That their role was not purely decorative was proved by aristocrats like the Marquis de Dion, who extended his class's sporting proclivities in a new direction by founding the Automobile Club and becoming a leading motor manufacturer. It seems true to say that by around 1900 landed and industrial wealth were integrated with each other, and that the topmost strata of French society formed a cohesive and powerful social group. (Robert Anderson, *France 1870–1914*, 1977, p.33)

*Extract (d)* (Italy)
Steelworks and railways were not built solely, or even mainly, for economic reasons; and the 'economy' affected every aspect of social life, as is clear from the peasants' living conditions. Above all, the rulers of Italy were not essentially concerned with economic growth or prosperity. In 1881 . . . there were about 200,000 'independent' landowners, rentiers and entrepreneurs, and about another 100,000 'professional' men – doctors, lawyers, engineers and the like. Often there was no real distinction between these two groups. Landowners and rentiers did not usually inherit until they were in their forties; until then, it was proper to follow a gentlemanly profession, like the law or the army . . . But sometimes the distinction was real enough, particularly after 1876 when the 'professional' classes enjoyed more political power, and when income from land began to decline. In any case, the two groups together formed the élite, who dominated Italian society, and about whom we know far too little. These 'independent' classes were, of course, outnumbered by their less prosperous 'petty-bourgeois' fellows: smaller landowners, shopkeepers and the 'dependent' middle classes, e.g. clerical workers. There were 100,000 Italians holding respectable white-collar jobs in the private sector, and there were also 250,000 in non-manual public employment, including around 75,000 teachers. A government post was the next best thing to unearned income, and the number of clerical employees on the railways never failed to surprise foreign observers.

Only in Northern Italy were there significant numbers of commercially-minded businessmen, mostly engaged in activities linked to agriculture, or in banking and insurance. Even in these sectors professional managers often had to be imported from successful growth economies like Britain . . . Italy lacked an entrepreneurial middle class, nor could the deficiency be supplied from below. Her skilled artisans were being squeezed by international competition, and in any case lacked the finance, contacts and literacy essential for founding successful businesses. On the other hand, she was over-endowed with a host of officials and clerks, squabbling among themselves for the spoils of office; and the holders of economic power were still mainly a landowning 'gentry' class, living off the peasants. Over most of Italy the upper and middle classes were not 'modern', not educated or travelled or enlightened. Many of them disliked and feared industry. They prized unearned income above earned, relied on rents or governments for their prosperity, and clung firmly to 'traditional' values. They even preferred to settle their quarrels by duel, to great public acclaim. In short, they were not 'middle class' at all, but aristocrats *manqués*.

And the real aristocrats were still numerous. Sicily alone could boast of 208 princes, 123 dukes, 244 marquises, and 104 counts; and the mainland South (the old Kingdom of Naples) did even better, with 172 princes, 318 dukes, 366 marquises and 81 counts. There were 321 patrician families in Rome, 28 of them with the title of prince. The other regions, especially Tuscany and Piedmont, were also well stocked with noble blood. Throughout Italy there were 7,387 noble families, plus 318 '*signori*' in Piedmont and 46 hereditary '*cavalieri*' in Lombardy and Veneto.

What role did these aristocrats play in society? The Prefect of Naples, when asked this question by Carpi, gave an uncompromising answer: 'The ancient and modern nobility is powerless, uneducated, generally poor and with little influence . . . incapable of any initiative whatsoever, not at all diligent, and consists of a large number of needy families, a few moderately well-off ones, and a rare wealthy one.' This seems fair comment for Naples, but the Italian aristocracy was by no means a spent force elsewhere, especially in the countryside. The princes and noblemen may not have enjoyed the social prestige or political power of their Russian, Prussian or English counterparts, but they still owned vast tracts of land, especially in Sicily and the *Agro Romano* near Rome: ten families owned 17 per cent of all Latium. The acquisition of Church lands enabled some of them to *extend* their landholdings in the 1860s and 1870s; this was true even of the Papal aristocrats in Rome, including those closest to the Vatican.

Moreover, as cities grew larger, there were plenty of opportunities for aristocratic landowners to benefit from property ownership. This was particularly the case in Rome, where the building boom was most intense. Via Veneto, for example, was built on the site of the Villa Boncompagni Ludovisi, which Henry James had thought the finest park in Europe. Aristocrats were welcome on the boards of the banks that financed those operations. Then there were forests to be sold off for railway sleepers, and rich heiresses to be married. In hard times, too, there were certain Court posts, in diplomacy or the army, where outdoor relief was available for the upper classes; at least one-third of the diplomats in the foreign service were noblemen. Even politically some aristocrats survived . . . In short, aristocratic landowners retained much of their wealth, and formed an important, if often underestimated, part of the social élite. (Martin Clark, *Modern Italy 1871–1982*, 1984, pp.28–30) ∎

**Specimen answers and discussion**   1   Berghahn first of all shows the way in which many members of the bourgeoisie were gaining enormously in wealth, while, in contrast, some landed families were doing extremely badly. However, he then goes on to point out how rigid German society was and how difficult it was for the bourgeoisie to penetrate or replace the aristocracy. This, then, is a very finely balanced picture in which the strengths of both bourgeoisie and aristocracy are brought out. Overall, it coincides quite closely with the picture given by Mayer – the landed class are tenaciously maintaining their position (despite often adverse economic circumstances).

2     A rather similarly balanced position is given by Macartney: advances by the bourgeoisie, but the aristocrats holding on to positions of power, in some cases through themselves engaging in the commercial and industrial exploitation of their holdings. Here again we have considerable support for the Mayer thesis.

3     Anderson definitely differs from Mayer. He does not see the bourgeoisie deferring to the aristocracy but, as in my formulation, sees bourgeois and aristocrat merging, with the bourgeois buying land and the aristocrat involving himself in commerce and business. The element that is reminiscent of Stone is the way in which he points out that a class can be split politically between government and opposition, between conservatives and liberals.

4     You will have noticed (perhaps with some anguish!) that none of these accounts by first-class historians is simple. Unfortunately the realities of social structure and of the distribution of wealth and power do not conform to concise summaries, let alone political slogans. The special point which Clark brings out is that, apart from a few areas in the north (and even here there was a marked absence of entrepreneurial talent), Italy, unlike the other three countries (we shall have to look at Russia again more closely), did not have a genuine rising bourgeoisie. On the other hand, he does point out that in many areas the landed aristocrats and the professional classes were really all one class. Clark paints a picture of opposition to industrial growth and suggests that the middle interests were not truly middle class but really failed aristocrats. Finally, he stresses the continuing importance of the major aristocrats. In one sense, then, Italy would seem to be a prime example in support of Mayer's thesis of the persistence of the old regime and of the landed aristocracy; at the same time the detail of the Italian situation as presented by Clark is rather different from that generalized about by Mayer. The existence of a large number of petty bureaucrats is important, and may be compared with Kocka's comments on Germany. □

## 1.3     Class and stratification

My concern in this section is to establish a picture, or map, of the social composition of the various countries which went to war in 1914. Then we can compare these pictures or maps with how the countries looked after the war, with a view to trying to determine if the war itself had any effects. I shall be talking about 'classes', but since I do not endow 'class' with the central explanatory power of Marxist analysis, and since I do not follow Weber in making a distinction between 'class' and 'status', many sociologists would maintain that what I am really talking about is 'social structure', or to use a more pompous phrase, *social stratification*. I am not interested in getting entangled here in argument over whether what I call 'class' and 'classes' should really be called, respectively, 'social stratification' and 'status groups'. You will notice that in a passage I am going to quote shortly, Professor Berghahn runs together in one brief phrase the words 'class', 'status' and 'group'. The basic point is that, as an overwhelming mass of evidence shows, all of the societies we are concerned with did, in 1914, break down into distinctive social aggregates, distinguished from each other by, for example, different levels of wealth, power, freedom of various sorts, and by different patterns of living conditions and cultural behaviour. Whether we call these classes or not is for each individual to settle: *but be sure you know what you have settled!*

However, it is vital that I remind you of three distinctive features of the Marxist approach, partly because, as already explained, you should be aware of them when you encounter them in the various secondary authorities, and more particularly because they are central to some of the primary documents relating to European socialism which you will be studying.

Marx made a distinction between a class 'in itself' and 'for itself'. A class was only fully mature when it recognized its own interests, which were in conflict with those of other classes, and acted 'for itself' in support of these interests. You will find writers talking of a social aggregate 'acting as a class'; the implication is that an aggregate is not really a class unless it recognizes its own interests and acts in accordance with them. (I, on the contrary, would argue that you can have a distinctive social aggregate, recognizable as a class, in which, however, different individuals may act politically in very different ways.) Marxists speak of individuals or groups being 'class conscious', by which is meant actively aware of their (as seen by Marxists) class interests. (I believe that individuals can be aware of belonging to a class, without actually being conscious of it in the technical Marxist sense, and therefore I sometimes use the phrase 'class aware'.)

It was very much part of Marx's original political philosophy that the future lay with the working class, or 'proletariat', and that this class had a special destiny in the creation of the classless society.

Lastly, there is the Marxist belief in revolution. Mayer, we saw, chides the bourgeoisie for not fulfilling *its* destiny in carrying through revolution against the aristocracy: this leaves out of account the possibility, strongly urged by a whole school of French sociologists, that what actually happens in the development of human societies is not that one class overthrows another, but that the more powerful elements of one class join with the superior class, thus steadily transforming its character. This, to come back round to where we were, is to me a more plausible explanation of what was happening in the upper reaches of society in 1914 – the successful members of the bourgeoisie were joining the aristocracy (itself, of course, suffering from some aspects of economic change), thus creating a new upper class with many of the characteristics of the old aristocracy, but much of its wealth coming from bourgeois activities. The process had reached different stages, and had particular peculiarities of its own, in the different countries.

The whole issue of class and social structure, then, is quite a difficult one. Yet, we simply cannot enter into questions about the effects of war if we are not able first of all to pin down the nature of social structure and class relationships in the various societies we are studying. To give you an example of how leading historians of today deal with the subject, I am now going to quote a further passage from Berghahn, the one I mentioned a few sentences ago.

**Exercise**   Carefully read the passage that follows and when you have finished answer the following questions:

1   Is Berghahn speaking here of class, or social structure, or what?

2    What does he identify as the factors contributing to social distinctions in Germany before World War I?

> Sooner or later the workers and their families discovered that opportunities of economic betterment and upward mobility were strictly limited, and limited by socio-cultural as well as political barriers. It is more difficult to be precise about the former than about the latter, largely because the mechanisms of social and cultural stratification in Wilhelmine Germany were fairly subtle. Furthermore, they were not merely rooted in tangible differentiations of wealth, income and power which have been mentioned above, but also in *perceptions* of class and status of one group by another. This is an area of social history which social historians of Germany have only just begun to explore. Nevertheless, there is little doubt that there existed marked differences in the way in which people organised their life outside their workplace. Here traditions, customs and social consciousness weighed heavily. From childhood on, people had been socialised into a milieu in thousands of small ways and these experiences had an important influence on their perceptions of the world around them. Depending upon their position within the social structure, men, women and children would eat, speak and dress in a certain way. They had their own peculiar habits of furnishing their rooms and of spending their leisure time. Cultural and social differences of this kind provided as much of a frame of reference by which people 'recognised' others inside or outside their own groups as did their job or income. (Berghahn, *Modern Germany*, 1982, p.10) ■

**Specimen answers**  1    It's not, I think, entirely clear. Berghahn uses a succession of different phrases to indicate the way in which German society divided up into aggregates with different levels of power, wealth, lifestyle, and so on: 'socio-cultural barriers', 'political barriers', 'social and cultural stratification', 'class', 'status', 'group', 'social structure', and finally, again, 'groups'. Personally, I would call all of these 'class', but Berghahn obviously wants to avoid the sort of misunderstandings that might arise if he used that word, with readers assuming that he was using it in the Marxist or Weberian sense; it may indeed be that he feels that that is the only way in which it should be used. Anyway, the point is not to haggle over such details, but to be aware of the approach that is being followed and then – the real purpose of the whole exercise – get as accurate a picture of German society in 1914 as we can.

2    In essence, Berghahn identifies three types of circumstance which give rise to, and confirm, social distinctions:

(a)    the basic 'tangible' distinctions of wealth, income and power;

(b)    what he calls '*perceptions* of class and status of one group by another' – that is to say attitudes and language about social distinctions are a part of social distinctions themselves;

(c)    the different ways in which people organize their lives, their habits, customs, lifestyles; Berghahn is saying that because from childhood people lived in certain kinds of houses, observed certain customs, and so on, this helped to shape them into a particular distinctive social group.

**Discussion**    These last two points are very important. Historians today are very conscious that social distinctions are a matter of attitude, language and custom, as well as a simple economic 'relationship to the dominant mode of production'. □

Can we then now move towards getting some overall idea of the social structure, or better, social structures, of the European countries in 1914? How many major social groups (if warily, like Berghahn, we prefer to use that phrase rather than the blunt 'classes') were there? Already from what you have read in this unit, and in previous units, you should be able to provide such a list.

**Exercise**  Starting with the wealthiest and most powerful at the top, and going down to the poorest and least powerful at the bottom, give a list of the main social groups in the various European countries in 1914. Where, from what you have already read in this unit, there is some argument about the nature of a particular social group, add that as a comment. ■

**Specimen answer**  Well so far (with variations of name) we have encountered the following:

| List | Comment |
| --- | --- |
| Aristocracy or landed class Bourgeoisie Gentry | But there are arguments over whether the bourgeoisie had already supplanted the aristocracy (traditional Marxist view; also the view of Roberts, a non-Marxist, who, on pp.63–4, says bourgeoisie are taking over and have fundamentally different assumptions from aristocracy), or whether the most successful elements in the bourgeoisie have joined the aristocracy transforming it into a new upper class, with variations in the different countries (my own view). Some landed families are undoubtedly going down in the world, generally the smaller landholders. |
| *Mittelstand*, middle class, or lower middle class | There are Kocka's arguments that part of the *Mittelstand* really belong to the bourgeoisie, and part to the working class. Other questions which you may not have thought of are: where do doctors, teachers, lawyers, successful small businessmen figure? Are they members of the bourgeoisie, or what? Is there an 'upper middle class'? |
| Peasants | Do these include farmers, independent smallholders, landless labourers, and so on, or should each be fitted into different classes (e.g. farmers into the middle class, landless labourers into the working class)? |
| Working class | Are they 'above' the peasantry, 'below' or level with them? Are they bottom of the heap, or are there yet more unfortunate people below? |
| Riff-raff, 'under class', or residuum | This aggregate has not appeared in our discussion so far. Mayer talks of the persistence of the old regime exclusively from the point of view of, as he sees it, the continuing dominance of the dominant class in that regime. But the old regime had its cohorts of jobless, landless, beggars, and unfortunates. Such groups still existed in the societies of 1914, together with a whole range of other dispossessed and unfortunates created by growing industrialization. □ |

A really big question hangs over what is so often, and so loosely, referred to in Britain, and in British writing, as 'the middle class'. Quite evidently the sort of people Kocka was talking about are very different from the great bourgeois figures that Mayer says were avid for the titles and trappings of the nobility: the small shopkeeper who owns his shop, the skilled artisan who owns his workshop, certainly the minor civil servant tied to his desk, and even the small-town businessman employing, say, a couple of dozen, all of these are very different from the owner of the iron foundry which dominates the employment in a town of 50,000, or a banker with an interest in several major financial institutions.

These matters are sorted out for us with magisterial succinctness by one of the leading authorities on late nineteenth-century France, Professor Jean-Marie Mayeur.[1] But here again, I fear, we run into the dreaded problem of foreign languages. Students have been telling me, ever since I taught at Edinburgh University a quarter-of-a-century ago, that to require a knowledge of languages from history students is a cruel and unnatural punishment, that an understanding of languages (or at least the few elementary points we are providing you with) is a badge of the privileged rich; on the contrary, language is an essential tool of the historian.

There is an excellent translation of Mayeur's *The Beginnings of the Third Republic 1871–1898* in which, addressing this question of the different groups contained within what is sometimes loosely called the middle class, he says:

> . . . at the top of the social ladder reigned the upper middle class. The aristocracy still had a prestige in 'society' which should not be underestimated, but it retained social power only to the extent that it had merged with the upper middle class. Matrimonial alliances and the acceptance of directorships made this merger possible. (Jean-Marie Mayeur, *The beginnings of the Third Republic 1871–1898*, 1984, pp.65–6)

My first comment must be that this view postulates members of the aristocracy 'merging' with the bourgeoisie, rather than successful members of the bourgeoisie merging with the aristocracy. That is an interesting way of rephrasing the position which I have myself enunciated; it, of course, differs significantly from Mayer's position. But what I have to draw your attention to is the original French, where both times in the English translation 'upper middle class' is a rendering of, in the French, *la haute bourgeoisie*, the 'high bourgeoisie'. Perhaps there is no great problem there. Let us continue. A little further on in the English version:

> It is relatively easy to trace the frontier which separated the upper middle class from the ordinary middle class. The scale of incomes establishes a primary distinction.

In the original French 'upper middle class', of course, is 'high bourgeoisie'. 'Ordinary middle class' is a translation of *la bonne bourgeoisie*, the 'good bourgeoisie', or the 'sound bourgeoisie'. Let us continue:

> between this 'ordinary bourgeoisie' and the people came the immense 'bourgeoisie in embryo' of the lower middle classes.

[1] Note that in this course we refer to A. J. Mayer, J-M. Mayeur and C. Maier. Confusing!

Though the French phrase remains *'bonne bourgeoisie'*, the English translator, obviously having doubts, has switched from 'ordinary middle class' to 'ordinary bourgeoisie'. The translator's problem becomes clearer when we realize that 'the lower middle classes' in the English translation is, in French, simply 'the middle classes' (*les classes moyennes*). The French, you see, recognize both a bourgeoisie (in various sections) *and* the middle classes (plural) below. Bear this careful French usage in mind every time you are tempted to speak of one monolithic middle class (or, for that matter, bourgeoisie) unless you do really mean the very powerful group at the top. Below 'the middle classes' are the people who, as Mayeur reveals elsewhere, comprise the 'agricultural' or 'peasant' classes, and the 'working class'. Mayeur discusses 'the middle classes' as follows (the translation here is mine):

> They are characterized by their wish to be bourgeois, but, whether because of an insufficient income, or because of a lack of culture and proximity to popular origins, they are on the fringes of the bourgeoisie. It is the absence of manual work which distinguishes them from, in the sharpest sense of the term, the popular strata.

## 1.4  Social structure of France in 1914

So far what I have been saying about class and social structure has consisted of a number of general statements and some extracts from various distinguished secondary authorities. In the end, as with all historical topics, what we know about social structure is based on primary sources. I will now concentrate on France in order to bring together two or three different kinds of primary source, together with one secondary source. The question of social structure obviously involves numbers: How many aristocrats? How big is the bourgeoisie? Where precisely is the divide between middle class and lower middle class (if there is one) – or, in French terms, between bourgeoisie and middle class? How large is the working class compared with the peasantry? Statistics contribute to our knowledge, but they certainly don't tell us everything. Here now is an exercise based on a simple statistical table.

Turn to document I.6 in *Documents 1*. As students of the Open University's Arts Foundation Course will recall, you have to establish certain points about a historical document before you can begin to make use of it. The figures in this table of incomes were used in a proposal to establish an income tax in 1894–95, so we know the dates they refer to and that they are fairly reliable. The figures were used again in a book published in 1907, so presumably they were thought still to be relevant to the immediate pre-war period we are concerned with. Open University students will also remember from the Arts Foundation Course that to make sense of the document, we need to have some idea of what, say, 2,500 francs, and 100,001 francs mean in terms of purchasing power. Converting into pounds isn't perhaps a very fruitful exercise since, of course, the purchasing power of the pound was rather different in 1894 or 1907 from what it is today. Let us simply say that 2,500 francs is a very bare subsistence income, perhaps equivalent to about £75 a year in Britain at that time.

Now, from the point of view of any questions we might wish to ask of it, this document, like all documents, has many imperfections. In particular, if we want to know the complete story on the distribution of wealth in France it is grossly inadequate, and it is also somewhat inscrutable on the nature of the social structure. On the other hand it does tell us something rather directly about the equality or inequality in the distribution of incomes, and by making some simple deductions we can make a quite striking statement about how many people had a percentage of the total income and the size of that percentage. (This, actually is the document used by Mayeur to support his point about there being a clear divide between the high bourgeoisie and the good bourgeoisie.)

**Exercise**     Try now to answer these questions:

1     Where does the document fail in telling us about distribution of wealth?

2     Where is it inadequate in giving us a picture of social structure?

3     What does it tell us about equality or inequality of income distribution, and what calculations can we do to make striking statements about who held what proportion of total income?

4     How do you think Mayeur used this to demonstrate his point about the divide between the high bourgeoisie and the good bourgeoisie? ■

**Specimen answers**     1     The document refers only to incomes. Powerful people often depend far more on property, stocks and shares, and so on, rather than straightforward income.

2     The document provides 'categories of income', but these are not in any way related to any of the social groups we have been discussing. We might presume that the first and lowest categories apply to the working class, but we certainly can't be sure about that.

3     The gross inequality in the distribution of incomes is (I hope!) immediately clear. Out of a total of 11,000,000 people, more than 9,000,000 have the lowest category of income. A mere 3,000 have incomes nearly fifty times as high as this majority group. But if we look at the third column, the actual total amount of money 'earned' by the different income categories, we can, by adding the two richest groups together, see that more than half the total income (674,000,000 francs added to 572,000,000 francs) is earned by a mere 12,800 people (9,800 plus 3,000).

4     Mayeur suggests that the good bourgeoisie are situated in the income levels 10,001 francs to 50,000 francs, while the high bourgeoisie are divided off around the 50,000 mark. His basic argument (English translation, p.62) is that: 'It is relatively easy to trace the frontier which separated the upper middle class from the ordinary middle class. The scale of incomes establishes a primary distinction.' You may well feel with me that it does not quite do that, and that it is only because he brings to bear a considerable amount of specialist knowledge that Mayeur is able to interpret (correctly, I believe) the statistics in this way. Even statistics (like other primary sources) do not offer transparent truth: they require the interpretative skills of the historian. □

To discuss social structure in the subtle way of a historian like Berghahn, we need literary documents as well as purely statistical ones. I now want you to consider document I.7 in *Documents 1* which consists of extracts from a book by a distinguished French writer, Jules Bertaut, who produced both 'factual' historical and sociological studies, and also literary works. This book, as he explains at the beginning of the first extract, was written in the months before the war, though not published until 1918. It is in fact a fictionalized account, yet based on true experiences of a real French town. The contents list will give you some idea of which social groups Bertaut felt were worth considering, and in what order, in this general study of a provincial French town. I should explain that chapter IV on 'The Wanderers' (*Vagabonds* in French) refers to the high-level government administrators (or civil servants, or 'functionaries', as the French call them) who are allocated by the central government to work in various provincial centres, and who move from one to the other without establishing permanent roots. Angelina in chapter IX is a famous courtesan of the previous century whom I have left in to give some of the flavour of the entire book.

**Exercise**  Now read through these extracts in *Documents 1* (I.7) and then write a paragraph summarizing the social structure as it is presented in them, starting at the top, and commenting on any points relevant to our discussion so far. Say in particular if there are any social groups (or classes) that you would expect to find which are not mentioned by Bertaut. ■

**Specimen answer**  It would seem that at the very top stands Baron Jampy, a Parisian-based aristocrat. The continued importance of the old regime aristocracy is made clear through the attention given to Monsieur de Geneville, and through the information that, however powerful, Monsieur Pellegrin-Simonnet has not quite been assimilated into the true aristocracy. But beyond that, it is clear that the group represented by the 'grand bourgeois' Monsieur Pellegrin-Simonnet is very powerful. He has made it into the exclusive Artistic and Literary Circle (note incidentally the reference to the Jockey Club of Paris – France had, and has, just as many snobby, exclusive clubs as Britain). Though there isn't much about them in the extracts I have quoted, it is clear if you pay close attention that the next group of importance is that of the grand functionaries – the top civil servants. Then note that Bertaut gives three kinds of bourgeoisie, apart from the grand (or high) bourgeoisie: the independent bourgeoisie, the middle bourgeoisie, and the petty bourgeoisie. His comments on these groups suggest that they are not particularly powerful: they prefer the easy life to making money. However, a leading local political figure, Barouille, comes from this class. Then he mentions the petty functionaries, whom he obviously doesn't like (he's clearly liberal-conservative in sympathies); I suspect that he exaggerates their real influence, though he's probably right that they formed a conservative force for the preservation of their own interests. From the list of contents you may have picked up: (a) the Prefect, who in fact goes with the high functionaries (but of course you do not have this information and I am not expecting you to provide it); the teachers, who go with the middle or petty bourgeoisie; (c) the clergy, who are scattered across a range from the bottom of the middle class to the high bourgeoisie; (d) the magistrates, who go with the high functionaries; (e) the liberal professions, who run from the top of the independent bourgeoisie into the high bourgeoisie; and (f) the military community, which is very much seen as a group apart. The only other groups mentioned in the body of his text are that elusive entity 'the people' and the riff-raff. Whether by 'the people' Bertaut means the 'working class', or whether they are the same as the riff-raff, is not clear. Anyway, one striking omission, which I hope you noted, is of the working class, named as such; the other omission is of the peasants.

**Discussion**  Now it may be that in a small town of this type there is no real organized working class; there may be artisans and labourers of various sorts, rather than a factory-based working class. And, of course, one would probably not find peasants actually living in a town. □

There are other interesting points in this quite rich document and some of them will be referred to when we come to other topics. Remember, any one historical document will have many different uses depending upon the questions you are asking of it. *Documents 1* (I.8 and I.9), among other things, tell you something about the conditions endured by the French working class (other documents again discuss working-class political organizations). I don't propose to talk you through these documents. Do just note that while there is no reason to doubt their general veracity, the book *The Tragic Life of Workers*, was written by two brothers very sympathetic to the working-class cause, and published by Jules Rouff, the publisher of the standard *Socialist History* under the direction of the great French socialist leader Jean Jaurès. *The Shop Girls of Paris* is a good example of the kind of progressive, investigative writing of the time deliberately designed in a propagandist way to arouse social consciences and create a demand for political action.

**Exercise**     Read the following extract from Robert Anderson, *France 1870–1914*, then answer the following questions:

1   In what ways does Anderson, while critical of Marx, show that he has absorbed certain Marxist ideas?

2   Do the French peasantry form a class?

3   Are any other classes mentioned by Anderson in this discussion?

> The largest group of all, the peasants, do not fit into any horizontal scheme of social stratification. In a well-known passage, Marx explained how the peasants 'form a vast mass, the members of which live in similar conditions but without entering into manifold relations with one another . . . the great mass of the French nation is formed by simple addition of homologous magnitudes, much as potatoes in a sack form a sack of potatoes'.
>
> Marx was correct in showing why the peasants did not act as a class, but misleading in his implication that they were an undifferentiated mass. The true picture is complex, and demands some preliminary definitions. The term 'peasant' was commonly applied to all who worked on the land, and even to rural artisans and the inhabitants of the countryside generally. 'Peasant farming' in the more limited sense of a system of family holdings worked with little outside labour was characteristic of France, but by no means all the 'peasants' were 'peasant farmers' – there was a substantial force of landless or near landless labourers. Moreover, the peasant farmer was not necessarily a peasant proprietor: much land was rented, and peasant farming could co-exist with large-scale landownership . . .
>
> The statistics for 1892 show that 75 per cent of all farms were farmed directly by their owners; but because many of these holdings were small, they accounted for only 53 per cent of the land area. The remaining 47 per cent was owned by landlords, who let it out either for a cash rent (*fermage*, 36 per cent) or on a crop-sharing basis (*métayage*, 11 per cent). Many of these landlords were bourgeois with one or two farms, or squires with an estate confined to one commune, but there were also rich landowners with an accumulation of estates which made them leading figures in their departments, although the British style of landed magnate holding sway over a vast tract of territory was unknown in France. (Anderson, *France 1870–1914*, 1977, pp.39–40) ∎

**Specimen answers and discussion**

1    He uses the phrase 'act as a class'.

2    Anderson brings out the great variety of types within the peasant aggregate – here he is in disagreement with Marx. But this very variety reinforces, he feels, Marx's view that the peasantry do not form a class. You will recall Clive Emsley's arguments that many peasant families had little sense of belonging to a French nation (let alone to a national peasant class). None the less I would maintain that the bulk of the (smallholding) peasantry was 'class-aware', conscious that their rewards and their style of life were different from those of landowners, clergy, lawyers, shopkeepers, artisans, and that in this sense they did form a 'class', or certainly a distinctive social group, while the landless labourers are analogous to the town-based riff-raff. You are fully entitled to disagree.

3    Other classes mentioned are: the landholding class, and the small 'bourgeois' landholders; in my terms, the landed sectors of, respectively, the upper class, and the upper middle class. Although other factors come in (such as ethnic compositions), class structure is closely related to the nature of the economy. In trying to pin down the distinctive features of the class structures of the different countries in 1914, you will find it useful to raise the points made about the different economies (and about nationality) in the previous unit. France, remember, had a much smaller working class and a less fully developed industrial bourgeoisie than Britain, and a much larger agricultural class (more than half of the population). □

## 1.5   Social structures of Italy, Austria, Germany, Russia and Britain

You have already received a picture, from Martin Clark (extract (d) on pages 142–3) and from Clive Emsley in the previous units, of Italy as a relatively 'underdeveloped' society: small working class, very large peasantry, and a lot of bureaucrats desperately conscious of their status.

**Exercise**    In *Documents 1* (I.10) there seems to be a pretty clear conception of the existence of a working class. How, in the exact words of the document, is that working class defined? ■

**Specimen answer**    'Italian citizens of both sexes who render service of work by the day or who in general do work which is predominantly manual for third parties or also on their own account, provided that, in this latter case, they do not pay, in whatever form, taxes to the State higher than 30 lire a year.'

**Discussion**    The key points of the definition are that the work is manual, and that the earnings are limited. When we discuss class structure we must remember that classes are constantly changing. Since the period discussed by Clark, more land workers have moved to the towns, thus a larger working class, more typical of developed industrial countries, is in the process of *formation*; the working class is being *recruited* from the country areas. These notions of class formation and class recruitment are important ones. Classes are not some permanent abstraction detached from the main processes of demographic, economic and social change. This document is an official document setting out the nature of Italian social insurance legislation. □

Austria-Hungary was an even more variegated state than Italy (again with more than half the population deriving a living from the land). But for the moment just note from paragraphs 3 and 4 of *Documents 1* (I.11) that a factory-based industrial working class is developing in parts of Austria. Document I.11 consists of extracts from the autobiography of Adelheid Popp, who was born in 1869 near Vienna; the book was published in German in 1910, with an introduction by the famous German socialist and feminist Auguste Bebel, and then in English in 1912, with an introduction by the British Labour leader Ramsay MacDonald.

Now turn to *Documents 1* (I.12), an extract from a book on the nature of capitalism by the distinguished German economic historian Werner Sombart, published in Germany just before the war, and in Britain soon after the war started.

**Exercise**     Carefully read document I.12 with the following two questions in mind, writing answers to them when you have finished your reading.

1     What rather strange word appears in the very first line, and again in the first line of the last paragraph. Remembering that it is always a vital part of source criticism to explain any strange or difficult terms, try to give a modern English rendering of this word.

2     What German social group, or class, is being celebrated here? Is Sombart agreeing with Mayer, or with my view of the amalgamating of two classes? ∎

**Specimen answers**     1     'Undertaker'. We would now always use the French form of this word, 'entrepreneur', which of course means businessman, industrialist or capitalist.

2     Sombart is celebrating the successful German upper middle class or bourgeoisie. He seems to see them as separate (by virtue, for instance, of their methods and industry) from the older aristocratic class, so he appears to be agreeing neither with Mayer nor with my view of the classes amalgamating. □

In Unit 3, Clive Emsley told you that Germany was the only country apart from Britain with less than half the population deriving their living from the land. Germany's working class, therefore, is next in size to that of Britain – but don't neglect the German peasantry, who play a more significant role than British farmers or British agricultural workers. We've already learned a little about Russian society. However, important as the qualifications made by Stone are, I think we would be wrong not to seize upon the fundamental facts that great landowners of Mayer's old regime type still, under the autocracy of the Tsar, possessed great powers, and that despite apparent gains the lot of the peasants as a whole, a few lucky exceptions apart (those who became elders or scribes, or government officials), was extremely bad, and in some ways getting worse.

These are basic points. Further details can be derived from the following comments by a leading expert, Hans Rogger. I heartily recommend you to read them carefully.

> At first blush the structure of authority in the countryside looks exceptionally democratic. It seemed to give wide scope to local self-government and custom and to avoid the formalism and legalism that illiterate or semi-literate peasants have at all times and places found remote, incomprehensible, and difficult. At the lowest level, the village community (*selskoe obshchestvo*), acting through the assembly of heads of households, exercised much of the authority formerly vested in the landlords or, in the case of the state peasants, in the Ministry of State

Domains. The village community elected and paid its elder and scribe, set local dues, apportioned state taxes or other obligations and saw to their collection. It selected the required number of conscripts for the military; admitted, banished or released members; decided on divisions of households and property in large families; apportioned the arable and common lands among member households, and for each ten of the latter sent one delegate to the assembly of the canton (*volost*) . . . They also kept records and vital statistics, called out peasants to work on schools and roads, to fight fires and floods.

But the elected officials of village and canton-elders and their deputies, clerks and tax-gatherers, the judges of cantonal courts who heard civil cases involving no more than 100 rubles and punished minor offences – accepted their posts with more resignation than joy. Having to do the state's work took them away from fields and families and did nothing to make them popular with their fellows. These could be flogged at their order, deported to Siberia for 'vicious conduct', denied a passport to leave the community or hired out to make good their share of its financial obligations.

Nor did peasants think of themselves as favoured and protected by an administrative and legal system to which they alone were subject. Village government was based on their separateness from other citizens . . . and helped to perpetuate their distinctness and inferiority. The village representatives were not the peasants' representatives and protectors. Contemporary accounts are full of complaints about them: that elders had men whipped for insolence; that clerks (often the only literates in rural government and therefore powerful) cheated and insulted peasants; that since the best men shunned the village posts, the worst took them up for selfish reasons, and that a bucket of vodka or other bribe could influence elders or judges . . .

The gains made by the peasantry as a class, though statistically impressive, were not enough to satisfy those who most hungered for land, or to keep pace with the explosive pressure of population. From 1877 to 1897 the rural population grew by 25 per cent and did so again in the next twenty years. Land in peasant possession had increased only by 15 per cent in 1905 and 19 per cent in 1916. The average size of an allotment held by peasant households declined from 13.2 desiatinas in 1887 to 10.4 desiatinas in 1905 (one *desiatina* = 2.7 acres). Calculated on the basis of average allotment size per male peasant, the loss was 47 per cent between 1860 and 1900. What allotment land there was and what was purchased in addition had to be divided among households whose number rose in the half century after 1861 from 8.5 million to 12.3 million. According to another calculation for the same period: population grew by more than 50 per cent; the amount of additional land acquired through purchase by 10 per cent.

The peasant's sense of having been cheated – the so-called cut-offs (*otrezki*) kept by the former masters were roughly one sixth the area they surrendered – was deepened by the frequently poor quality and location of holdings and the retention by his noble neighbour of woodland and meadow. The peasant was also made to 'redeem' his allotment. He had to repay the state for the compensation the latter had made to the gentry (and to itself in the case of state peasants) for losses of land and labour. The redemption payments – fixed above market value of the land and stretched over forty-nine years (forty-four for former state peasants) – were a reminder of servile status; so was the village community in which title to the allotted land was vested along with joint responsibility for dues and taxes.

The *mushik* (literally, the little man) was no longer subordinate to the serf-master or an agent of the Ministry of State Domains. He was not yet a free individual who could move or dispose of his property at will. Allotment lands could be distributed or redistributed among members of the community, but they could neither be sold nor mortgaged. Redemptions dues and taxes were a heavy burden. Together with over-population, a low level of agricultural techniques, an exhausted soil, inadequate rainfall, frequent crop failures, a slump in grain prices and a steep rise in land values, they were the classic ingredients of what had become a deep-seated depression of most of peasant farming. (Hans Rogger, *Russia in the Age of Modernization and Revolution 1881–1917*, 1983, pp.71–2, 76–7)

Britain at this time had the most developed industrial working class of any nation in the world, quite simply because industrialization had come to it first. Because of the development of financial and administrative institutions, Britain also had a very developed lower middle class (similar to the German *Mittelstand*). Document I.13, takes the form of extracts from a couple of letters written by John Galsworthy, grandson of a London property developer, whose offspring moved steadily up in the world, buying land, and entering into such highly prestigious professions as that of barrister (as Galsworthy himself did). Already immensely rich, and having received a traditional upper-class education, Galsworthy was at this time just about to embark on his career as a successful novelist.

**Exercise**    Read *Documents 1* (I.13) and say what view of the upper class Galsworthy presents. ■

**Specimen answer**    Galsworthy sees the upper class as an amalgam of the older aristocratic and gentry and business elements. There are very fine distinctions, but basically they seem one integrated class. Middle-class elements, particularly businessmen, but also professionals, remained firmly middle class – below this new upper class identified by Galsworthy, but clearly above the new lower middle class. □

## 1.6    The significance of class

From Mayer, whether his precise account of the processes taking place is correct or not (I think not), we can see that in all countries the main positions of economic and political power are held by a relatively small number of families grouped at the top of society. Class, or social structure if you prefer, is very important to the way wealth and income are distributed. Berghahn, Kocka and Mayeur give us some of the more subtle, but very important, influences of class: the way people lived, the resentments they felt, the forms of organization they adopted, were very strongly influenced by their place in the social structure.

Of course, people are grouped together in other ways than just by social group or class.

**Exercise**    Name the other kinds of associations or affiliations or groups that people can have which might affect their outlook, behaviour and life chances? ■

**Specimen answer**    Nationality, town, village, other local community, religion; possibly also sex.

**Discussion**    Clearly in Austria-Hungary the question of nationality is of great importance, probably more important than that of class. Berghahn steers a nice position in regard to Germany, and his analysis would apply in greater or lesser degree to the other developed continental European countries. As the most advanced industrial society Britain probably was more affected by class than by the other distinctions.

> . . . there were two currents which tended to cut across the stratification of Wilhelmine society in terms of a specific class culture. These cross-currents complicated the overall picture because they did not act to reinforce existing divisions along class and infra-class status lines, and they were: regionalism and denomination.
>
> The importance of regionalism and local consciousness cannot be emphasised too strongly . . . Local uniformity of a particular accent has occasionally been taken as proof that regionalism was a stronger bond than class. Wilhelmine Germany was deemed to be less class-ridden than Edwardian England where the accent immediately betrayed a person's social background. It may be that a Bavarian felt particularly Bavarian in Berlin or Cologne; but this did not mean that he or she had lost the capacity or propensity to place other Bavarians within the Empire's overall social structure. He might be pleased to meet a fellow-businessman from Munich in Prussia. Yet he was as unlikely to befriend a Bavarian factory worker outside Bavaria as he was to have social intercourse with him back home.
>
> Religious belief was the second factor which cut across class and status barriers . . . (Berghahn, *Modern Germany*, 1982, pp.10–11) □

Class is related to political belief and activity, though not always in a completely direct way. As you saw from document I.11, the growth of the working class in Austria was giving rise to a socialist movement; there were similar movements in other countries. But, inevitably when you think about it, the active members of these movements were a rather small minority of the working class as a whole. Just where the other classes, and indeed the working class itself, stood in relation to conservatism and liberalism is something best explored in the next unit.

# 2  HIGH CULTURE AND POPULAR CULTURE

## 2.1  Historical study of culture

Class was bad enough, you may think, but culture! Like Goering you may well want to reach for your gun. It has always been a fundamental characteristic of history teaching at the Open University that we believe that history embraces all the activities of human societies in the past – political, economic, social and cultural. But for those of you who like your history to be about political parties, trade unions, international treaties, and rates of inflation, let me develop this point.

The question of the effects of war on culture is a very central one in any comprehensive discussion of war and social change. To get a feel for the nature, and limits, of the debate, I want you now to read the fourth paragraph of 'The birth of the modern: 1885–1914' by G. D. Josipovici, reprinted in the Course Reader. Please do make a point of reading this now since in the space of a few lines it sets up a very important issue.

Now, if you can put your hand on your heart and swear to have read that extract, read the following paragraph, which is from an essay entitled 'The First World War and the literary consciousness' by R. Gibson: (in Cruickshank, ed.):

> It would clearly be wrong to attribute the modern humanists' malaise exclusively to the impact of the First World War. The traditional bases of humanism were in any event being gravely eroded by the effects of spectacular advances in science and technology, by the challenging new ideas of anthropologists and sociologists, and, most particularly, by the revolutionary theories of Freud. At the same time, the effect of the war should not be underestimated either. It provided its own irresistible impulse to forces which were already dynamic, brutally stripping away illusions and confronting Man with the frailty of his body and the fragility of his beliefs. Man has, ever since, been left to come to terms with the daunting conclusion that the principal cause, as well as the principal victim, of war is Man himself.

One cannot understand the twentieth century if one does not have an understanding of its most important cultural movement, modernism. The twentieth-century historian who does not know something of Proust, Joyce, Picasso, Klee, Schönberg and Stravinsky, has no business being in business. What I am speaking of here is, of course, 'high culture', and I am for the moment making a case for the necessity for studying high culture.

Purely on this limited issue of high culture, Mayer makes another less general, more traditionally historical, argument for the study of high culture, in the extract from Chapter 4 'Official high cultures and the avant-garde' of *The Persistence of the Old Regime* (reprinted on pp.67–71 of the Course Reader).

In a moment I am going to ask you to read that section, but first I want you to read the whole of the Josipovici chapter. As you may find this quite heavy going (though personally I find it a brilliant exposition of a difficult topic), I will indicate the main points you should get from the essay.

As a preliminary, let me stress that our concern here is with the condition of modernism on the eve of World War I in order to provide a basis upon which we can subsequently assess the effects, if any, of that war on the further development of modernism. Josipovici has to delve far back into the nineteenth century, but our concern is purely with the artists still practising in 1914, and above all with ones who went on writing over the World War I period. We are not at this stage concerned with the writers who only came to the fore after World War I (T. S. Eliot, for instance). Let me therefore list the artists (in addition to the five already mentioned, the novelists Proust and Joyce, the painters Picasso and Klee, and the composers Schönberg and Stravinsky) who are relevant to our studies: Braque (painter), Kafka (novelist), Jarry (playwright), Debussy (composer), Diaghilev (choreographer). The other names mentioned by Josipovici are important simply in explaining the early development of modernism. There are one or two other names that I wish to bring in, such as Thomas Mann, the German novelist, Anton Chekhov, the Russian playwright, and Richard Strauss, the Austrian composer.

The key points about the nature of modernism made by Josipovici are:

1   Modernism is a reaction to decadent, self-indulgent Romanticism. (In making this point, it should be noted, Josipovici is grossly unfair to the opera composer Wagner, stressing the weaknesses of his self-indulgence and 'magic' but, of course, passing over the immense strengths of this creator of great music drama.)

2    Modernism recognizes the limitations upon art and the clear differences between the various forms of art: painting is brush strokes, poetry is groupings of words, and so on.

3    Modern art seeks to make the viewer or reader work hard by showing him the familiar in a new light and by drawing him into the actual processes through which the work of art is produced.

4    While modernism may have begun as a reaction against Romanticism it is in reality nothing less than a complete break with centuries of tradition in art. There are three main aspects of this which I shall number points (a), (b) and (c).

(a)    Modernism recognizes that the traditional Western way of looking at things is only one way among many (here direct historical influences are important, the discovery of Japanese art, African sculpture, and so on).

(b)    Traditionally, the artist was concerned with either, or both, expressing himself and imitating external reality. The modern artist, instead of seeing his work as an expression of himself, deliberately separates himself from his work. This can be seen, for instance, in the long series of novels produced by Proust (of great interest to us, since the first one was published just before the war, the second just at the end of the war, and the remainder in the post-war years) *À la recherche du temps perdu* (conventionally translated as *Remembrance of Things Past*), which, in one of its aspects, is not a traditional novel, but is a discussion of how the central character, Marcel, might write a novel.

(c)    Modernism also breaks sharply with the idea of imitating the external world: it breaks 'with four centuries of mimesis' ('mimesis' simply being an elegant way of saying 'imitation'). Modern artists are aware that they produce according to particular conventions, particular rules of the game; they are not presenting a slice of external reality. Proust is a good example again in that he breaks sharply from the nineteenth-century tradition of presenting rounded characters whose every action is consistent with the character carefully delineated by the author. Proust seeks to show that we never really know what other people are like, or indeed what we ourselves are like, and that in fact we all act in all sorts of inconsistent ways, there being no definite, clearly perceived, 'external' character. Proust also shares with modernist writers a preoccupation with the conventions of art: what art is, the nature and purposes and possible achievements of art, these are questions which run through Proust as also through much of the work of Thomas Mann.

**Exercise**    I want you to read the piece by Josipovici, and then the section by Mayer already indicated. As you read through Josipovici make sure, for your own studies, that you note where the main points I have made occur in his text.

1    Note down what Josipovici says about actual geographical centres of modernism.

After you have read both Josipovici and Mayer, note down answers to the following:

2    Remember that earlier I said Mayer offered a reason for historians to study high culture. What is it?

3    Write a sentence or two pinning down the ways in which Josipovici and Mayer agree and disagree in their views of the significance of modernism. ∎

**Specimen answers**    1    Josipovici says that 'the modern movement . . . was an urban movement . . . to be found in all the great cosmopolitan centres of Europe: Vienna, Munich, Prague, and especially Paris'.

2    Mayer says that the dominant class which he is writing about uses high culture, on the one hand, to exalt its regime and validate its moral claims, and on the other hand to display its wealth, taste and status. (This, then, becomes the fourth argument for historians giving attention to the study of culture, or in this case, high culture.)

3    Both writers seem to agree in their belief in modernism, that it is, as it were, 'a good thing'. Perhaps because he is not basically concerned with the historical and social aspects, Josipovici rather gives a picture of the steady advance and triumphs of modernism, whereas Mayer is arguing that this old regime which he believes is still dominant preserves the older pre-modern or 'historicist' as he calls it, culture, and that the avant-garde, the proponents of modernism, are, before 1914, largely unsuccessful.

**Discussion**    This is a very important issue. It is on the whole true that much modernist art appealed only to a minority of a minority, and that much (though by no means all) was scoffed at even by the educated audiences at which it was aimed. It is relevant to the point made at the end of the Josipovici piece that while the Post-impressionists gained wide acceptance in artistic and intellectual circles in Paris, they did not do so in London. Proust was deeply respected within his own intellectual coterie, but he could not find a commercial publisher for his first volume, and had to have it published privately. □

Excellent as the Josipovici essay is, it has at least one omission. Josipovici leaves out developments in science and technology, which apart from their important effects on material life and the nature of warfare, also affect high culture and modernism. Critically important are the undermining of the notion of a stable physical world associated with Newtonian physics, through the discoveries of Heisenberg, Schrödinger, and Einstein, and of the stable human personality through Freud's claims to have discovered the deeper, sub-conscious human drives. For these points, and a good explanation of the differences in the ways in which new ideas affect élites (the proponents of high culture) and more popular audiences, read chapter 7 of Roberts's *Europe 1880–1945*, to the foot of page 233.

## 2.2    Culture as historical evidence

A fifth reason for studying cultural artefacts is, of course, that, like everything else created by the age the historian is studying, they can often prove valuable sources.

It has often been argued that certain works of art and literature, some within the realm of high culture, some perhaps more properly belonging to popular culture, reveal that there was 'a will to war' in European society before 1914. The phrase is both metaphysical and question-begging, but there simply can be no question that many works aiming at a limited, intellectual audience, as well as many aiming at a much wider audience, expressed attitudes of jingoism, national rivalry, and a happy expectation of war.

One very striking example is the French poet and essayist Charles Péguy, who was born in 1873 and came from a poor rural family. He was both a socialist and a supporter of traditional French rural life. But well before 1914 he had turned towards the exaltation of heroism, patriotism and military glory. In 1913, in his poem 'Prayer for we others', he wrote:

> Happy are those who have died for the charnel earth,
> But provided that this was in a just war,
> Happy those who have died for four corners of earth,
> Happy those who have died a solemn death . . .

In a series of novels about military life in North Africa, Ernest Psichari expressed a viewpoint which can be summed up in this short quotation from *The Call to Arms* of 1913: 'Guns are the most real of realities, the only realities of the modern world.'

Péguy, despite his humble origins, perhaps belongs in the world of high culture; Psichari is a more popular writer appealing to all who are literate. *Documents 1* (I.14 and I.15) are both extracts from popular writings, one German, and one British, which demonstrate expectancy of war.

Militarism, glorification of violence, expectation, and even anticipation of war, are very marked characteristics of the pre-war movement in the visual arts known as Futurism, and also in the British offshoot known as Vorticism. These movements are illustrated in the art pack and its associated audio-cassette, where I shall try to identify the influences of war on culture. Here my basic objective is simply to establish that modernism was already in full view well before 1914.

## 2.3  Religion and popular culture

Changes in the nature of religious belief as it operated in the realm of high culture can be traced in Roberts, pages 74 to 81. Roberts also touches on religious practice and belief as an important part of popular culture. In general, his is a picture of decline in religious practice and belief. It is true that in industrial areas religion had never meant much to the under class. Read the section on 'Religion' in Roberts now; however, bear in mind these points which, in my view, Roberts does not stress sufficiently:

• In rural areas, however poverty-stricken, traditional religious practice and belief continued to be a fundamental element in everyday life.

• Among respectable working-class families in all countries religious observance was certainly one element in everyday life (active socialists, particularly in Germany, as Roberts says, were usually exceptions; however, in Britain, many socialists continued to be practising Christians).

• Even where there were strong anti-clerical movements, as in France, and, towards the end of the period, in Italy, opposition to what was thought of as clerical dictatorship did not necessarily mean abandonment of an acceptance of the tenets of Catholicism.

Traditional religious belief was under attack well before 1914, but across Europe as a whole religious belief was still very much a part of the fabric of everyday life. We have to be clear about this before we can, in the next book, assess the effects of World War I on religion.

## 2.4   Other aspects of popular culture

Popular novels such as we have already mentioned come within the realm of popular culture. So also do popular newspapers, popular songs, trade-union banners, brass bands, folk dancing and spectator sports, such as football. Spectator sports are a product of the later nineteenth century; popular newspapers of a sort have a longer history, though the modern mass-circulation daily newspaper is really only a product of the very end of the century. Just, however, as high culture in the twentieth century was to be strongly characterized by modernism, so popular culture in the twentieth century was characterized by one strikingly new cultural medium.

**Exercise**    What is this new popular medium? ■

**Specimen answer**    The specific new medium is the cinematographic film, actually an invention of the 1890s and, of course, still silent in the period we are studying. □

Later developments in the technologically based mass media are the development of sound radio, development of talking film, of colour film, and eventually of television. It will be another task of our course to discuss how far, if at all, war affected the development of these mass media; and also to discuss the use of these media in wartime.

The question of how far film had already developed *before* 1914 is one which must be treated with some care. It would be fairly widely agreed that it was in the period 1908–14 that film in the more advanced European countries became an important field for commercial investment, and that it was in the same period that film moved from being a small component of music hall or fairground shows to providing a complete evening's entertainment in 'picture palaces', either converted theatres, skating rinks, and so on, or, increasingly, specially built, with fancy trimmings designed to attract wealthy middle-class patrons in addition to the working-class ones who were the mainstay of cinema audiences. Document I.16 in *Documents 1* gives some interesting statistics for Britain. France was perhaps slightly more developed, Germany probably in roughly the same position as Britain, and the other countries somewhat behind.

Programmes were still often made up of a large number of short items, but already the American industry was beginning to provide real feature films, with sufficient prestige to attract top European, as well as top American, theatrical performers – for example, the Italian opera star Lina Cavalieri. All the elements, then, of commercial silent cinema seem to be there. However, cinemas had not really spread far outside the main urban centres; audiences remained overwhelmingly working class; much of what was shown was of rather simple interest, and rudimentary in quality, feature films which developed a proper story still being pretty rare; and many commercial speculators felt that film was merely a passing fad out of which money should be made as quickly as possible.

## 2.5   Conclusion

In much French historical writing, academic and popular, the period from roughly 1890 to the outbreak of war is *'la belle époque'*, the beautiful epoch. Roberts on page 151 refers to the economic growth which provides the basis for this label. Obviously, from the material we have already studied, whether the time was really 'beautiful' or not for the individual family would depend very much upon their class position. Document I.12 in *Documents 1*, together with some of what you have read from Berghahn, would suggest that there also was a class in Germany full of optimism and conscious of doing very well; such a class could also be found in Vienna, Prague, in some of the urban centres of Italy, and certainly throughout most of Britain. For industrial workers in steady employment, standards everywhere were higher than they ever had been before. It is doubtful, however, whether the label *'la belle époque'* could ever be applied to East and Central Europe or to Russia.

Certainly, as with all historical labels, the phrase *'la belle époque'* is one that must be used with some caution. Probably it is safest to confine it to its country of origin. For upper class, for upper middle class, for others lower down the scale out on an isolated binge, there were in all countries equivalents of the *Folies Bergère, Moulin Rouge,* and *Chez Maxim,* whose heyday this era undoubtedly was. France had one additional reason, as we have seen, for feeling particularly pleased with itself. Whether we speak of modernism, or of the avant-garde, Paris took precedence over all other European capitals; the Diaghilev ballet might be Russian, but it was in Paris that it had its first great triumphs.

## References

Anderson, R. (1977) *France 1870–1914: Politics and Society*, Routledge and Kegan Paul.

Berghahn, V. (1982) *Modern Germany: Society, economy and politics in the twentieth century*, Cambridge University Press (second edition 1987).

Clark, M. (1984) *Modern Italy 1871–1982*, Longman.

Cruickshank, J. (ed.) (1968–70) *French Literature and its Background*, Oxford University Press.

Kocka, J. (1984) *Facing Total War*, Berg.

Macartney, C. A. (1969) *The Habsburg Empire 1790–1918*, Weidenfeld and Nicolson.

Mayeur, J-M. (1984) 'The beginnings of the Third Republic 1871–1898' in Mayeur, J-M. and Rebérioux, M., *The Third Republic from its Origins to the Great War, 1871–1914*, Cambridge University Press.

Rogger, H. (1983) *Russia in the Age of Modernization and Revolution 1881–1917*, Longman.

Stone, N. (1975) *The Eastern Front, 1914–1917*, Hodder and Stoughton.

# UNIT 5   THE PROCESSES OF CHANGE

*Arthur Marwick*

**Open University students of this unit will need to refer to:**

Set book: J. M. Roberts, *Europe 1880–1945*, Longman, 1989

*Documents 1: 1900–1929*, eds Arthur Marwick and Wendy Simpson, Open University Press, 1990

# *1 HOW CHANGE COMES ABOUT*

The general aim in this unit is to establish a firm basis for your subsequent analysis of the exact place of World War I in the major social changes which took place in twentieth-century Europe. In essence it aims to establish what changes were *already* taking place *before* war broke out.

## 1.1   'Structural' and 'non-structural' factors

My title for this section may or may not mean something to you. If it does, it may help you to answer my first question. But even if it doesn't, have a fair crack at trying to answer it.

Exercise   Obviously Russia in 1914 was different from how it had been in, say, 1800; Britain was different from how it had been in 1850, and so on. How does historical change come about? Write down as many headings or points as you can. ■

Specimen answer and discussion   I would have expected you to note down points like the following: through industrialization, through the application of technology; through economic growth and international trade; through population growth (or decline); through the emergence of new social classes and groups; through social and political reform (acts of parliament, decrees of an absolute ruler, and so on); through pressure from, say, trade unions; through new ideas being put forward in reaction against old ones. You might also have said, through revolutions, or, anticipating the major concerns of this course, through wars, or, you might have added, through imperial conquest and exploitation, through the discovery of gold and new raw materials.

I don't know whether that's the sort of thing you put down, whether you got more points, or less. One could always go after the less usual (as far as modern Europe is concerned) and bring in, say, plagues and famines. Or one could go into much more detail, talking about the influence of particular political ideas, such as liberalism or socialism, or mentioning the importance of agitators, propagandists and revolutionaries; one might talk about the special importance of newspapers, or of railways, or of the electricity industry, or of town-based metal industries. One might wish to mention the significance of the challenge of Darwinism and the rise of secularism to traditional religion.

But then would we not be moving from the causes of changes to the changes themselves? Always a difficult problem in historical study where the search for primary causes is bedevilled by the fact that in the human past different types of development, causes and effects, are closely interrelated. We can see that industrialization causes changes, but what causes industrialization? I have in my sub-heading used the metaphor (drawn from mathematics) 'factors', but actually I could as readily have said 'change', thus thoroughly begging the question!

Still, I think my original list was, as these things go, a pretty fair one to start off with. Of course, you may have answered in a totally different way, and that I will discuss shortly. □

Exercise   Confining yourself just to my original list, and ignoring the elaborations, can you now put some of these headings and points into the category 'structural', and the rest, for the moment, into the category 'non-structural'. If you would like a little help, you could look at Roberts's table of contents, and the outline for chapter 11 given on pages vii–viii. You will see I have used his own major sub-heading 'Structural change'.

Can you give a brief explanation of what is meant by 'structural' in this context? ■

**Specimen answer and discussion**

I'll start with my explanation of the difference. Structural factors refer to the broader forces in society which, irrespective of the intentions of individuals or groups of individuals, bring about changes affecting, willy-nilly, large sectors of the population. Industrialization, application of technology, economic growth, population growth, and the emergence of new social classes and groups, involve changes in the very *structure* of society. The other factors brought about (or intended to be brought about) by particular individuals or groups (parties or trade unions, for instance) deliberately acting to some kind of policy or plan, are 'non-structural'. The distinction can never be absolutely hard-and-fast. Obviously the application of technology does involve something in the way of deliberate human choices (as indeed does growth of population), but clearly in their effects industrialization together with applied technology has ramifications for whole societies which go far beyond the conscious decisions of individuals or groups. Thus, my original list divides up as follows.

| *Structural* | *Non-structural* |
|---|---|
| Industrialization | Reform |
| Application of technology | Trade-union pressure |
| Population growth or | New ideas |
| decline | Revolutions |

There are problems in the second column. Traditional Marxists would regard revolutions as essentially the product of structural forces. And it is difficult to argue that great new movements of ideas, such as Romanticism, or individualism, or socialism, can be categorized with political reform and agitation as the product of the deliberate intentions of single individuals or groups. Traditional Marxism maintained that structural, basically economic, changes come first, and that ideas, the 'superstructure' in traditional Marxist phraseology, are a product of these; however most modern Marxists are inclined to accept at least relative autonomy for the major movements in ideas. The point of all this, remember, is that if we are to establish what, if any, changes are brought about by war, we have to be clear about what forces of change are in operation anyway, whether there are wars or not. It will help if we make a distinction between *three* sorts of factors which can produce change: (1) structural (you now know what these are); (2) ideological – the great movements of ideas, such as Darwinism and modernism; and (3) what I am going to call 'guided', though say 'political' if you prefer that more traditional, though less exact, word. What I mean here is not the profound, long-term structural factors, and not the great movements of ideas, but the actions of, for example, politicians and trade unionists, which are in a very distinctive sense conscious or deliberate – they result in 'guided' change, as distinct from structural and ideological change, which can very reasonably be considered together as 'unguided change'. Of course, as in all academic work there is an element of artificiality in this. But then the search for ultimate first causes in historical study is not a rewarding one. □

## 1.2   Marxism and 'modernization'

There are totally different ways of handling this issue. Marxism, as you know, has an all-embracing theory of how change comes about, that is through the development of new modes of production and through the conflict that engenders between the existing dominant class and the rising new class. Marxism, in effect, is an example of an approach which stresses the centrality of structural factors to the exclusion of almost everything else. Other approaches stressing structural elements have been developed through Max Weber and more recent sociologists and political scientists. One such approach involves the concept of 'modernization'.

> . . . modernization is the process of change towards those types of social, economic, and political systems that have developed in Western Europe and North America from the seventeenth century to the nineteenth, and have then spread to other European countries and in the nineteenth and twentieth centuries to the South American, Asian, and African continents.

The importance of all this is that if we are to have a serious discussion of whether the two world wars have brought change we have to have a clear idea in our minds of how change does come about. You will remember from my quotations from Kocka at the beginning of the previous unit that Kocka's Marxist philosophy contributed to his answers about the effects of World War I on the *Mittelstand* in Germany: he was arguing that the processes of change which Marxists see as 'normal' had become distorted in pre-war Germany and that the war, in some sense, restored these processes to their 'proper' working. Those who conceive of change as essentially caused by structural factors will tend to dismiss the effects of wars as being of minor account compared with longer term structural forces. One simple formulation which is sometimes put forward is that the effect of modern war is to 'accelerate modernization'. We shall wish in this course to scrutinize such bland statements. 'Accelerate' is a metaphor borrowed from the physical sciences. Beware of all metaphors: they, at best, describe; they do not explain.

# 2  THE AREAS OF SOCIAL CHANGE WITH WHICH THIS COURSE IS CONCERNED

What kinds of change are we talking about? This is really rather crucial if we are to make any progress with our analysis, though it is a rather regrettable fact that even quite distinguished historians sometimes write books concerning historical change without ever defining precisely which areas they are dealing with, or what exactly they mean by 'change'. In this course it is very simple: we have to look at (a) the international and geopolitical consequences of war, and (b) the implications of war for social developments *within* the countries we are studying.

Here now is a list of the areas of concern in this course:

### (a) International, geopolitical and strategic

It is a commonplace that wars affect the drawing of boundaries between states – victorious powers annex territory, defeated ones lose it. More than this, even where political frontiers remain unchanged, the power relationships between countries may be changed significantly. (In terms of actual territory, America did not increase at the end of World War II, though Russia did; both countries, as is well known, emerged as 'super powers'. It could also be argued that Australia's position in the world altered – from being broadly still within a British sphere of influence in the 1930s, it was now very much in an American sphere of influence.) Such geopolitical matters may seem at the furthest extreme from social and cultural ones; but in fact geopolitical changes have ramifications throughout society.

### (b) Social

This includes the following areas:

*1  Social geography*
This includes population (clearly very directly affected by the destruction of war), urbanization, distribution of agriculture and industry.

In wars people are killed, family life is disrupted, disease and famine spread. Some contemporary historians consider population change to be the most basic structural factor in historical developments.

*2  Economic performance and theory*
This includes activities and structures, the nature of work, exploitation of science and technology. A central question (particularly in the study of war) concerns the extent to which governments themselves should directly intervene in the economy.

Wise in our generation, we know that all other questions, whether expenditure on welfare services or opera, depend upon economic performance.

*3  Social structure*
We know that there have been changes in social structure over the twentieth century. But the exact nature of these, and the role played in them by the two wars, are matters for precise analysis.

*4  National cohesion*
Some nations, for example Britain and France, were nationally very homogenous in 1914, others such as Russia and Austria-Hungary were not. It is a commonplace that modern wars are likely to offer opportunities for national minorities to assert themselves.

*5  Social reform and welfare policies*
This is very much a twentieth-century phenomenon. Has the experience of war played a part?

*6  Material conditions*
It is another commonplace that living standards generally have risen through the twentieth century: could war, that most destructive of all human activities, possibly have played a part?

7   *Customs and behaviour*

This is a difficult heading, which overlaps with aspects of the next three headings (particularly with respect to popular culture and family life), yet one that serves as a useful focus for some of the items of potential change which stand out most strongly in popular memory, but are often neglected by historians, including costume and dress, eating and drinking habits, hours of work and recreation, the role of authority structures such as church and family. Do wars disrupt traditional patterns of behaviour, and bring in new customs? Are the disruptions greater in less developed, more agrarian societies, than in the more industrialized ones?

8   *Women and the family*

By using this heading the writers of this course do not wish to imply that these two topics are indissolubly linked, nor that war and the status of women cannot be treated as an independent topic. What is beyond dispute is that in all the debates over the possible effects of war the questions of women, and of women's traditional role within the family, have figured very prominently.

9   *High and popular culture*

In introducing (in Unit 4) the Josipovici article in the Course Reader, I indicated the nature of the major debate over war's relationship to modernism. With regard to popular culture, questions arise as to how far films, broadcasting, popular newspapers, and so on, took their basic impetus from the experience of war.

10   *Political institutions and values*

You already know that the European countries in 1914 varied greatly with respect to the rights enjoyed by their citizens, whether they had autocratic or representative institutions, and whether their values were broadly liberal or authoritarian, religious or secular. Did it need war to dethrone the autocracies or, on the contrary, is war a fundamentally undemocratic activity?

# 3   HOW DO WE MEASURE CHANGE?

The list above is of the ten main areas within which, in the aftermath of war, we shall be hoping to identify social change or the lack of it. How, indeed, do we measure whether or not change has taken place in these areas?

**Exercise**   It was suggested in Unit 1 that there are two broad ways in which change can be measured. What are they? Add a sentence or two explaining the two different approaches. ■

**Specimen answer and discussion**   The two ways are quantitative and qualitative. When measuring economic performance, material conditions, demographic changes, who actually has the vote, and so on, precise statistics are indispensable. Indeed, we should always seek to quantify. However, when we are dealing with questions of political or moral values, quality of life, culture, and so on, clearly we shall be making *qualitative* judgements, relying on the more traditional type of discursive written document. □

# 4 STRUCTURAL FACTORS EXAMINED

Let us distinguish between two broad types of structural factor: (a) demographic; (b) industrial and economic.

**Exercise**  Turn to Roberts page 22 and read from the beginning of the paragraph 'This political framework . . .' to the end of the section on page 29, keeping the following questions in mind.

1   As structural forces for change, do demographic factors operate on the short term or on the long term?

2   Given that birth rates were now falling, why was population in general still rising?

3   What major long-term consequence of the main demographic changes does Roberts identify with respect to social conditions, quality of life, and so on?

4   With regard to population growth Europe splits into two halves. What are these?

5   What is the relationship between population growth and great power status? Which country was most adversely affected by this relationship?

6   Within countries, what was the most noticeable shift in population?

7   Does Roberts make any suggestions about possible effects of war on demographic trends? Can *you* think of any possible effects? ∎

**Specimen answers and discussion**  1   Long term. The reason for asking this question is to bring out that it may be that demographic trends operate on a totally different timescale from any possible effects of war which, obviously, one would expect to be apparent within the war and post-war periods themselves. However, also consider the response to question 5.

2   The population was still rising because of falling death rates, *above all among infants in the first twelve months of their lives.*

3   Human beings began to expect, and demand, more in the way of better living conditions, amenities of life, and so on (first paragraph on page 26). I posed this question because it is sometimes argued that wars raise expectations; we shall have to consider that argument within the long-term context which Roberts is setting.

4   Higher population growths in the poorer southern and eastern countries; lower ones in the richer northern and western ones.

5   A large and growing population is necessary for sustaining the military power upon which great power status ultimately rests. France, with a practically negligible rate of population growth, was increasingly in a serious position (which helps to explain some of her phobias in respect to her powerful neighbour, Germany).

6   A shift from the country areas to the towns – though note Roberts's very careful words on the subject.

7   Although Roberts discusses demography throughout practically the whole period of this course, he does not refer to the two world wars. However, one might predict that the large destruction of life in wartime, and in particular the destruction of potential fathers, and also the separation of husbands from wives,

might have adverse effects on population growth. On the other hand, Roberts does cite medical advances and rises in living standards as important factors behind population growth. It may be (this has yet to be determined) that wars encourage such improvements and thus, paradoxically, enhance population growth. □

Because Roberts is writing a comprehensive work of history endeavouring to bring out the complex interrelationship between historical forces as they actually operate, he is not able to separate out the different 'areas of change' and 'factors of change' in the way in which, in order to simplify and clarify, I have done. However, the section from page 29 to 48 broadly sets out the main structural factors, other than the demographic ones which we have just discussed. Remember that our main purpose is to try to determine how far the main structural factors which have shaped Europe in the twentieth century were already clearly in operation before 1914, and how far we have to seek their critical origins in the period after 1914, the period of the two world wars. Roberts writes with clarity and lucidity but the purpose of his book (to provide a general history of modern Europe) is, of course, slightly different from that of this course (to illuminate the interrelationship between war and society). Rather than set a series of questions on this passage from Roberts, I shall simply offer a series of headings which, I hope, will help to drive home the relevance to our studies of the points Roberts is making, with just the occasional question to highlight particularly relevant issues.

**Exercise**    With this summary beside you, read through the section in Roberts headed 'The economy before 1914', noting answers to the questions I ask as you go along.

The first three paragraphs summarize what Roberts in the fourth paragraph refers to as 'the foundations of Europe's wealth' – basically in fact geographical factors.

In the next three paragraphs he introduces the question of the basic economic system, capitalist, large scale, and involving specialization. He notes that with population growth European countries more and more had to import food; but he also discusses the different types of improvement in domestic food production happening in the different countries.

Roberts then (on page 34) moves on to the growth of industry, the fundamental dynamic factor in shaping European society. Very quickly he makes two contrasting points, one suggesting that pre-1914 Europe is still rather different from the Europe of the later twentieth century, and one suggesting that in essence it is the same.

1    What are these points? Write them down now.

Roberts's discussion of the basic economic system continues with an identification of the traditional bases of industrial production, and their uneven distribution and of the resumption (after the so-called 'depression') of industrial expansion in the 1890s.

2    What does Roberts say about growth rates in Russia?

3    On page 39 Roberts goes on to discuss 'new industries'. He mentions three. What are these?

Then we have a passage running from page 42, 'The relations of . . .', to page 44, '. . . and a capital-importer', comparing industrial advance in the different

European countries. Germany is in some ways surpassing Britain, France is remaining behind.

Note the three classes into which Roberts divides the European economies (page 44).

Roberts then goes on to a very important discussion (running to the end of the section) of the way in which the European economies are both closely interrelated with each other and with the wider world economy. Again Roberts seems to be saying on the one hand that here we have basic economic structures which were to dominate the rest of the twentieth century, and on the other he seems to be saying that the conditions existing before 1914 were to be seriously changed after 1914.

4    Pick out two phrases used by Roberts which suggest that conditions obtaining in 1914 were to be changed after 1914. ■

**Specimen answers and discussion**

1    On the one hand he says that it is important to remember how much of an older economic world was still interlocked with the new industrial world, while on the other he claims that 'the industrial Europe of 1940 can be seen in that of 1880'.

2    Russian rate of growth was very high (p.38) (though of course Russia was still very 'backward' in the sense that total output was still small). We have to bear all of this in mind when considering the effects of war and revolution on Russia.

3    Chemicals, electricity, internal combustion engine.

4    Roberts refers to a 'golden age' of intricate international integration (p.44) – the implication being that the golden age did not exist after 1914. He also, on page 46, refers to economic life being 'more completely self-regulating' (before 1914) than *since*. □

# 5 THE AGENTS OF 'GUIDED' OR 'POLITICAL' CHANGE

We must now look more closely at the elements producing 'guided' or 'political' change. Ideas directly affect society through political and industrial movements (that is to say, largely through political parties and trade unions) which are themselves often formed in response to structural changes. But political movements have to respond to everyday contingencies and their achievements, furthermore, are often tied up with the quality and character of the political 'actors' and leaders.

Across the Europe of 1914 quite a range of political and social ideas were held, and sometimes vigorously advocated, by different individuals and groups.

Once again, I'm afraid, we are in an area where (as with class) the happy tossing around of labels is no substitute for careful historical exposition. The same label (for example, 'liberalism' or 'socialism') can mean different things in different countries, or in different periods, or indeed to different people in the same country at the same period. The names taken by political parties do not necessarily represent a total, or even partial, commitment to any particular set of political ideas (the majority party in French parliaments throughout most of the period we are studying called itself the Radical Socialists, though it was certainly not socialist, and it is a moot point how far it was radical). In this section I want to explore the relationships between the major political philosophies and the actual policies of rulers, political parties, trade unions, and the many associations and pressure groups which play a part in social change. Politicians and parties, even the most purely opportunistic, operate within their own framework of ideas and values, reacting of course to particular events, crises, and necessities: out of these reactions spring what I have termed guided change.

At this point, I shall suggest a list of the main political and social philosophies effective in the Europe of 1914, with notes on their complexities and on their relationship to actual politics.

### Conservatism

Across the countries of continental Europe this term implied support for the principles and institutions of what Mayer calls the old regime, and resistance to change. It involved support for monarchy, aristocracy, and whatever church establishment these two upheld. The most celebrated conservative in late nineteenth-century Europe was Bismarck (see Roberts pages 218–22); Bismarck, like some, though by no means all, other conservatives was prepared to concede social reforms in order to maintain the unity of the nation and contain opposition. No party on continental Europe actually gave itself the label 'Conservative'. The only Conservative Party was that of Great Britain and the British party was, ironically, a good deal less conservative than its European counterparts – it shared most of the dominant values of British society of the day, including representative government and moderate social reform. We sometimes describe conservative reform within the maintenance of the existing social order as 'paternalist'.

### Liberalism

This word does sometimes figure in party labels, though often with a qualifying adjective (as in the German 'National Liberals'), but it covers a range of meanings at least as wide as that of conservatism. In its broadest sense liberalism is the philosophy of those who oppose the old regime, support representative govern-ment, and uphold the ideas of individualism and private enterprise. By 1914 most liberal parties, whatever their exact label, accepted that the establishment of elementary rights for the poorest sections of the population did necessitate some social reform, but in essence liberalism maintained that government intervention in social and economic matters would be likely to curtail individualism. Essen-tially the Radical Socialists, or Radicals as they are usually termed, in France were a liberal party, committed to republicanism, representative government, private enterprise and anti-clericalism.

### Nationalism

This is a particularly tricky one. Sometimes 'nationalism' is spoken of as a 'force' in history – this is nationalism conceived of as a 'natural', and perhaps scarcely conscious, wish to associate oneself with one's own community and nation, and repulse attempts of alien communities to rule over one. Here, on the contrary I am speaking of a conscious political and social philosophy. Nationalism as a political movement was often associated with liberalism – both believed in representation, self-determination, and the rights of the individual. For subject nationalities, such as the Czechs or the Ruthenes, nationalism, on the whole, continued to have this association. But in countries where the nation was already practically synony-mous with the state, such as Germany, France and Britain, nationalism could as often be allied with a kind of jingoistic conservatism. Liberals in Britain supported subject nationalities abroad, but on the whole favoured internationalism rather than a belligerent assertion of British claims. In discussing popular culture in the previous unit, I pointed out the way in which an aggressive nationalism was assuming an important place in French life in the years before 1914. In Germany, an aggressive nationalism, deeply subservient to existing autocratic and militaristic institutions, was dominating German liberalism by the beginning of the century. Critically absent from German political life was any party analogous to the French Radicals, or British Liberals, or indeed to mainstream, moderate elements in British conservatism. On this point, let me quote here the leading authority:

> . . . nationalism had always been an important part of liberalism's historical development in Germany. Liberals had been instrumental in defining national issues and in making them a central element in German political life. By setting the search for national unity within a broader ideological context, liberals had given political meaning to the concept of nationality; by mobilizing popular support for the cause of national unity, liberals had provided nationalism with an institutional base. Both ideologically and institutionally, therefore, liberalism was the means through which cultural nationalism and traditional patriotism were transformed into a political commitment to national unification. Throughout the first two-thirds of the nineteenth century, liberals disagreed among themselves about the character and relative importance of this commitment. Most liberals assumed, however, that the freedom of the German *Volk* at home was inseparable from the freedom of the German *Volk* to define itself as a nation. The struggles for nationhood and for political reform seemed to be against the same enemies and for the same goals.
>
> After 1866, the relationship between liberalism and nationalism was fundamentally altered. The first and most obvious reason for this was the way in which the Bismarckian 'revolution from above' had severed the link between foreign political success and domestic political progress. Even though some liberals tried to maintain that there was an inevitable connection between unity and freedom, the lesson taught by Bismarck's triumphs became increasingly apparent: nationalism was not an inherently liberal concept and national goals need not be part of a progressive political ideology. On a number of levels and in a variety of ways, national issues were separated from a commitment to domestic reform. In school books and public rituals, periodicals and popular literature, the nation was presented as an autonomous source of values, a pre-eminent focus of loyalties, a political end in itself. As early as 1871 Treitschke had begun to argue that nationalism should be the primary source of cohesion in German life. 'Immature youth,' he wrote, 'is inclined to think of parties with the idealistic enthusiasm which a grown man reserves for his country.' Nationalism, not liberalism; the army, not the parliament; war, not domestic politics – these were to be the formative values, institutions, and experiences through which social solidarity and political stability could be maintained. (James J. Sheehan, *German Liberalism in the Nineteenth Century*, 1978, p.274)

But, to repeat, in many parts of Europe, particularly those ruled by Russia and Austria-Hungary, nationalism as a political creed was closely intertwined with liberalism, democracy and, often, socialism. Roberts, who – though not a Marxist

– clearly sees a close association between the evolution of liberal ideas and values, the development of capitalism and the rise of the bourgeoisie, suggests repeatedly that the greater the acceptance of liberal values the greater the stability and potential for orderly development in a given society. His point is that it is not enough for a few politicians to put forward, or pay lip-service to, liberal ideas; these have to be deeply embedded in society. I shall shortly ask you to identify particular phrases used by Roberts in making this point.

*Socialism*

Socialism is a word to be found in European writing well before the publications of Karl Marx, and thus independent socialist traditions developed quite early in both France and Britain. In its essence, socialism takes the community rather than the individual as its basic unit, and calls for the community to organize all aspects of social and economic life on behalf of the community as a whole; this, of course, conflicts sharply with the faith in private enterprise and *laissez-faire* fundamental to nineteenth-century liberals, and increasingly upheld by conservatives. Marx brought to socialism the ideas we have already discussed, particularly those of class conflict, of the inherent contradictions within capitalism leading inevitably to its supersession, and of the need to achieve that supersession through revolution. The main European socialist parties in 1914 accepted the doctrines of Marxism. Roberts, page 244 'Socialism before 1914 . . .' to page 250 '. . . and educate the workers', gives a basic, and perhaps slightly unsympathetic account. He possibly makes too much of the various splinter groups, but note in particular what he says about the relationships between socialism, anarchism, and syndicalism, about the revisionist debates at the turn of the century, about the special features of the British Labour party, about the dominant role of the German Social Democratic party, and about how particular interpretations of socialism (for example, whether it should be revolutionary or reformist) affected the actions and policies of political parties and trade unions. Please now read these pages of Roberts.

# 6   LEVELS OF SOCIAL AND POLITICAL CHANGE, AND THE POTENTIAL FOR FURTHER CHANGE

In the previous section I tried, in my capacity as teacher, to summarize quite complex material under a series of simple headings. Inevitably such a procedure must seem authoritarian: *I* am telling *you*, without any opportunity for discussion. In the end, all discussion of political values, as of any other historical topic, must be grounded in primary sources. But, as you know, we can't simply go to primary sources 'cold' as it were. The more one knows of the context, the more one can squeeze out of the sources. There is no way in a course of this sort that you are going to be able to read all the important secondary material, let alone seek out all the primary material. Teaching general history is inevitably a compromise. This section is going to take the form of critical, guided reading of three chapters from Roberts, and a discussion of some primary texts. As indicated in its title, there are two aims for this section, both, of course, intimately linked with the overall course aims:

1    to help you to establish what change had already taken place in the different European countries, in order that you will subsequently be in a position to assess the effects of World War I;

2    to help you to assess what further change would have taken place anyway had conditions of peace been maintained (again, obviously, as a basis for subsequent study of the effects of war).

Your main reading now is Roberts chapters 5 and 6, together with a further quick reading of chapter 7. We shall have to take the different countries in the order given by Roberts.

**Exercise chart**    Allocating at least a couple of pages for each country write in, as main headings, the names of the countries discussed by Roberts, deleting Spain, however, but keeping Italy. Then, for each country, and numbering from 1 to 10, list the areas of social change identified in section 2 of this unit. Under each of these headings, and leaving approximately equal space between them, write these two sub-headings: (a) levels of change in 1914; (b) potential for further change. Now before you begin to read Roberts, draw upon what you have already read in this course to fill in what points you can on this 'exercise chart'.

When you come to read Roberts, you'll find that chapter 7 is not very helpful on topic 7 'Customs and behaviour' – I expect you'll only be able to fill in odd fragments here. Likewise with topic 9 'High and popular culture'. Indeed, if I were writing an essay on, say 'Social and cultural change in Europe on the eve of the Great War', I think I'd apply this heading to the whole of Europe, rather than break it up country by country. None the less, let's stick with the plan and see what we come up with. In the end, the central issues we are leading up to here are: Did World War I affect the development of *modernization*? Did it affect the growth of mass culture? ∎

Before you start your reading I want to make a few comments on the first section of chapter 5:

●    Roberts, in my view, exaggerates the extent to which British society was uniquely different from that of other European countries. In particular, although I disagree with the emphasis of Mayer's interpretation, I think Mayer is right in perceiving a common pattern with respect to the formation of the European upper classes.

●    The (correct) figures for numbers of voters which Roberts gives in the second paragraph on page 136 do not in fact suggest the 'democratic mass politics' of which he speaks; in fact, in my view, Roberts greatly overstates the extent to which Britain was a democracy in 1914. In reading Roberts, you should bear in mind that in 1911 only 59 per cent of the adult male population (there were just under 8,000,000 adult males in a total population of 40.8 million) had the vote, and it was clear from the complicated registration procedure that the franchise was still a privilege which a man earned through his respectability and proven value to the community, not a democratic right. As the law stood under the terms of the most recent Reform Act, that of 1884, there were seven different types of franchise, of which the two major ones, accounting for 84 per cent of those registered to vote in 1911, were the occupation and household franchises: the former qualified the occupier, as owner or tenant, of any land or tenement of the clear yearly value of £10; the latter the inhabitant occupier, whether as owner or tenant, of any dwelling defined as a separate dwelling. Half a million among the wealthier sections of the electorate had two or more votes; in the election of January 1910 two especially well-qualified brothers between them cast thirty votes. The principles upon which the system was based were clearly expressed in the rhetorical question posed in the House of Commons in July 1912:

> Is the man who is too illiterate to read his ballot paper, who is too imprudent to support his children, to be placed on the same footing as the man who by industry and capacity has acquired a substantial interest in more than one constituency?

The British franchise in 1914 was not democratic, and was not intended to be.

● On page 141 Roberts refers to 'a mass of legislation' being enacted in the last two decades of the century. Near the top of page 147 he refers to the Liberal government after 1906 'founding the modern welfare state'. Roberts does not make it clear whether this 'founding' differed from the previous 'mass of legislation'. Certainly, Old Age Pensions and National Insurance were new, but my own view is that Roberts exaggerates their significance. We shall look at extracts from both of these acts shortly.

**Exercise**  Now start your reading of chapter 5, reading fairly quickly through to the bottom of page 144, but noting down answers to the following two questions, as well as filling in any relevant points in the exercise chart you have already made (if you take this drafting and filling in of the chart seriously you will be giving yourself superb practice in systematic note-taking).

1   What does Roberts say with respect to Mayer's point about the persistence of the old regime?

2   In what quite extensive passage does Roberts set out his views on British political values?

The pages from 145 to the end of the first paragraph on 148 give you the most direct picture of what was happening in Britain immediately before the war. Read this with care, before concluding the section with Roberts's brief account of the Irish crisis. Note further points in your exercise chart, but also answer this question:

3   Roberts makes two very strong pronouncements about political and social reform in this period. What are they?

Now go on to the section on France. Note down relevant points in your exercise chart, paying particular attention to the state of the franchise, and the potential of French socialism as an impetus to change. Also answer this question:

4   What impression does Roberts give of French political values?

Read to the end of the third paragraph on page 167 of the next section, noting the broad contrasts between Spain and Italy, and also the use once again of the word 'structural' at the beginning of the second paragraph on page 167. Now, skipping the detailed material on Spain, move to the beginning of the second paragraph on page 174 'Italy's trials . . .' For your chart, note in particular both the size of the electorate, and whether steady expansion of it was taking place. Read fairly rapidly to the middle of page 182 '. . . repression would end'. The last few pages give quite a sharp picture of Italy on the eve of the war. Note in particular what is said about Giolitti, the most noteworthy Italian protagonist of the 'liberalism' of which I have already spoken.

5    What phrase does Roberts use to bring out his feelings about the importance of deeply embedded liberal values?

6    Turn to *Documents 1* (I.17), Giolitti's ministerial report of 8 February 1909, and bearing in mind what you have just read in Roberts, as well as my discussions earlier in this unit, answer the following questions:

(a)  List the social reforms which Giolitti says his government has carried through. How do these reforms compare with the ones carried out in Britain, as described by Roberts?

(b)  Roberts tells us that one of Giolitti's other reforms was in fact a failure; from the document itself we can see that Giolitti failed to get some of his other proposals approved. What are these?

(c)  Such failures highlight something Roberts tells us about the general weaknesses of Italian governments within the Italian parliamentary system. What is this?

Remember to make appropriate comments (don't worry about duplication) in your exercise chart.

Now read Roberts's section on 'Imperial Russia' in chapter 6, concentrating especially on page 192 'A more sinister side . . .' onwards.

7    Again in keeping with one of his principal arguments, Roberts has a phrase about shared values. What is this?

8    Roberts gives us an example of guided action in the area of economic development. What is this?

9    Compare the extent of extra-parliamentary, or revolutionary, action in Russia with that in Italy, particularly from the point of view of what it achieved, if anything, in either country.

10    Roberts singles out one extremely important social reform just before the outbreak of war. What is that?

11    Turn to *Documents 1* (I.18). Read this carefully, and bearing in mind the comments of Roberts, say: (a) exactly what this document is; (b) how far it suggests that Russia was now on course for peaceful constitutional development, and how far it suggests the opposite. Now turn to *Documents 1* (I.19 and I.20). Read them quickly, and without bothering for the moment about their detailed provisions, say: (c) in the light of Roberts's comments, what hope they offer of reform within the Tsarist system.

Now read the section on 'The Habsburg Monarchy'. In particular note for your exercise chart what is said about the franchise, and what is said about national cohesion.

Now read the section on 'Imperial Germany'. Again, for your chart, note what is said about voting rights, and pay particular attention to the significance of Prussia as a powerful state within the German empire. With regard to 'the abdication of German liberalism' (second paragraph on page 217), remember the comments of Sheehan I quoted earlier.

12    What does Roberts say about German political values?

13(a)    In the second paragraph on page 225 Roberts, given his general point of view, makes a rather surprising pronouncement about the possible achievements of the SPD. What is this?

(b)    Turn now to document I.21, the Erfurt programme: what elements in this programme justify the description of it quoted by Roberts that it was a 'revolutionary party, but not a party that makes revolutions'? Remember what you have already read about socialism on pages 244 to 250.

Finally, read from page 250 to the end of chapter 7. Make appropriate notes in your chart.

14    Which documents that you have already looked at are relevant to this issue? ■

**Specimen answers and discussion**    I shall take the short questions first, giving my version of the exercise chart at the very end.

1    Roberts says that the *ancien régime* was transformed by 1914, with both Prime Minister and Chancellor of the Exchequer men of relatively humble origins. Thus, according to Roberts, significant change in the class structure at the top of society is already taking place. (Personally I think he exaggerates both the extent and the novelty of the change.)

2    The extensive passage comes in the second paragraph on page 132, where he stresses acceptance of the existing system, settled procedures for legislative change, assertion of individual liberties, and dislike of political violence.

3    On page 145 Roberts says 'Radicalism seemed firmly in the saddle at last' and 'It has rightly been called "a landmark in our social history"'.

4    Roberts suggests that after sharp disagreements in the early years of the Third Republic in the nineteenth century, French political values had become pretty settled by 1914 with, he suggests, widespread acceptance of both the Republic and parliamentary government.

5    At the very end of the chapter Roberts comments: 'In the long run, both Spanish and Italian constitutionalism were to fail because the *ideological and social presuppositions of liberal democracy were lacking*.' [my italics]

6(a)    Giolitti lists a weekly day of rest; strengthening of funds for workers' disability and old age; provision of housing for those on low incomes; rehabilitation of prisoners; low-interest loans for aqueducts and public health installations; attention to the problem of abandoned children; enquiries set on foot with regard to land workers in the south.

Although clearly some of these, particularly the social insurance fund for disability and old age, are along the same lines as the British reforms, many of them do sound rather minor.

(b)    We know that the social insurance fund exists from the document on that subject we have already studied. Roberts says that railway nationalization was a failure; the bills on public works and on university professors are to be re-submitted, so obviously they were not approved.

(c)    Because of the fragmentation of Italian political parties there was never a strong single-party government; in the Italian system, known as *il transformismo*, the permanent coalition governments shifted in composition, buying off critics by

bringing them into government. Thus Italy lacked the strong government necessary for pushing through social reform.

7    On page 187 Roberts remarks that: 'Russian society lacked the values and
ideas which were the common-places of western capitalism.'

8    At the foot of page 193 he describes the deliberate forced industrialization
undertaken by the Russian government at the instance of Witte at the Ministry of
Finance.

9    According to Roberts there was 'a near-revolutionary crisis' in Italy between
1896 and 1900, and he gives a graphic description of this on pages 181–2.
However, the mention of hunger and brigandage suggests to me a 'primitive'
protest of an underdeveloped society, rather than organized revolution; Roberts
himself uses the phrase 'the crisis had in fact almost blown itself out'. The
assassination of the king must be taken seriously, but again it seems to have been
an act of revenge rather than a planned take-over of government. For the years up
to 1914 Italy, it seems, was relatively stable. In contrast, it was in the middle of
these years, in 1905 to be precise, that mass riots, strikes and organized agitation
took place in Russia. However, Roberts, on page 196, makes the point that
without the crisis of the Russo-Japanese war these would have made little
headway. As it was, the combination of agitation and this crisis brought the
limited changes described by Roberts on pages 197–8. Great, but apparently
somewhat despairing violence continued sporadically in Russia.

10    Stolypin's agrarian reforms which cancelled all arrears of redemption payments (payments dating back to the abolition of serfdom), the abolition of joint
family holdings, and the granting of assistance to peasants who wished to buy
their own land (pages 200–1) – this, incidentally, creating the class of rich
peasants, or 'kulaks', that we will hear so much about later.

11(a)    At the height of the revolutionary crisis of 1905, an Imperial Manifesto was
issued announcing the setting up of a *Duma* with real legislative powers, the
extension of the franchise and the granting of real civil liberties. On the eve of the
opening of the *Duma*, this document (I.18), a set of Fundamental Laws, was
issued which codified the main constitutional enactments of the preceding
months.

(b)    Some basis for future development is provided in the clauses safeguarding
individual rights, that is, clauses 30 to 40, and in the very establishment of the
*Duma* (chapter IV). However, the continued autocratic powers of the Tsar are very
clearly marked as are the limitations on the powers of the *Duma*, particularly
through the existence of the non-elected State Council.

(c)    The Bolsheviks boycotted the first *Duma* and subsequently were forcibly
prevented from playing any active part in Russian government (pages 199–200).
Thus, whatever significance this programme might have for the future, it had no
direct effect on Russian policies before 1914. The Kadets (the main voice of the
kind of liberalism I have already described) was the majority party in the first
*Duma*, but subsequently was effectively excluded from any influence on government policy. Thus this programme too had no direct impact before 1914.

12    Roberts says that despite the fact that many of the assumptions of civilized
politics were present in Imperial Germany, it cannot be classed among the
constitutional states with widely shared liberal values; there never had been a
strong liberal tradition based on respect for individual rights (bottom of page 215

and page 217). There was no acceptance of divergence of political aims within a consensus of agreement about ends (bottom of page 217). Note that Roberts concludes by re-stressing the existence of 'civilized standards'.

13(a)    Roberts seems to be saying (on page 226) that the SPD could only have 'big' achievements if it were positively revolutionary (strange given his obvious predilection for constitutionalism).

(b)    The first six paragraphs are a straight statement of orthodox Marxism: in this sense the SPD was a 'revolutionary party'. Thereafter, the document turns to the need for political rights, for action through a more democratic parliament, and then lists a series of practical legislative items. These are the policies of a party committed to constitutional action, not to 'making revolutions'.

14    The relevant documents are the extracts in *Documents 1* from the autobiography of Adelheid Popp (I.11), the extract from the survey of conditions among French women shop assistants (I.9), and also the Erfurt programme (I.21) which you have just looked at, which calls for equality between the sexes. □

**Exercise chart: specimen answer**    If you have made a serious effort at this, I think you will have found it a valuable exercise. Compare your chart with mine. I expect I will have some points that you have not thought of. Actually, having one's attention drawn to points which, even after conscientious effort, one has omitted, is one of the best ways in the world of fixing such points firmly in one's mind. Furthermore, I hope you will find my version of the chart a very useful point of reference for your further studies.

## UNITED KINGDOM

| | | **Levels of change in 1914** | **Potential for further change** |
|---|---|---|---|
| 1 | Social geography | Roberts emphasizes decades of 'industry and the growth of cities' (p.130), and 'a growing, ever more tightly packed population' (p.133). He is not very explicit on the growth of suburbs, simply saying that in 1880 'the great shift to suburban areas had not yet taken place' (p.133). In fact this 'great shift' was well under way by 1914.<br><br>Middle-class families were getting smaller, and the population was growing older. | Further urban and suburban growth is clearly to be expected. Signs of a significant drop in the birthrate ('natural increase', p.133) are not, according to Roberts, apparent in 1914. |
| 2 | Economic performance and theory | Wealthiest nation in Europe (in the world, second only to the United States); the world's greatest trading nation. Being overtaken in certain areas by the United States and Germany. The financial centre of the world. Not now as technologically innovative as Germany and the United States or even, with respect to the internal combustion engine, France. | Despite the worries about technology, there was no real reason to believe that Britain could not continue its impressive economic advance, and its dominance of world finance. |

## UNITED KINGDOM (cont'd)

| | | Levels of change in 1914 | Potential for further change |
|---|---|---|---|
| 3 | Social structure | Britain had a clearly articulated, and widely recognized, class structure. In Roberts's view, the bourgeoisie had effectively taken over as the dominant class; in my view, the upper class was still strongly coloured by aristocratic elements, while incorporating the more successful bourgeois elements. A substantial white-collar element had been added to the more traditional professional and business middle classes. The British working class was the oldest and most fully developed in the world. Class divisions were extremely sharp, inequalities gross, and the wage for most working men in employment inadequate to the needs of raising a family. | Liberals, and many Conservatives, were favourable to legislation designed to reduce inequalities; though still very weak, the Labour Party also agitated for such policies. The world's most highly developed trade union movement was an important force in making claims on behalf of the workers. Overall general economic trends had been towards rising living standards for the majority of society; however, in a time of rising prices, wages were static in the years immediately before the war. There was much deference to the existing social structure, and any drastic change in it seemed most unlikely. On the other hand, modest ameliorations could legitimately be expected. |
| 4 | National cohesion | Despite modest Home Rule movements in Scotland and Wales, Great Britain was, compared with most continental countries, a remarkably cohesive and homogeneous country. The striking exception, of course, concerns Ireland. | The attitudes of Unionists were threatening, and certainly there was a serious Irish crisis when war broke out; however, it was not necessarily apparent that a peaceful accommodation within the framework of the United Kingdom was out of the question, though, equally, communal tensions between Protestants and Catholics had a long and bitter history. |
| 5 | Social reform and welfare policies | A range of social welfare measures had been introduced at the end of the nineteenth century (most particularly in the realms of housing and workmen's compensation), and a further distinctive burst of legislation took place after 1906. Referring to social insurance, Britain had now certainly caught up with Germany, and in most respects was in advance of other European countries. | Roberts speaks of the founding of the welfare state, with the obvious implication that further developments gradually extending the welfare state were inevitably on the way. I would be inclined to point to the severe limitations in the post-1906 legislation and suggest that accepted ideas on private enterprise, self-help, and so on, must be a limitation on the expectation that further major reforms would inevitably follow. |

## UNITED KINGDOM (cont'd)

| | Levels of change in 1914 | Potential for further change |
|---|---|---|
| 6   Material conditions | For the wealthy and much of the middle classes material conditions were extremely good. For the working class, and some of the lower middle class, life was lived at little above a bare subsistence level; there was a large residuum (about a third of the total working class) existing at less than subsistence level. | It is hard to see how any sharp improvement in these conditions was immediately in prospect though, no doubt, given the introduction of old age pensions, and so on, it was not unreasonable to expect gradual amelioration. |
| 7   Customs and behaviour | A general point made by Roberts, which would seem to apply with particular force to Britain, is that 'new economic opportunities and easier communications already [that is, in 1914] made the physical break with the parental home easier' (p.239). Detail, however, is lacking. Other points I picked up were: religion is very much an observance of the middle and lower middle classes, with little impact on the working class; life in the urban slums was often brutal; *but* popular education is spreading – popular newspapers and the cinema have arrived. So, one might add, has the great spectator sport, association football. Roberts suggests that Britain was still a deferential society, though not as deferential as formerly. If you have any acquaintanceship at all with Edwardian photographs you will know that fashions and style of dress very firmly underpinned class distinctions. | Further decline in religious observance, further growth in mass culture might be expected, but the impression is very much not that of a society in which a rapid change in social customs was to be expected. |

## UNITED KINGDOM (cont'd)

| | | Levels of change in 1914 | Potential for further change |
|---|---|---|---|
| 8 | Women and the family | Employment opportunities for women were expanding, as was women's education. Contraception was reducing the burdens of childbearing borne by upper-class and middle-class women. Since 1894 women property owners were able to vote in local elections. Women did not have the parliamentary vote, but very active suffragist and suffragette movements were in being. | Clearly the long-term expansion in women's opportunities was likely to continue. Obviously the women's movement would keep up the pressure, though militant suffragette action had lost the cause a lot of sympathy. Conservative leader Balfour had said that any further extension of the franchise would have to involve women. In fact, in 1914 (apart from the Labour Party) there was no strong support among political leaders for a general extension of the franchise. Resolutions in favour of votes for women had several times passed the House of Commons, but had never received the necessary government support. Finland and Norway already had votes for women, as had several American states. The issue was undoubtedly a major one in 1914. No doubt votes for women would have come some time (though one must note the very strong arguments against made by both men and women), but it does not seem to me that it was an immediate prospect – however, this is a controversial issue and you can only come to a satisfactory conclusion of your own by reading some of the important works on the subject. The beginning in the last quarter of the nineteenth century of the permanent long-run fall in the birth rate and in family size has been singled out as a process with a good claim to be the most important change in women's lives in the whole of history. This, obviously, was a long-term process of change which could be expected to continue. |

## UNITED KINGDOM (cont'd)

| | | Levels of change in 1914 | Potential for further change |
|---|---|---|---|
| 9 | High and popular culture | Even within the élites, modernism was greeted with considerable derision; in the realm of popular culture, cinema and the new popular press were already beginning to establish themselves; religious belief was still strong in the rural areas, but had never been strong in the towns. | Modernism had arrived, and popular culture was expanding, but there was no reason to expect any striking changes and certainly not that cinema would become acceptable to the middle and upper classes. |
| 10 | Political institutions and values | Widely shared liberal values, but the franchise definitely not democratic (two-fifths of men and all women without the vote). Despite the strong Irish Nationalist movement no self-representation for the Irish people. Despite some moves towards collectivism, ideas of private enterprise and *laissez-faire* still strong. The British two-party system tended to produce strong governments capable of carrying through positive social-reform measures. | Given the series of reform acts and the Liberal commitment to some form of Irish Home Rule, gradual change seemed perfectly likely; on the other hand, as Roberts brings out with regard to Ulster, Conservatives (or Unionists), aided by their entrenched majority in the House of Lords, and their support in the British army, were determined to sabotage any hint of a break-up of the United Kingdom. A slow movement towards collectivist policies was clearly discernible. |

## FRANCE

| | | | |
|---|---|---|---|
| 1 | Social geography | As already noted, France's population, relative to other European countries, was already in decline. The drift from the land was slow. | France's relative population decline was already apparent in 1914 and seemed set to continue. There was no reason to expect any upset or acceleration in the slow change in the balance between town and country. |
| 2 | Economic performance and theory | On the world scene, France did not count to the extent that Britain and Germany did; none the less, Roberts (pp.150–1) speaks of 'expansion and growing prosperity'. French technological innovation is exemplified by the Panhard car. | With a strong agricultural sector France, in many respects, had a balanced economy: there was no reason to believe that steady economic expansion would not continue. |

**FRANCE (cont'd)**

| | | Levels of change in 1914 | Potential for further change |
|---|---|---|---|
| 3 | Social structure | The French social structure, in essence, was not dissimilar to that of Britain. On the whole the upper class neither had the wealth nor the aristocratic tone of the British; within the middle classes there were rather more small businessmen and tradesmen; the French working class was small and ill-organized compared with the British; most critically, France had a very substantial peasant class. | The working class was growing, but there was no real reason to expect substantial changes in the near future. |
| 4 | National cohesion | Local loyalties were strong, and many of the inhabitants of rural areas were only slowly beginning to think of themselves as French. Still, compared with Central and East European countries, France was nationally a very cohesive country. The loss of Alsace-Lorraine (taken by the Germans in 1870) was felt quite bitterly. | It was to be expected that France would continue to become a more integrated nation. There seemed little prospect of the regain of Alsace-Lorraine. |
| 5 | Social reform and welfare policies | France's most notable achievement in comparison with Britain was that of the establishment of universal education. For the rest, French individualism, the absence of strong single-party government, and the preoccupation of French 'liberals' with anti-clericalism, militated against extensive social-reform programmes. A more prosperous country, France did not even have the patchy reforms we noted in Italy. | Given that there was no sign of effective pressure from the socialists, major social reform seemed unlikely. |
| 6 | Material conditions | In general, living standards were lower in France than in Britain, but France did not have the same vast pool of urban misery. | It was to be expected that steady economic expansion would bring a gradual raising of living standards. |

## FRANCE (cont'd)

| | | Levels of change in 1914 | Potential for further change |
|---|---|---|---|
| 7 | Customs and behaviour | The key contrasts with Britain which I picked out were that: religious affiliation, or lack of it, counted for a great deal in ordinary life (Roberts, of course, does not say much on Catholic–Protestant clashes in Ireland, or those parts of England and Scotland with large numbers of Irish immigrants; the Chapel traditions of Wales would also be worth noting); that pre-industrial, pre-liberal/democratic elements were still strong in France. Roberts picks out the telling example of the continuance of public executions in France (abolished in Britain in the 1860s). In general he states (end of last paragraph on p.150): 'France changed less than England or Germany between 1880 and 1914.' | I think we are bound to conclude that any great change in customs and behaviour seemed most unlikely in the France of 1914. |
| 8 | Women and the family | In the world of education and the intellect, opportunities were probably greater for French women than British – note the achievements of Madame Curie mentioned by Roberts on page 252. But the women's movement was not nearly as advanced in France as in Britain and, on the whole, Catholicism stressed women's domestic role even more strongly than was the case in Britain, with its variety of nonconformist faiths. | Slow advance would undoubtedly continue, but the prospect of votes for women was remote. |
| 9 | High and popular culture | France, or at least Paris, led the world in the sponsorship and acceptance of modernism. Cinema was at roughly the same stage in France as in Britain, with possibly a greater interest being taken in it by the intellectual middle class. Religion still had a strong hold on popular belief. | Further cultural innovation could confidently be expected in a Paris-dominated France. |

## FRANCE (cont'd)

| | | Levels of change in 1914 | Potential for further change |
|---|---|---|---|
| 10 | Political institutions and values | Although liberal values had perhaps been diffused more slowly, the French parliamentary system was democratic in a way that the British was not: all adult males (though, of course, no females) had the vote. | Despite some manifestations of extreme right-wing nationalism, on the whole the trend in France was towards greater stability, and greater acceptance of the system. And there was no good reason to believe that that would not continue. On the other hand, there seemed little likelihood of French socialism influencing high politics in a way that it was possible for the British labour movement to do, since French socialism followed the German example in totally dissociating itself from parliamentary government. |

## ITALY

| | | | |
|---|---|---|---|
| 1 | Social geography | Italy (Roberts, pp.174–5) was deeply divided geographically and demographically. A fundamental factor was the large and growing class of desperately poor peasants (p.175): the economic and social gap between north and south had 'widened terrifyingly by 1914' (p.175). | The expectation could only be that, particularly with further industrialization in the north, the north–south divide would continue to get worse. |
| 2 | Economic performance and theory | In the crisis years of 1896 to 1900 there had been privation and even starvation. Modest economic growth took place thereafter, but the desperate economic plight of the south was not dealt with. About the best that one can say for Italian economic performance is that it was not as bad as that of Spain. | Given Roberts's comments on renewed political instability at the end of the period, and Martin Clark's comments on Italian economic organization and entrepreneurial enterprise which you read in the last unit, steady economic advance in Italy did not look particularly likely. |

## ITALY (cont'd)

| | | Levels of change in 1914 | Potential for further change |
|---|---|---|---|
| 3 | Social structure | The Italian social structure only rather faintly resembled that of France or Britain; you learned from Martin Clark of Italy's lack of a substantial commercial or industrial bourgeoisie and of the very 'undeveloped' nature of its class structure. At the same time, a working class recognizably like that of other countries was steadily developing. | Given the backwardness of large areas, particularly in the south, rapid change in the class structure was not likely. |
| 4 | National cohesion | The fundamental divide is that between the north and the south; furthermore, many who now thought of themselves as Italian nationals, were still living under Austrian rule. | There seemed to be no realistic prospect of change. Industrialization in the north simply aggravated the contrast with the south. |
| 5 | Social reform and welfare policies | Italy did have workers' social insurance for disability and old age. The other reforms were relatively minor in character. Indeed, Roberts (p.184) suggests that Giolitti's reforms can be interpreted as 'mere tactical expedients'. | I do not think it can be said that Italy was steadily moving forwards in the realm of progressive social reform. |
| 6 | Material conditions | Even the petty aristocracy who doubled up as professional workers were not particularly rich. Very widespread poverty and deprivation was a characteristic of Italian society. | The evidence does not indicate the prospect of any rapid improvement. |

## ITALY (cont'd)

| | | Levels of change in 1914 | Potential for further change |
|---|---|---|---|
| 7 | Customs and behaviour | Roberts stresses the pervasive significance of the Catholic Church (p.174). Italy was a country of widespread disorder and violence. It lacked, says Roberts (p.185), 'healthy political *moeurs*', that is, 'customs'. If you know anything of Italian literature (or opera) of the period, you can flesh this out as implying 'primitive' notions of honour and revenge, lack of respect for human life, lack of 'civic virtue'. A majority of Italians might well be included among those 'millions of Europeans' still living in 'a theocentric universe' (referred to by Roberts on p.227). | Apart from the fact that industrialization was advancing in the north, signs of change are notably absent. |
| 8 | Women and the family | Roberts doesn't say much but, reading between the lines, I think we can deduce that the condition and status of women in Italy were considerably lower than in France. | Since the latest franchise reform concerned solely men, it seems unlikely that votes for women was on any short-term political agenda. |
| 9 | High and popular culture | Italy was the home of the Futurist movement in painting, irrationally glorifying war, but definitely modernist in style. However Italian Realism (in literature and opera) was scarcely in the vein of modernism; nor was Italian nationalistic literature. Traditional culture was a political concern (largely, one presumes, because of the importance of tourism). Religion exercised a powerful control over popular belief. In many parts of Italy opera was genuinely a part of popular culture. | If one is required to make some comparative statement about Italy I think it would have to be something like: 'In the eyes of the intellectuals of Paris, Vienna, St Petersburg, Berlin and London, Italy was perceived as having a great past culturally, but little future.' |
| 10 | Political institutions and values | Liberal values were not deeply embedded, according to Roberts. The Italian socialist movement seemed too divided to be effective. Throughout most of the period, the franchise was a limited one; however, in 1912 Giolitti introduced universal male suffrage for those over thirty. | Certainly Roberts's view is that, given the lack of deep-rooted liberal values, constitutional government was in a very shaky position in Italy. Given the time it had taken to achieve the age-qualified manhood suffrage of 1912 there is no good reason for believing that a move to full democracy was an immediate prospect. |

# IMPERIAL RUSSIA

| | | Levels of change in 1914 | Potential for further change |
|---|---|---|---|
| 1 | Social geography | The essence is contained in the sentence on page 187 beginning 'Most Russians were poverty-stricken peasants . . . their misery increasing year by year as their numbers grew.' | Yet, by 1912, Stolypin 'had broken the back of the worst problem facing the country' (p.201). But Stolypin was dead, murdered. None the less, says Roberts, 'in 1914 Russia was at last beginning to move into modern history' (p.201). Whether the problem of peasant land hunger had really been solved is open to doubt. |
| 2 | Economic performance and theory | This is a crucial matter, and subject for some debate. Roberts stresses Russia's rapid industrial growth and, of course, the guided economic policies of Witte. On page 187 he goes to the core of the matter in stating that 'It is wrong to assume that collapse in revolution was the inevitable fate of Imperial Russia.' Though undoubtedly industrializing rapidly, Russia remained a very inefficient and backward country; however, the weight of expert opinion would in general agree with Roberts's analysis. Technologically, Russia was very dependent upon the inventions of others. Russia's performance on the world market was not impressive. | From the main argument in the column opposite it can be contended that Russia was already well on the road to economic modernization. |
| 3 | Social structure | The Russian upper class were landowners, and the small Russian middle class were also largely landowners. The divide between these on the one side, and the peasants on the other, was greater than could be found in any other European country. There were few institutions through which the middle class could express itself. The working class was small but concentrated into one or two areas. Its conditions and status were very much governed by its peasant origins. | Stolypin's reforms were improving the condition of the peasants; both the middle class and the working class were growing. Growth, however, in 1914 seemed to be suggesting instability and possibly open conflict, rather than the evolution of a stable society – though, arguably, the continuance of economic growth might have provided the conditions for just that. |

## IMPERIAL RUSSIA (cont'd)

| | | Levels of change in 1914 | Potential for further change |
|---|---|---|---|
| 4 | National cohesion | The Russian Empire consisted of a large number of subject nationalities, generally quite firmly repressed. The fundamental laws of 1906 restored autonomy to Finland. | The prospects of self-determination for the subject nationalities did not appear to be great in 1914. |
| 5 | Social reform and welfare policies | Any social provision in Russia came through the peasant commune, the very agency that Stolypin was trying to break up. Of social welfare strictly defined (as distinct from agrarian reform of the type fostered by Stolypin) there was practically none. | Future developments in social reform would depend upon whether there was any likelihood of liberal elements being brought into government: from the standpoint of 1914 the possibility seems remote though, of course, steady economic advance might have brought a change here. |
| 6 | Material conditions | Roberts does not mince words: most of the peasants 'lived in squalor, misery and ignorance' (p. 187); 'most Russians grew poorer' (p. 194). | Perhaps under Stolypin's reforms, there would have been continuing improvement. In different ways, both the Bolsheviks and the Kadets had plans for social improvements: but, as we have noted, in the normal course of events, the chances of either being in power seemed remote in 1914. |
| 7 | Customs and behaviour | There are only hints in Roberts, for example (p.177): 'This huge mass remained an enigma, a vaguely threatening background to the activities of a highly civilized and westernized élite. The peasants seemed inaccessible to progressive influences . . . they lived in a tradition of subjection and exploitation . . .' | If one believes that a Western model entailing 'progressive influences' is ultimately likely to triumph, then clearly there was much scope for change – though little prospect of it as an immediate reality. |
| 8 | Women and the family | University education (Roberts, p.252) had been long established for women in Russia. However, neither women's rights, nor a strong movement in support of them, are noticeable in that country in 1914. | Both the party programmes which we have studied called for equal rights for both men and women. To that extent, there was the possibility of change in the future. Once again, as I have said several times, it would depend on whether the opportunity came for such party programmes to be put into practice. |

## IMPERIAL RUSSIA (cont'd)

| | | Levels of change in 1914 | Potential for further change |
|---|---|---|---|
| 9 | High and popular culture | Russian achievements in literature, drama and music were considerable; perhaps as an international centre of high culture Russia was no more backward than Britain, but it does have to be noted that the great successes of the Diaghilev ballet took place not in St Petersburg or Moscow, but in Paris. In popular culture Russia was highly traditionalist; orthodox religion dominated popular belief. | Russia was not seen by contemporaries as being on the threshold of staggering cultural innovations. |
| 10 | Political institutions and values | Political and individual rights were granted by the fundamental laws of 1906, but the powers of the autocracy were still very great. Because of the general hopelessness of the Russian situation, Russia, the most illiberal of all the countries studied here, had the most convinced revolutionary Marxist movement. | The exclusion of the social democrats (Bolsheviks and Mensheviks) was perhaps not altogether unexpected, but the exclusion of the liberal, reformist party, the Kadets, suggests that possibilities of steady constitutional change were not great. |

## THE HABSBURG MONARCHY

| | | | |
|---|---|---|---|
| 1 | Social geography | Roberts (p.205) brings out very clearly the enormous differences between areas in Hungary 'almost as backward as Russia', or where '"age-old tribal communism" could still be found', and in Austria, 'virtually untouched by the market economy', on the one hand, and those of urban Bohemia and 'the cultural élite of Vienna or Budapest', on the other. | The existing system appeared well tempered to maintaining these differences. |

**THE HABSBURG MONARCHY (cont'd)**

| | | Levels of change in 1914 | Potential for further change |
|---|---|---|---|
| 2 | Economic performance and theory | Roberts (going back to page 44) puts Austria-Hungary in his third category of nations, those predominantly agricultural, with a relatively undeveloped industrial base. On the world scene Austria-Hungary was certainly not a major trading power. | Obviously, as is brought out in the extract from Macartney you read in the last unit, economic development was taking place, with considerable potential for further growth. But it is debatable whether the monarchy's multi-racial composition, and repression of subject minorities, was really compatible with sustained economic growth. |
| 3 | Social structure | Class structure is inevitably interrelated with the nationality problem. In many areas the structure is essentially the dichotomous one of landowners and peasants, but Macartney indicated the development of the standard model of the most successful bourgeoise elements joining with the aristocracy. The urban working class was still small in 1914, though, as we have seen, capable of supporting socialist organization. | Obviously, following Macartney, social structure was slowly changing, but there were no great signs of a steady modification of the link between nationality and social position. |
| 4 | National cohesion | Obviously, the Habsburg monarchy, *par excellence*, was the state without national cohesion. At the same time, despite vigorous nationalist movements, the situation in 1914 did seem to be that, however shakily, and however threatened by such external states as Serbia, the monarchy was managing to hold together its disparate nationalities. | The picture seems to be the rather paradoxical one of rational improvement scarcely seeming possible, while actual collapse was far from imminent. |
| 5 | Social reform and welfare policies | Because of the complexities of the institutional set-up and the difficulties of organizing strong governments, adequately financed, welfare provision in Austria-Hungary was almost non-existent. | In the light of all that has been said, it is clear that the possibilities for change were not great. |

## THE HABSBURG MONARCHY (cont'd)

| | | Levels of change in 1914 | Potential for further change |
|---|---|---|---|
| 6 | Material conditions | Factories, as we learned from Adelheid Popp (*Documents 1*, I.11), could offer wages which were attractive to rural workers. In general living standards throughout the Dual Monarchy were low. | Though working-class organization was growing, prospects for change were small. |
| 7 | Customs and behaviour | Little possibility of generalizing: enormous gulfs between 'backward' peasant cultures and sophisticated metropolitan cultures; a multiplicity of national customs. | No major transformation on the horizon. |
| 8 | Women and the family | Obviously in Adelheid Popp herself, and in the commitment of Austrian Social Democrats to equal rights for women, we have important signs of change in Austria-Hungary. In general, however, national and religious issues tended to cut across the advocacy of women's rights. | Given that the arguments were being made, obviously the potential was there. But, as in the other issues, the position of 'the Dual Monarchy as "despotism tempered by slovenliness"' (Roberts, pp.205–6) must militate against any realistic prospect of change. |
| 9 | High and popular culture | In Vienna and Prague the Dual Monarchy had two of the greatest European cultural centres, with Budapest not far behind. Yet it may be that the high culture of Austria (the music of Richard Strauss, the paintings of Klimt) exemplify particularly well Mayer's case that the ruling old regime sponsored traditionalist art forms. Against that we have to put the facts that the major works of Freud originated from Vienna and that Kafka came from the Austrian lands. In popular culture and belief, religious and nationalist loyalties are dominant themes. | Who can say? I make this rhetorical question seriously: Vienna, in many ways, may be the declining, decadent city, yet as a cultural centre it rivalled Paris: the conditions of production for high culture are not easily pinned down. |

## THE HABSBURG MONARCHY (cont'd)

| | | **Levels of change in 1914** | **Potential for further change** |
|---|---|---|---|
| 10 | Political institutions and values | The nationalities problem inevitably intrudes upon that of political rights. Roberts puts matters neatly in the passage from the last paragraph on page 205 to the end of the second paragraph on page 207, when he points out that behind the appearance of liberal attitudes and institutions, the practice throughout the Dual Monarchy was in fact extremely illiberal. | At the very beginning of the third paragraph on page 207 Roberts indicates that the monarchy did not have within itself the powers to carry through reforms. |

## IMPERIAL GERMANY

| | | | |
|---|---|---|---|
| 1 | Social geography | The German birth rate began to fall in 1904, but the population still grew: 'The great flow to the cities . . . produced a huge industrial proletariat' (Roberts, p.214). | Everything pointed to the continuance of these trends. |
| 2 | Economic performance and theory | The testimony is overwhelming that with respect to economic performance and technological advance Germany is eclipsing all other European countries. | There could be no reason in 1914 to feel that this would not continue. |
| 3 | Social structure | The German upper bourgeoisie was doing extremely well, as Berghahn and the primary text by Sombart (document I.12) (not that we have to believe him) would seem to suggest. Yet, that fusion between traditional landed elements and the more successful elements from the bourgeoisie, which was already characterizing France and Britain (I would maintain) had not fully taken place in Germany where, as Berghahn points out, traditional lines of social distinction were very strong. To the older middle class was being added the new *Mittelstand* – the developments here, I have | The aims of the German Social Democratic party suggest a peaceful way towards transforming this autocratic and sharply divided society. However, it would not be easy to say that, faced with the evidence of 1914, such a transformation was likely in German society. |

## IMPERIAL GERMANY (cont'd)

| Levels of change in 1914 | Potential for further change |
| --- | --- |

suggested, not really being as unique as Kocka suggests. After Britain, Germany had the most fully developed working class in the world. At least adult working-class males had the vote within the German imperial system, more than can be said with respect to the British working class. Yet the German working class, or certainly the German working-class movement, was treated much more obviously as being outside respectable society than was the case in Britain.

**4 National cohesion**

The German Empire was, despite the local differences well identified by Berghahn, nationally a very homogenous entity. The problem for the rest of Europe was that the industrious German nation was scattered widely over many other countries outside the ambit of the German Empire. In particular, of course, Germans dominated one part of the Austro-Hungarian Dual Monarchy.

Though Pan-German sentiment (that is, sentiment in favour of a greater Germany including *all* Germans) was quite strong, there were no obvious indications of future change here.

**5 Social reform and welfare policies**

Because of the policies of Bismarck Germany had the most fully developed social welfare system in Europe, only being equalled and overtaken by the British legislation of the post-1906 period.

Because of the hostility of the established political nation towards the working class, it must be considered a possibility that no further social measures favourable to the working class were likely to be enacted. On the other hand, the tradition was firmly there, and there is, equally, no serious reason for doubting that steady progress might well continue.

**6 Material conditions**

Material prosperity in Germany was second only to that in Britain.

There was no reason to believe that living standards would not continue to advance.

## IMPERIAL GERMANY (cont'd)

| | | Levels of change in 1914 | Potential for further change |
|---|---|---|---|
| 7 | Customs and behaviour | The only hints I could track down in Roberts were: the 'military tone' of German life (p.224); and Germany's consciousness 'of herself as part of a European and Christian civilization' (p.226). The cinema and the popular press, of course, had come to Germany as to Britain and France. | Growth in mass culture, but otherwise no spectacular developments would have seemed a reasonable prediction in 1914. |
| 8 | Women and the family | Educational advances for women at least equalled those of France, and were more strongly marked than those in Britain. Otherwise, the traditionalist, authoritarian attitudes of Prussian-dominated Germany must be seen as inimical to the interests of women. | The existence of a strong Social Democratic party arguing for equality for women must be strong testimony on the other side; however, I'd be inclined to extrapolate from what I have just said in the column opposite that the potential for change in the role and status of women was not great. |
| 9 | High and popular culture | Germany was Europe's most dynamic nation in 1914 with several traditional cultural centres (Berlin, Munich, Dresden) to rival Paris. | Further developments in both modernism and popular culture seemed highly probable. |
| 10 | Political institutions and values | Liberalism was not deeply rooted in Germany; in the delicate relationship between nationalism and liberalism, nationalism triumphed. Germany had the largest and best organized Social Democratic party in Europe; it was, on the one hand, committed totally to Marxist theory, but, on the other, against revolutionary action.<br><br>In the *Reichstag*, the parliament of the German Empire, deputies were elected on the basis of one man one vote. The crucial problem (I hope you spotted this!) was that within the German Empire the individual state of Prussia, because of its enormous military prestige, exercised an overwhelming, and most undemocratic, influence: the voting system for the Prussian parliament | The German Social Democratic party was growing in strength, but since it was effectively excluded from the political nation, and since it did not show the willingness of the British Labour Party to try to influence existing institutions, and since there was a vacuum in Germany where in other countries the parties representative of liberalism existed, the possibilities for steady change in Germany were probably not high. |

## IMPERIAL GERMANY (cont'd)

**Levels of change in 1914**

**Potential for further change**

was quite undemocratic, and angled towards the traditional elements in Prussian society. The powers of the *Reichstag* were in fact limited; the prestige of the Emperor and of the Prussian military caste very high.

# 7 *FINAL DISCUSSION OF DOCUMENTS*

You will recall my disagreement with Roberts over whether the social policies of the Liberal government in Britain after 1906 amounted to the 'founding of the welfare state'. The two key acts in the Liberal government's social welfare legislation were the Old Age Pensions Act of 1908, and the National Insurance Act of 1911 (Part I dealing with Health Insurance, Part II with Unemployment). Extracts from these two acts are printed as *Documents 1* (I.22 and I.23). Turn now to these documents and let us work through them together.

*Old Age Pensions Act, 1 August 1908*
Chapter 1 clauses (1) and (2) are straightforward. Clause (3) could be seen as favouring Roberts's case since all the money to meet these pensions is to be allocated by parliament, this is to say by the central government out of taxation, without any contribution from the potential beneficiaries. Clause (4) also marks something of a break from the nineteenth-century past where the principle of the Poor Law was that anyone who accepted Poor Law relief immediately forfeited the rights and privileges mentioned here.

Chapter 2 begins to stiffen things up: there is in particular a very tough means test in clause (3).

Chapter 3 begins (in my opinion) to show quite definite nineteenth-century overtones. As (1b) makes clear, you have to have shown yourself to have been a dedicated worker if you are to qualify. On the other hand, if you have shown yourself thrifty by, for example, contributing to a provident society, that will certainly be no disqualification. Clauses (2) and (3) rule out those whose moral character is doubtful.

*National Insurance Act, 16 December 1911: Part II, Unemployment Insurance*
Remember that this act is in two parts, the first concerned with insurance against ill health, the second with insurance against unemployment. Roberts may very well be right that the very fact of enacting legislation concerning these two issues can be regarded as 'founding the welfare state'.

With regard to Part II, Unemployment Insurance, I want you now to read the Sixth Schedule, and the third paragraph of the Seventh Schedule.

**Exercise**   1   The Sixth Schedule seems to present a pretty comprehensive list of working-class occupations. Are there any missing? Why these occupations and not others?

2   With regard to the Seventh Schedule, comment on the length of time for which unemployment benefit may be received. ■

**Specimen answers and discussion**   1   Manifestly absent are the coal-mining, railway and other transport, textile, and chemical industries.

In fact, to cut a long story short, this is not a comprehensive coverage of working-class occupations, but a concentration on trades where, because of weather conditions or fluctuations in demand (as with the manufacture of ordnance and fire-arms), 'seasonal' unemployment was likely.

2   The maximum coverage is for under four months. Unemployment insurance was intended as a temporary alleviation in trades where temporary interruptions were to be expected. □

To me these are piecemeal, limited reforms, pervaded by nineteenth-century attitudes. That is why I find Roberts's language exaggerated. Note what is at stake here with regard to the main issues of our course. If the pre-1914 legislation is all Roberts says it is (and you will have to make up your own mind), this would probably lead one to downgrade any possible significance attaching to the war in bringing about social reform. If, however, relatively little had been achieved by 1914, then the war might stand out as that much more significant. You see again how initial attitudes can colour later conclusions.

Now I want you to turn to *Documents 1* (I.24), a statement of the SFIO, 1905. You will recall what Roberts said about the different splinter groups within the French socialist movement, and about the unification of that movement (p.248). This is the document which represents that unification; note the Marxist terminology.

**Exercise**   Now, as a final exercise, write a full commentary on part of *Documents 1* (I.25), The Charter of Amiens, 1906, saying what it is, commenting on any points in the body of the document, and assessing its historical significance in the study of war, peace and social change.

> The Confederal Congress of Amiens confirms Article 2 of the Constitution of the *Confédération Générale du Travail*: 'The C.G.T. unites, independently of all schools of politics, all workers conscious of the need to strive for abolition of employers and wage earners.'
>
> The Congress holds that this declaration is a recognition of the class war which, in economic life, rallies workers in revolt against all the forms of exploitation and oppression, material as well as moral, practised by the capitalist class against the working class.
>
> The Congress adds to this affirmation of general principle the following specific points:
>
> In the process of making its everyday demands syndicalism seeks to coordinate the efforts of the workers, to better their conditions through achieving such immediate improvements as shorter working hours, wage increases, etc.
>
> But this activity is only one side of the work of syndicalism. It is

preparing that complete emancipation, which can be accomplished only when the capitalist is expropriated; it commends the general strike as a means of action, and it believes that the *syndicat*, which is now the nucleus of resistance, will in future become the nucleus for production and distribution, the foundation of social reorganization. ■

**Specimen answer**    This is part of the Charter adopted at the Congress in 1906 of the principal confederation of French Trade Unions, the CGT. The CGT, it should be noted, did not have any organic relationship with the French socialist party equivalent to the relationship between the British Trade Union Congress and the Labour Party. However, the Congress did take place at a time when efforts were being made to bring unity to the French working class and socialist movement.

Paragraph 1 confirms an existing article of the constitution of the CGT, an article which incidentally brings out the independence of the trade union movement from political parties, including the socialist party, but which basically stresses that the CGT does not seek to unite all workers, but only those workers class conscious in the Marxist sense, that is to say conscious of the need to abolish a fundamental feature of capitalism, the separate existence of employers and wage-earners. The second paragraph takes further and emphasizes the classical Marxist nature of the CGT: the CGT overtly recognizes the existence of the class war. However, after this affirmation of general principle, the charter goes on to specific everyday points, shorter working hours, wage increases, and so on. We then, in the final paragraph quoted here, go on to the distinctive essence of French trade unionism, the belief in what in English is known as 'syndicalism'. There are two points: the basic means of bringing down capitalism is the general strike, and the individual trade union branch, the *syndicat*, which at present is the basic unit of resistance, will in the future become the basic unit of the socialist organization of society. It may be noted that this particular notion of syndicalism does not appear in the policy statement of the united SFIO of 1905.

Thus the historical significance of this document is that it shows that France's principal trade union organization before World War I was not aiming at uniting all workers, but only the class-conscious ones, and that while basically Marxist it was not directly associated with, and indeed in its policy of syndicalism differed from, the French socialist party. Its belief in class war and the general strike effectively set it apart from the constitutional processes of the French Republic. In so far as it had the practical aims of improving hours and wages it could have some effect in bringing about social change before World War I; but, in general, short of a revolution or general strike, it could not be effective in bringing about social change within the context of the French parliamentary institutions which existed in that period.

**Discussion**    Obviously, compare your answer with mine. This was partly simply intended as practice in the handling of documents, but also intended to drive home that the basic issue I have been concerned with in this unit is to set the scene for our coming discussion of how far, if at all, changes were brought about by World War I. □

## Reference

Sheehan, J. J. (1978) *German Liberalism in the Nineteenth Century*, The University of Chicago Press.

# UNIT 6   THE ORIGINS OF WORLD WAR I

*Ian Donnachie*

**Open University students of this unit will need to refer to:**

**Set book: J. M. Roberts,** *Europe 1880–1945*, Longman, 1989

*Documents 1: 1900–1929*, eds Arthur Marwick and Wendy Simpson, Open University Press, 1990

Course Reader: *War, Peace and Social Change in Twentieth-Century Europe*, eds Clive Emsley, Arthur Marwick and Wendy Simpson, Open University Press, 1990

*Offprints Booklet*

# INTRODUCTION

In this unit you will be introduced to the complex forces that contributed to the outbreak of World War I, examining its political, social and economic origins. The aim of the unit is also to develop your understanding of the historical – and continuing – debate surrounding the origins of the war, enhanced by an examination of the relevant historiography, and a close reading of several important contributions to the debate.

How did the events of summer 1914 come about? Why did the great powers allow a regional conflict between Serbia and Austria-Hungary to escalate into a continental war? This final unit of Book I examines the origins of World War I and the historical debate surrounding them.

Firstly, I want to look with you at the major causes of the war, so let me pose a few key questions immediately:

• How far did the war spring from pre-war society, and did domestic conditions in different countries contribute to the outbreak of war?

• Were nationalism, militarism and imperialism essentially to blame?

• How did related diplomatic manoeuvres influence the course of events?

• How much actual blame attaches to particular countries or individuals?

• How far have views changed, and why?

These central issues dominate *any* discussion about the origins of the war, though naturally the emphasis might vary between historians.

My second objective – remembering your study of the course this far – is to highlight the value of historical debate as a tool for resolving a major controversy in twentieth-century European history. Scholars debated and analysed the origins of the war virtually from its outbreak, and since the Armistice at least, historians of many nationalities and biases have generated a voluminous literature. So another set of questions springs to mind, including:

• What did historians closer to events have to say and what conditioned their interpretations?

• How far have such views altered in the light of subsequent events and more recent historical research?

• What new interpretations have emerged recently, notably from a more vigorous emphasis on domestic rather than external affairs in Britain, France, Austria-Hungary, Germany, Russia, and other countries?

I hope that by the time you've worked your way through this material you'll have thought through these two sets of questions, have some awareness of an intriguing historical debate, and be better equipped to understand the origins of the war itself in the light of your work in the first five units.

Before proceeding you should read Roberts, chapters 4 and 8, paying particular attention to the comparisons drawn between each of the countries described and already stressed in Units 2 and 3.

# 1 RECONSTRUCTING THE ORIGINS OF THE WAR

The origins of the war are clearly complex and interrelated, as the questions posed on page 207 indicate. Some were essentially political – others more socio-economic – though, as you can appreciate from earlier units, both are inevitably related.

You know enough already about the nature of European societies, armies, governments and the processes of change to appreciate that some of the contributory factors were *long term*, while others were more obviously *short term* in impact. Let's now build, through a reading of the relevant sections in Roberts, on what you know of European society before 1914 to reconstruct for ourselves the origins of the war. To make anything of the historical debate you need to know the background and I've designed the following readings and exercises to help you summarize the basic points about the origins of the war.

**Exercise** Having read chapters 4 and 8 in Roberts and using the sub-headings in his list of contents as a guide – as well as bearing in mind the concepts you've met in the course so far – make a list of the major areas of tension and potential conflict between European societies before 1914 indicated by Roberts. This will provide a useful basis for further analysis and discussion. As you make your list try to link together those sources of tension which interrelate (for example, imperialism and colonization). ∎

**Specimen answers and discussion** The most obvious sources of tension I identified were the following:

1 Industrialization and trade rivalry (these two clearly go together, especially during the new phase initiated by rapid economic development in Germany after 1870);

2 Imperialism and the scramble for colonies (as seen in the 'new' imperialism after 1880);

3 Nationalism and tension between different ethnic/cultural groups (closely related to (1) and (2) above);

4 Strategic considerations and the arms race (in defence of all three above);

5 Diplomatic manoeuvres and alliances (likewise);

6 Domestic social and political factors (social unrest, the emergence of social democracy, challenges from the Left and Right);

7 The specific situation in Austria-Hungary and the Balkans.

In fact, the list above while perfectly sound, is highly traditional and very commonsensical, but needs to be elaborated on and will be qualified later. □

You should have got all of those points and probably could add more details from your reading of earlier course units and Roberts. Inevitably one's tempted even at this stage to start thinking about *rank* orders as they affect different countries – which is just what historians involved in the great debate have done – with the balance shifting from one set of explanations to another depending on the arguments or sources being deployed. Let's for the moment look in more detail at these seven sources of conflict.

## 1   *Industrialization and trade rivalry*

This is an obvious starting point for a discussion of economic rivalry between the major powers and you've already seen something of the differing levels of economic development in Europe in Unit 3. Throughout the nineteenth century different countries had industrialized at different times and at different rates – Britain having the established lead. By the late nineteenth century British industrial success was still based on several dynamic key sectors – coal, iron, engineering and textiles – still selling relatively strongly in international export markets. These included Europe, North America and other areas of colonization and recent settlement in Africa, Australasia and other parts of the British Empire, notably India and the Far East.

But the late-starters, Germany, France, and the USA (belatedly Russia and Japan), caught up fast and were soon in a position to challenge Britain's hegemony. Although the industrialization of Britain's rivals and the drive for new colonies at the end of the nineteenth century do not in themselves explain the 'new imperialism', they were nevertheless powerful influences.

## 2   *Imperialism and the scramble for colonies*

This should bring you logically to imperial rivalry, which as Roberts indicates in chapter 4 (and you've read in Unit 3), was a major feature of European societies, power politics and diplomatic manoeuvring in the 1880s and 1890s. It became a significant issue mainly because of the fact that by the time the late-starters got in on the act there was little of the globe untouched by earlier colonization, especially by Britain.

Although France was already a significant colonial power before the new 'new imperialism' of the 1880s, it acquired more colonies at that time and other countries including Germany and 'little' Belgium, for example, were also bene-ficiaries of the same drive. The 'scramble for Africa' and the European partition of the continent were merely part of what was happening internationally in export markets during a period of intensifying imperial rivalry. Despite the fact that the African continent had an established reputation as the white man's burden – a graveyard for European colonial officials and merchants – and the trading potential was relatively limited, the great powers persisted. Elsewhere the United States had her frontier in the West, while Tsarist Russia looked east to Siberia and beyond: both shared the imperialist aspirations of the other great powers.

## 3   *Nationalism and racialism*

Both nationalism and racialism – important in themselves as far as the more complex origins of the war are concerned – help explain much of the drive to both industrialization and imperialism. The search for new sources of raw materials was closely related to the search for new markets.

Nationalism was a powerful force among European societies during the second half of the nineteenth century. The 'older' nation states (Britain and France being the obvious examples) and the 'newer' ones (Germany and Italy, both thanks to unification) were dominated by élites whose prestige and the will to possess power was influenced by the theories of Charles Darwin on evolution and natural selection. Thus Western civilization (especially upper- and middle-class ideology and morality) would be spread to supposedly 'inferior' races worldwide.

Mutual suspicion *between* European societies also had clear racial and ethnic undertones which could easily be manipulated by governments and élites in support of wider nationalist aspirations, for example, in the idea of revenge cultivated in France for the loss of Alsace-Lorraine after the Franco-Prussian War or the racial tensions in Austria-Hungary and the Balkans. Racial tension certainly contributed to the belligerent attitude that prevailed during the pre-war era. Yet, there is a good deal of evidence that the common people were sometimes pretty reluctant participants when war came.

### 4    Strategic considerations and the arms race

This is another aspect of the pre-1914 scene familiar to you from Unit 2. The arms race – notably the naval arms race of the 1900s – exacerbated tension between the great powers. Germany's leaders were obsessed with *Weltpolitik*, arguing force-fully that Germany could not be content with being a Continental European power, but must be a world power. Not only did she need colonies and world markets, but also a navy as powerful as that of Britain. The main advocate of this *Weltpolitik* was Admiral Alfred von Tirpitz who, supported by the Kaiser, set about the apparently hopeless task of building a fleet to rival those of other European powers. This began after the passage of the first Navy Law in 1898. Tirpitz argued that given Britain's widespread international commitments a German battlefleet only two-thirds the size of Britain's would suffice for victory at sea – provided the German fleet was concentrated in the North Sea. This argument was tied to the famous 'risk theory' which postulated the view that until the German Navy was ready, Germany would pass through a period of risk. During this time Germany must avoid war, at least until 1920. By then if Tirpitz's programme was up to schedule the German fleet would possess sixty battleships – an impressive deterrent to Britain and giving Germany the potential strength to defeat the entire British Navy in a war. While land warfare had become more industrialized and mechanized since the Franco-Prussian War of 1870, military thinking to a large extent was still dominated by strategy deploying cavalry and infantry. The German military, however, recognizing the problem of handling war on two fronts, favoured the Schlieffen Plan, giving rapid deployment in the West and using the most up-to-date communications and armaments essentially to subdue France. Overall, though, strategy had not caught up with technology and this would have a profound impact on the course of events after 1914.

### 5    Diplomatic manoeuvres and alliances

As Roberts indicates the era before 1914 was dominated internationally by diplomatic manoeuvres and alliances through which the major European powers sought to protect their own interests at home and extend their respective spheres of influence abroad. The main developments from the Dual Alliance to the Balkan crisis are as follows:

Dual Alliance (1879) – links Germany and Austria-Hungary

Three Emperors' Alliance (1881) – includes Russia

Triple Alliance (1882)

Mediterranean Entente (1887)

Franco-Russian Alliance (1894)

Austro-Russian Entente (1897)

Anglo-French Entente (1904) – Triple Entente emerges

Moroccan Crises (1905–06 and again in 1911)

Balkan Crises (1908–13)

These alliances and a complex series of related events gradually drove European societies into two opposing camps and helped aggravate other conflicts of interest. Certainly the war arose out of mutual distrust, a belief that a limited European war was unavoidable, the fact that the leading statesmen saw a limited range of options, and the expectations of both the military and the people that war was necessary to maintain national security and pride. None of the powers was willing to abandon its aims for the sake of peace.

Briefly, Germany wanted to escape the 'encirclement' and political isolation brought about by diplomatic manoeuvres and to assist troubled Austria-Hungary. The High Command (as we'll see) urged war in 1914 while a swift attack on France was still feasible. For its part Austria-Hungary held on to the notion of a supra-national empire; but this was incompatible with Serbia's ambition to bring fellow Serbs within a separate nation state.

Russia's relations with Austria-Hungary and Germany over the Balkans and other issues deteriorated rapidly after 1908. Hence the Tsar soon faced the threat of revolution inspired by social and political unrest at home and the prospect of large-scale war abroad. France, having teamed up with Russia and thus been rescued from the political isolation experienced since the Franco-Prussian War, hoped the alliance would bring pressure to bear on Germany. Both France and Germany failed to exercise any moderating influence on their alliance partners, Russia and Austria-Hungary. Finally, Britain vacillated between neutrality and taking sides: the Cabinet was indecisive, fearing Russian aims despite the alliance. A side issue – Belgian neutrality – was to prove critical.

### 6   Domestic social and political factors

Here the most significant points are:

- The impact of industrialization and the creation of an urban, industrial workforce with aspirations to higher standards of living;

- The emergence of an increasingly powerful middle class with strong economic and political aspirations;

- Pressures for social and political reform marked by social unrest and the emergence of what Roberts (in chapter 7) calls 'anti-traditional forces', including class, education, socialism and feminism;

- The reaction of governing élites varied from society to society – concessions through social welfare programmes in Bismarck's Germany or later in Britain under the reforming Liberal government, contrasting markedly with general suppression in Tsarist Russia (chapter 6).

The essential point is that an undercurrent of social unrest (in Austria-Hungary and the Balkans, and elsewhere racial tension) was fairly universal and was seen as posing a threat to established order and governments, whether controlled by upper or middle classes.

### 7   The specific situation in Austria-Hungary and the Balkans

The Balkans was a major area of real and potentially damaging conflict before 1914, and is often regarded as the principal 'cause' of World War I. The Balkan situation – partly precipitated by the decline of the Ottoman Empire – involved the interests of the great powers and the Balkan nationalists. The area had a long history of instability and during the Balkan crises of 1908–13 became the high-tension point of international power politics. The period was characterized by serious unrest and two wars, involving most of the major powers directly or indirectly. After the two Balkan wars, however, the region remained unstable – the powder-keg of Europe.

**Exercise**  Refresh your memory on these issues and conflicts by re-reading pages 100–5 and 267 to the end of chapter 8 in Roberts and the extract from *The Persistence of the Old Regime* by Arno J. Mayer in the Course Reader. It might help to construct a simple chronology of developments before 1914 for your own use. Do this now. ■

Having set the scene, let's move on and look at the historiography in a bit more detail.

# 2 THE HISTORICAL CONTROVERSY IN OUTLINE

Attempting to list – far less analyse – the many forces that contributed to the outbreak of World War I gives you a first-hand impression of just how complex this issue is. It comes as no surprise that even when the war had just started scholars were already examining its background, particularly the events leading up to the July crisis. In the aftermath of the war historians – with the benefit of hindsight – were in a position to reassess these views in the light of the war's impact on European societies.

Indeed, the origins of the war have so fascinated historians that a constant stream of detailed monographs and re-assessments has appeared in many different languages since the 1920s, and as new evidence has come to light about the attitudes of politicians, generals and informed onlookers.

Many prominent historians – British, German, French, Italian and American – have contributed to the debate about the origins of the war and it's my intention now to introduce some of them to you. To get some initial flavour of the controversy I want you to read the introduction to James Joll's book, *The Origins of the First World War* (1984, pp.1–8, which is reprinted in the *Offprints Booklet*), paying particular attention to the views of historians mentioned.

**Exercise**  Read the first four paragraphs of Joll's introduction and note down your answers to the following questions.

1   Why are the origins of the war so well documented?

2   Who did the victors blame?

3   Why was the Kaiser seen to occupy such a key role?

4   What was the attitude of the Dutch to the Kaiser and how did the Allies react?

5   Why was there a shift in emphasis about responsibility for the war during the 1920s and what explanations were then offered? ■

**Specimen answers**  1   The war is well documented because the debate about responsibility for its outbreak was of great political importance.

2   The victors blamed the Germans – as articulated in Article 231 of the Treaty of Versailles.

3   The Kaiser was seen to be morally to blame partly because of a 'blind instinct for revenge' on the part of the public in Britain and France, and partly because of his role as Emperor and Commander-in-Chief.

4    The Dutch had remained neutral throughout the war and later granted the Kaiser refuge. Both the French and the British – especially Lloyd George – reacted angrily, demanding his surrender.

5    Responsibility shifted from the person of the Kaiser because 'the attitude of the Netherlands government' made it impossible to pin the blame on him directly. The explanations therefore shifted more towards the 'old diplomacy' (*Aussenpolitik*) – particularly the secret diplomatic manoeuvres which were such anathema to President Wilson. (It is worth noting that the idea of Germany as a natural trouble-maker was also less fashionable for a while.)

**Discussion**    On a close reading you should have got most of these points. If not, go back and check over the text. To my mind this is a skilful and concise introduction to the problems surrounding the search for historical explanations about the origins of the war, and shows why the 'war guilt' of Germany should figure so powerfully from the outset. This, of course, embraced nationalism, militarism and imperialism, closely related to domestic economic and social conditions – though Joll does not go into such details at this stage.

The Kaiser himself was 'war guilt' personified, so it was understandably easy to pin most of the blame on him, as the victors sought to do. In an autocratic, militaristic society – as Germany appeared to many in 1914 – the Commander-in-Chief must ultimately be responsible for going to war.

The shift in emphasis to a more sophisticated interpretation was, in a sense, an extension of the German 'war guilt' clause. Blaming the system of alliances and the 'old diplomacy' seemed logical in a Europe whose map had been redrawn and in a situation where the United States had emerged as a major world power. Notice here that nineteenth- and early twentieth-century diplomacy was regarded as highly secretive – especially by socialists and social democrats – as Lenin stressed in a document I'll ask you to examine in due course. The establishment of the League of Nations helped to encourage the idea of 'open diplomacy' and consensus, though how effectively so is something you might like to address at a later stage in the course. □

Moving on, Joll introduces you to some of the historical studies of the war produced since the mid-1920s and shows how the debate broadened out from specifically diplomatic explanations.

**Exercise**    Read the next three paragaphs of Joll's introduction and make notes to answer the following questions:

1    What helped advance the historiography of World War I?

2    What were the major contributions to this?

3    The motives for publication are suggested. What are they?

4    Joll mentions a major impediment to the work of historians. What was it?

5    What was the main thrust of much of this work?

6    What view of the controversy about the war did these historians explore?

7    What new element entered the debate after World War II and what were the central questions addressed?

8    How did German historians react and what were Fritz Fischer's main arguments?

9    What sorts of questions did this new generation of historians pose about Germany's role? ■

**Specimen answers**    1    Most governments involved in the war published volumes of documents from diplomatic archives. Some of the documents had been secret until then, but they were often heavily edited.

2    The major contributions were:

● Tsarist treaties, published by the Bolsheviks;

● Numerous volumes published by the Germans, showing the operation of the 'old diplomacy' and that, apparently, no specific blame attached to them (1922–27);

● Documents on the origins of the war, published by the British (1926–38);

● French diplomatic documents, published 1930–53;

● Austro-Hungarian documents published by Austria (1930);

● Italian documents, mainly published after World War II;

● Further archival material published by the Soviets in the 1920s and 1930s.

3    The motives were essentially to prove that the various governments had nothing to hide, and, in the case of the Germans, to try to refute allegations of 'war guilt'.

4    The biggest problem for historians was that material in government archives relating to the war was invariably closed to them until after 1945.

5    The main thrust was an examination of the diplomatic relations between the great powers.

6    Historians were still basically concerned with the relative responsibility of each of the belligerent governments.

7    The new element in the debate was the linking of the causes of World War I with the causes of World War II. The questions posed included asking if the Treaty of Versailles contributed to the collapse of the Weimar Republic and the rise of Hitler; and if there was a continuity between German foreign policy (or *Aussenpolitik*) and 'war aims' between 1914 and 1939.

8    Some German historians found the 'war guilt' theory painful. There was thus considerable controversy when Fritz Fischer seemed to confirm it in 1961.

9    Fischer's main points at this stage were:

● That Germany had extensive annexationist aims before and during World War I;

● That Germany deliberately went to war to achieve those aims (as the last German Imperial Ambassador to London indicates in a document we shall study later).

**Discussion**    This section of Joll's introduction is vital to your understanding of how the controversy developed. He shows how the publication of archival material helped historians look at the origins of the war in greater depth – particularly the diplomatic aspects. For a time though there was no great advance in the debate, no real attempt to address the political, social or economic issues in the way that historians would do today. This changed with the Depression, the rise of Fascism, the coming to power of Hitler, and World War II.

For many historians working in the post-war era after 1945 there seemed to be remarkable continuity between Germany's aims in World War I and those of Hitler during World War II. More significant, there was increasing interest in the domestic affairs of belligerent countries, and a shifting emphasis towards socio-political analysis of events, rather than an overt concentration on diplomatic activities and the doings of élites. The idea of Germany's 'war guilt' was slightly modified by this change in emphasis, but nevertheless continued to be fashionable among non-Germanic scholars.

At this point Fischer, then a professor in Hamburg, threw his hat in the ring – much to the consternation of colleagues who had been trying to play down the notion of 'war guilt', far less the idea of continuity in war aims. □

**Exercise**   Finally, read the remaining six paragraphs of Joll's introduction. In these he discusses Fischer's views and points the reader forward to a more detailed assessment later in the book. Here are some questions to answer:

1   What was his main thesis?

2   Why had this sort of view become fashionable among American historians in particular?

3   What was the basis of Arno Mayer's argument and why might this seem to have more general application?

4   According to Joll (the tenth paragraph) what factors influenced the decision to go to war in 1914?

5   Why might we feel that the reasons given by politicians at the time were inadequate? ■

**Specimen answers**   1   Fischer's main thesis was that it was *domestic* political and social pressures (or *Innenpolitik*) that determined German foreign policy and diplomatic activity before 1914.

2   During the 1960s and 1970s the relationship between US foreign policy (affecting the whole period from the Cold War to the Vietnam War) and domestic conditions was analysed by scholars and 'it seemed natural to apply' a similar model to earlier European conflicts.

3   As you know already, Mayer took the view that the war arose from a crisis in the politics and policy of the European élite before 1914 – a view that echoed the Marxist view of the war as a crisis of capitalism.

4   The decision to go to war was influenced by:

●   Recent international crises and diplomatic alignments;

●   The military–civilian relationship;

●   Long-term strategic plans and armament programmes;

●   Short and longer-term domestic, political pressures;

●   Public opinion.

5   We might feel the reasons given at the time were inadequate because of the extent of the catastrophe. But the leaders could not have realized that the war would be different from what they intended; that it would be longer and more destructive, and would have such cataclysmic effects.

**Discussion**   The eighth paragraph of Joll's introduction states the views of Fischer and some of his successors quite clearly: the *primacy of domestic pre-conditions* and the importance of related political, social and economic affairs (*Innenpolitik* as opposed to the previously fashionable *Aussenpolitik*). For example, German politicians, generals and admirals – as Joll and others have shown – were very conscious of the connection between domestic and foreign policy, not only believing that foreign ventures might contribute to a mood of national solidarity at home, but also because they feared the strength of the socialist opposition to warlike policies.

While the Fischer thesis applies to Germany and does not necessarily entail any wider view embracing other countries, the other belligerents had their own domestic problems. Given that some of these difficulties sprang from the pressures exerted by industrial capitalism, it would not be unreasonable to assume – as many Marxist historians have – that the war was the inevitable outcome of imperialist rivalries and the prevailing economic system.

As Joll says, it's far from easy to decide which, if any, of the factors was dominant. Probably there is no single explanation, but what we can do now is look in a little more detail at what historians have written about the origins of the war and how the controversy developed over time. An examination of Joll's references gives you some idea of the amount of attention the topic has attracted internationally and we'll be referring to the work of some of these scholars as we proceed. ☐

## 3 WORLD WAR I HISTORIOGRAPHY: A ONE-SIDED DEBATE?

We do not need to spend too much time on this, just enough to give you some flavour of the standpoints taken by historians in the period before the primacy of domestic circumstances became a significant element in the debate. Section 2 of this unit has shown you that historians before the 1960s tended to concentrate on diplomacy, the significance of national and imperial rivalries, militarism, 'war guilt' and, for the Marxists, war as a crisis of capitalism. Let's now look at a document and some extracts presenting different viewpoints about the war.

**Exercise**   Read *Documents 1* (I.26) and the extracts (a), (b) and (c) reproduced here and then answer the following questions.

1   Can you suggest the historical context in which Lenin's 'Appeal to the soldiers of all the belligerent countries' was written? There are enough clues in the document apart from the date.

2   Who does Lenin hold responsible for the war?

3   What points does Lenin make about diplomacy?

4   Can you suggest the provenance of extracts (a) to (c) (pre- or post-Fischer will do!)? What does each writer have to say about the origins of the war?

> *Extract (a)*
> We have now seen how within the space of five years Germany's policy and the growth of her armaments led her to arouse and alarm most profoundly three of the greatest Powers in the world. Two of them, France and Russia, had been forced to bow to the German will by the plain threat of war. Each had been quelled by the open intention of a neighbour to use force against them to the utmost limit without compunction. Both felt they

had escaped a bloody ordeal and probable disaster only by submission. The sense of past humiliation was aggravated by the fear of future affronts. The third Power – unorganised for war, but inaccessible and not to be neglected in the world's affairs – Britain, had also been made to feel that hands were being laid upon the very foundation of her existence. Swiftly, surely, methodically, a German Navy was coming into being at our doors which must expose us to dangers only to be warded off by strenuous exertions, and by a vigilance almost as tense as that of actual war. As France and Russia increased their armies, so Britain under the same pressure increased her fleet. Henceforward the three disquieted nations will act more closely together and will not be taken by their adversary one by one. Henceforward their military arrangements will be gradually concerted. Henceforward they will consciously be facing a common danger.

Ah! foolish-diligent Germans, working so hard, thinking so deeply, marching and counter-marching on the parade grounds of the Fatherland, poring over long calculations, fuming in new-found prosperity, discontented amid the splendour of mundane success, how many bulwarks to your peace and glory did you not, with your own hands, successively tear down!

*Extract (b)*

When the First World War broke out in 1914, a general conflagration had been several times averted in the course of the eight preceding years: in 1906 during the Algeciras Conference; in 1908–09 after the annexation of Bosnia-Herzegovina; in 1911 as a result of the Agadir *coup*; in 1912–13 during the Balkan wars and their aftermath; at the turn of the year 1913–14 in connexion with the Liman von Sanders mission to Turkey. Though they subsided peacefully, all these crises, far from easing, had aggravated existing conflicts, among which the relationship between Austria and Serbia was that most fraught with danger.

Austria projects as a Teutonic outgrowth towards the Carpathian, Danubian, and Balkan region, environed by non-related nationalities. After being for centuries, first the essential element and then the centre of what was long known as the Empire and which in 1804 was named by Francis II the Hereditary Empire of Austria, it had in 1866 – as a consequence of its unsuccessful war against the Prussia of William I and Bismarck – lost its hegemony over the Germanic world.

*Extract (c)*

The balance between the factors maintaining peace and those pulling towards war seemed no different in 1914 than it had been throughout the previous generation, and war therefore was no more likely to occur than it had been previously.

There was perhaps one difference in 1914, a difference of emphasis rather than of nature. In nearly all European countries the forces making for war were much what they had always been – silly old generals who had never seen fighting, pedantic diplomats who had been told by someone or other that they should guard the national honour, hack journalists who could pull in an odd penny by writing a jingoistic piece. These were diseases of an endemic nature present in every modern society and did no harm except to themselves. In Germany militarism went deeper. Here was the only society where army officers determined the moral tone of public life as well as of their own military circle. University professors and bank directors took pride in their rank as army reservists, a quirk rarely encountered in England or France. Military values determined the tone of German policy in a way that was not true elsewhere. Of course Russia too would have been a 'military monarchy', if it had been capable of being anything. But in the general deliquescence of the tsarist regime, the Russian system had ceased to have any character.

Germany had displayed a peculiarly militaristic character ever since the foundation of the second Reich in 1871. Generals had always set the social tone, and the constitution had always been twisted in favour of the army. But in earlier years, particularly during Bismarck's time, the army and its leaders had existed for defensive purposes. Bismarck had certainly taught that Germany would perish unless she were the most militaristic of the great powers, but that was all he had taught. Indeed, in Bismarck's view, Germany had to be militaristic because she was weak. Since then Germany had grown increasingly strong. Few Germans doubted that their country was the greatest of European powers. From this it was an easy step to feeling that she was receiving less than her due. Germans were aggrieved that they had come late to the distribution of colonies. Hence their demand for 'a place in the sun'. This was comparatively harmless. There were plenty of sunny places still waiting to be allotted, and Germany could have had them. Assertiveness, though not perhaps open aggressiveness, had become a predominant German characteristic before 1914. When this was added to the traditional respect which Germans accorded to their military chiefs, Germany became the most dangerous power in Europe.

Comparatively few Germans had conscious plans for a German domination of Europe, and still fewer tried to give such plans practical shape. Most Germans in positions of high authority did not appreciate how far they had drifted from the general European outlook. They were aggrieved and bewildered when others rejected the proffered hand which they supposed they were holding out. In their view, they would be delighted to protect the British Empire as they had long protected the Austrian Empire: delighted, most of all, to assist the Russian tsar against his revolutionary subjects. It was strange and exasperating when others did not share their view. They inclined more and more to rely on Germany's 'sharp sword' – the sort of out-of date military phrase used by public men in every country. All imagined a war of glamour and heroics, with swords and cavalry charges. They got something quite different.

It is the fashion nowadays to seek profound causes for great events. But perhaps the war which broke out in 1914 had no profound causes. For thirty years past, international diplomacy, the balance of power, the alliances, and the accumulation of armed might produced peace. Suddenly the situation was turned around, and the very forces which had produced the long peace now produced a great war. In much the same way, a motorist who for thirty years has been doing the right thing to avoid accidents makes a mistake one day and has a crash. In July 1914 things went wrong. The only safe explanation in history is that things happen because they happen. ■

**Specimen answers and discussion**

1    Lenin's appeal is addressed to the soldiers of all nations at a time when Russia had sustained huge losses. It was written in April/May 1917, a month or so after the Tsar had been forced to abdicate and a new provisional government had been established.

2    As far as Lenin is concerned the capitalists of all countries – including Russia – are to blame. Their motivation is huge profits from war industry, war loans and colonization.

3    Diplomacy was conducted and treaties with far-reaching consequences concluded in secret. These were especially detrimental to Russia.

4    *Extract (a)*
This might surprise you! It's certainly very Anglo-centric and definitely 'pre-
Fischer'. It's from Winston Churchill's *The World Crisis 1911–18*, published in
1923–31. Broadly it reflects the 'war guilt' of Germany, articulated by other writers
of the inter-war period like Renouvin and Schmitt. Germany is seen as belligerent,
generating an arms race between the great powers. In effect this forced Britain to
defend her interests, in concert with France and Russia.

*Extract (b)*
This short extract again pre-dates the revisionism of the 1960s and is from the
voluminous work of Luigi Albertini, whom you met earlier in Joll's discussion.
Although published in Italy in 1942–43 it was not generally read by scholars in
English until this edition of 1952. Albertini catalogues the various crises and
diplomatic manoeuvres that preceded World War I, and clearly attaches consider-
able importance to the decline of the Austro-Hungarian Empire in the rise of
Germany.

*Extract (c)*
Here we have a longer extract from A. J. P. Taylor's influential book *War By
Timetable*, published in 1969 and therefore post-dating Fischer's work. Taylor
takes a fairly broad view here and one feels he is almost apologetic throughout
much of this extract. He argues that diplomacy and the arms race had actually
helped to enforce peace, and that the war happened almost by accident. But
militarism was a strong force in German society, indeed, a bastion against
domestic upheaval and revolution. □

I would not have expected you to have got all these points, but at least to have
grasped the essentials. We could have chosen samples from the work of Von
Wegerer, Renouvin, Schmitt and others mentioned by Joll, written from different
standpoints but in much the same tone. As we saw earlier, the prime concern of
these and other writers was the allocation of blame to one or more of the
belligerents – based essentially on diplomatic and strategic considerations – rather
than paying much attention to domestic conditions. Lenin, of course, took a more
global view and more recently others writing from a Marxist standpoint have
contributed to the debate about the primacy of the domestic situation in the
various countries. They describe the war growing out of a series of political,
economic and social difficulties faced by capitalist societies before 1914 (see, for
example, the work of Mayer).

# 4   FISCHER AND THE 'POST-FISCHER SCHOOL'

In this section I want to look at the work of Fischer and some other historians who
followed in his footsteps, as well as introduce you to some of their critics. We saw
briefly in section 2 how Fischer stirred up a hornet's nest by suggesting that
Germany's war aims before 1914 were not all that different from those before 1939,
and that there was a clear link between war aims and the domestic situation. Let
Fischer now pick up the story for himself.

**Exercise**     Read Fischer's Foreword to his book *World Power or Decline* (1965, English translation 1974) reprinted in the *Offprints Booklet*, where he describes the impact of his work on the scholarly community and public opinion. Then answer the following questions:

1     Why did German history before Hitler seem 'unproblematic'?

2     How did conservative historians in Germany react to Fischer's views?

3     Who supported Fischer and what aspects did they explore?

4     What was the main thesis of *War of Illusions*?

5     Why was the Fischer controversy so influential in recent German historiography? ■

**Specimen answers**     1     German history seemed 'unproblematic' up to the 1930s mainly because
**and discussion**     German historians had seen World War I as the outcome of the Triple Entente's attempt to hem in Germany. When the Entente powers attacked, Germany was forced to defend itself. Much of German history seemed to follow on from there.

2     Critics reacted by:

•     distorting Fischer's conclusions;

•     attempting to re-instate Bethmann Hollweg – the devil of the piece as far as Fischer was concerned;

•     reproaching his sources;

•     dismissing his views completely.

3     Two main supporters of Fischer were Geiss and Böhme who studied aspects of the domestic and social implications of imperialism.

4     The main thesis of *War of Illusions* looked at a wide range of forces affecting German war aims, particularly that domestic considerations became more important as efforts to acquire overseas possessions foundered.

5     There are several important points about the controversy. Firstly, it greatly influenced historical thinking. Secondly, it stirred the political conscience of Germany and destroyed illusions. Thirdly, it helped Germany reappraise her past. □

Here we have the essence of the controversy and are provided with a good indication of how Fischer helped sharpen up the debate about the origins of the war. We can hardly expect to explore all the angles on the origins of the war which the Fischer debate engendered, but let's look in a little more detail at the vital question of domestic conditions and foreign policy. How closely did they inter-relate? In trying to answer this we can make a start by looking specifically at one of Fischer's (constructive) critics, Wolfgang Mommsen.

In an important and very involved article in the journal *Central European History*, Mommsen identified four main approaches to the history of Wilhelmine Germany:

*The 'socio-Marxist' approach*, which emphasizes the influence of particular pressure groups interested in and likely to benefit from imperialist politics.

*The 'moralistic' approach*, which is primarily a critical analysis of prevailing ideological, that is, anti-democratic attitudes.

*The 'Kehrite' approach* (from the work of Eckhart Kehr on the 'primacy of domestic policies'), which tends to explain political developments as the outcome of defensive strategies by the ruling classes against the process of democratization – with strong Marxist undertones. Mayer, as you've seen, applied this sort of approach to European history of the period.

*The 'functional–structural' approach*, which pays special attention to the functions and malfunctions of constitutional and governmental systems under the impact of social forces unleashed by the advance of industrialization and mass culture – or the impact of 'modernization'. Here the defensive strategy of the ruling classes is considered as just one factor among others – the main argument being that disproportions between the social and political systems lead to increasing degrees of social conflict.

According to Mommsen, while many historians who entered the debate tended to combine these approaches in one way or another, Fischer's approach could be most readily described as 'moralistic'. Personally, I think this is a bit simplistic and facile.

**Exercise**   Now I want you to read an extract dealing with Fischer's views from the same Mommsen article, reprinted in the *Offprints Booklet*, and then answer the following questions:

1   How does Mommsen summarize Fischer's views and what are the central facets of the argument?

2   Why is Mommsen critical of Germany's 'will to power' as seen by Fischer?

3   Why does Mommsen play down the importance of the 'War Council' of 8 December 1912?

4   How does Mommsen account for Fischer's apparent failure 'to give proper consideration to the forces of moderation'? ∎

**Specimen answers and discussion**   1   Aggressive nationalism was a powerful force throughout German society, especially among the ruling classes. Germany had been deliberately heading for a European war in order to become a world power and to re-assert its position after the relative failure of its attempts to acquire colonies and more political influence overseas. German war aims after 1914 could be traced back long before the war, as instanced particularly in its economic objectives.

2   Mommsen claims that Fischer is ambivalent about which groups in German society were pressing for war, and that his argument shifts from one to another without any apparent consistency: 'Was it the government, the emperor, the military establishment, the Conservatives, the industrialists, or the nation at large, any one of them, or all of them?' Important insights are gained, says Mommsen, but the overall thesis is far from clear.

3   Mommsen plays down the decisions taken on this occasion, saying that the 'direct effects' of the conference were negligible – saving an acceleration of preparations for a new armaments bill. This is a complex issue. Mommsen regards the so-called 'War Council' as feigning urgency.

4   According to Mommsen, Fischer draws conclusions from what people *said* rather than what they *did*, and arrives at too radical conclusions because he tends to isolate nationalist or imperial quotations from their context. This is an interesting angle on the Fischer thesis! This is a fascinating critique but to my mind it certainly does not negate Fischer's view about the primacy of the domestic situation in Germany before 1914. Looking back at our list of major areas of

tension and political conflict in section 2 we can see that many do indeed derive from social and economic conditions within different countries – including Germany – before 1914. □

Finally in this section we'll look at a valuable comparative study of Britain and Germany, which places the controversy about the origins of the war in a wider context. This is an edited version of Michael Gordon's paper published in the *Journal of Modern History*, and reprinted in the Course Reader. Before you read the article please note that the central section dealing with comparative economic and political development has been omitted because of a lack of space. The arguments in this section are broadly that:

● Rapid industrialization had a dramatic impact on the rate of social change in Germany compared to Britain.

● German society remained traditionally authoritarian. Even the bourgeoisie was far more 'feudalized' than in Britain.

● State-supported industrialization was aggressive and ambitious and contributed to an erratic and bullying *Weltpolitik*.

● In terms of national identity Germany was internally fragmented and there was no mass base for the nation state that emerged after 1871. Britain – with the exception of Ireland – had a sense of common nationhood.

● Britain (Ireland always excepted) was a successful unitary state; Germany was mainly an unsuccessful federal experiment.

● Political participation differed considerably. In Germany the élites refused to compromise their position of dominance – except through 'negative integration' after 1912. In Britain the political system was also hard-pressed to accommodate new claimant groups, but democracy was nevertheless conceded cautiously.

**Exercise**    Now read the substantive part of Gordon's article in the Course Reader. Glance through the footnotes and comment on the kinds of source cited. ■

**Specimen answer**    The sources are, in fact, almost exclusively secondary, either in English or in
**and discussion**    German, and published in international scholarly journals. This suggests a wide-ranging review article, taking a comparative perspective. Indeed, what Gordon does is apply (rather rudimentary) political science models to the researches and discussions of historians. □

**Exercise**    In order to tease out the main arguments let's take the article a section at a time, noting that I have summarized section IV for you.

*Section I*
1   What, according to Gordon, are the main features of *what he calls* the 'traditional model' in diplomatic history?

2   What is its main drawback?

3   Outline Gordon's interpretation of the Fischer school's views.

4   What are the two main problems about Fischer's views?

5   What elements made up Mayer's model of the comparative domestic situation? ■

**Specimen answers and discussion**

1   The main features of the 'traditional model' as Gordon sees them are dominated by the 'primacy of foreign policy'. He sees the 'traditional model' distinguishing strongly between domestic and foreign policy, treating the state as a unified body, governed by rules of statecraft. The state is seen as a 'rational, unitary decision-maker' with external interests of power and prestige dominating, and with little attention apparently paid to domestic conditions within the state itself.

2   The main drawback of the 'traditional model' springs from the ambiguity surrounding various interpretations of the primary sources relating to foreign policy. The same document can be used to validate two opposing views depending on how the evidence is deployed. Hence the value of a wider perspective embracing diplomatic and domestic history.

3   Gordon says Fischer's concern was to show how German foreign policy was influenced by maintenance of the 'social status quo', the prestige of the Wilhelmine Empire, and the needs of economic élites. The second stage, as Gordon sees it, was the extension of this argument to war aims – expansion abroad being seen as the only way to preserve the status quo at home. Gordon echoes views you've already met, but adds his own interesting gloss.

4   According to Gordon the major problems are, firstly, that Fischer has not been explicit enough about his methods and assumptions, and his choice of sources is sometimes highly selective. Secondly, his work is not always sufficiently comparative and would benefit from greater attention to developments in Britain, France, Austria-Hungary and Russia. Hence the Fischerists put *too much* blame on Germany.

5   The Mayer model – as you should by now appreciate – focused on the domestic situation in various European countries, providing a comparative view of domestic violence, counter-revolutionary activity and diversionary war to sustain existing élites. ☐

Personally, I think we need to be careful of Gordon's somewhat cavalier dismissal of the so-called 'traditional model' of international history. There were impressive continuities in the foreign policies of all the great powers involved – which cover a very long period – and some considerable political and social change. The best-known examples from the great age of alliances before World War I are the Austro-German or Dual Alliance (which lasted from 1879 to 1918), the Triple Alliance (1882–1915), and the Franco-Russian Alliance (1894–1917). We need to ask ourselves how these continuities can be explained solely – or even mainly – in terms of domestic politics.

**Exercise**   *Section II*

1   What were the key features of German foreign policy?

2   What were the key features of British foreign policy?

3   Why do they not fit the 'traditional model'? ∎

**Specimen answers and discussion**

1   German policy was characterized by a willingness to risk war – local or otherwise – to achieve the breakthrough in *Weltpolitik*. Controversy surrounds the idea that the policy sought a 'preventive war', but the scale could hardly be predicted in advance.

2   British policy was lacking in effectiveness and energy, inconsistent in its

backing of France and Russia on the one hand, while playing the role of 'disinterested mediator' on the other. Britain failed to flex her muscles sufficiently, given the strength of her power internationally. The ententes and other relationships could be regarded as 'dangerous half-way adjustments', which did not challenge the German menace strongly enough.

3    Gordon says that the relative positions of Britain and Germany internationally did not differ enough to justify such contradictory responses to the July crisis. Both, in a sense, were hemmed in by domestic difficulties and crises of confidence, but in many ways Germany seemed the more buoyant. □

**Exercise**    *Section III*

1    What domestic factors did Britain and Germany share?

2    Who were the 'enemies of the existing system' in Germany?

3    What contributed to unrest and tension in Britain?

4    Can you identify the main points of contrast between Britain and Germany set out here? ■

**Specimen answers and discussion**    1    The two countries seemed to share a series of problems: economic difficulties; social strife; political unrest; constitutional crises; and potential violence on a large scale.

2    The enemies of the existing system in Germany included: the Catholic centre; the Social Democrats (the SPD); and the trade unions.

3    In Britain the main tensions arose from: class conflict; the militancy of the unions; the suffragettes; the right wing of the Conservative-Unionist party; and the problem of civil unrest in Ireland.

4    Germany had a strong state apparatus, more rigid social structures, and a powerful élite dedicated to maintaining the status quo despite the emergence of social democracy. Britain was far more democratic, lacked any real state bureaucracy, and was ruled by a fairly broad-based and reforming government. It follows that foreign policy reflected the differing domestic circumstances. □

**Exercise**    *Section V*

1    In what ways did domestic conflict have a 'contrary impact' on Germany and Britain?

2    What were the main repercussions for German policy? ■

**Specimen answers and discussion**    1    British foreign policy was moderate and largely defensive, whereas Germany became increasingly aggressive in the run-up to 1914.

2    The main repercussions identified by Gordon are: an exacerbation of problems of national identity; greater social imperialism; mass propaganda; armaments programmes; and a nurturing of fears and grudges. These typified the *Weltpolitik* of the Wilhelmine era. Much of this was 'self-induced' before 1914, says Gordon. □

Mommsen and Gordon were only two of a clutch of historians who addressed the debate about the 'primacy of domestic politics' in the origins of the war. In Germany itself the domestic policies of Imperial Germany were examined intensively during the 1970s, with close attention being paid to economic aspects, social structures, public opinion and political culture. It is therefore true to say that in the long run 'Fischer's methodological emphasis on the need to focus on the inter-action of Imperial domestic and foreign policy has been at least as influential as his substantive conclusion that the German government was primarily responsible for the First World War' (Roger Fletcher in the introduction to F. Fischer, *From Kaiserreich to Third Reich*, 1986, p.16).

The most prominent of the 'post-Fischerists' – including Hans-Ulrich Wehler and Jurgen Kocka of the University of Bielefeld – contributed vitally important new studies of German history, the emphasis being on social history of the pre-war era. The Bielefelders had wider concerns than Germany's role in the making of World War I, but nevertheless they helped to consolidate Fischer's basic thesis and through their openness and tolerance rebut many of his critics.

# 5 A CONTINUING DEBATE: 'INNENPOLITIK' VERSUS 'AUSSENPOLITIK'?

As Roger Fletcher, editor of the English edition of Fischer's most recent work *From Kaisserreich to Third Reich*, has argued, by the 1980s the post-war revolution in German historiography 'was beginning to devour its own children'. Another generation had emerged in whose eyes Fischer was ancient history and the Bielefelders belonged in medieval mothballs. The 'new' social history, in common with similar work in Britain, France, the USA, and elsewhere, deployed a radical new toolkit of approaches and was obviously and deliberately critical of the work pioneered by Fischer, Wehler, Kocka and their school. The case against Fischer and the Bielefelders is summed up as follows:

> First, it portrays too static a picture of German history and does not sufficiently allow for social and political change. Secondly, it ascribes too much to the manipulative wizardry of the political élites and neglects the independent effect on the political system of the allegedly manipulated groups in German society. Thirdly, it exaggerates the extent to which the ruling groups in late nineteenth- and early twentieth-century German society were 'feudal' or 'pre-industrial' or 'traditional' in their outlook at a time when Germany was already a highly industrialized capitalist economy. (R. J. Evans, 'From Hitler to Bismarck: Third Reich and Kaiserreich in recent historiography', *Historical Journal*, vol.26, no.4, 1984)

The grassroots historians may indeed be critical of Fischer and the 'post-Fischerists', but as Fletcher says, German history in the twentieth century has now a diversity and fluidity that it lacked before the 1960s and the Fischer controversy has generated a vital debate internationally.

Undeniably the *Innenpolitik* argument remains in the ascendancy, despite some recent and extremely interesting efforts to reassert *Aussenpolitik*. For example, some fascinating questions are raised by the work of John Röhl and others about the influence of some key politicians, diplomats and military men in codifying Germany's war aims. (See J. Röhl, ed., *1914: Delusion or Design? The Testimony of Two German Diplomats*, 1973.) Did Germany 'blunder into war'? Was it by 'delusion or design'? Was it war 'by timetable', as Taylor and others have suggested? Most of the evidence, as Röhl shows, points to the culpability of a powerful nexus group within the German élite, and he cites the surviving testimony of several German diplomats and others close to the events of 1912–14. One example drawn from the Memorandum by Prince Max Lichnowsky, last Imperial German ambassador to London, will illustrate this particular angle.

**Exercise**      Read document I.27 in *Documents 1* and answer the following questions:

1   In what circumstances did Prince Lichnowsky take up his post in Britain and what does he have to say about British policy at that time?

2   What view is given about German policy and aims? ■

**Specimen answers**      1   As Lichnowsky explains, he arrived in London in November 1912 after the
**and discussion**       end of the First Balkan War. Britain desired peace with Germany but, he says, had to support France, her ally.

2   German policy did nothing to preserve peace. In fact, war seems to have been the aim. The only question was when? □

Lichnowsky's views are very typical of surviving evidence supporting the culpability of the Prusso-German military establishment in engineering the outbreak of war – the culmination of a longer-term bid for 'world-power' status, as Röhl describes it.

# 6 *CONCLUSION*

We've moved a long way from our general analysis of war origins, which took account of wide-ranging international forces, to recent German historiography of World War I. As Professor Berghahn says, the debate was always about the immediate origins and the last years and months of peace before 1914. While the *long-term* factors were clearly critical, there is hardly any disagreement now about who pushed Europe over the brink at the end of July. The debate continues over why Berlin and Vienna did it. Fischer continues to argue that the objective was to realize the expansionist aims of *Weltpolitik*. He continues to attach great importance to the 1912 War Council at which he believes the decision was taken to launch a major war eighteen months later. Fischer's opponents emphasize the defensive considerations of the Reich government and insist that Berlin first pursued a *limited* Balkan war strategy that went wrong. Many of the differences of view are essentially differences of emphasis – greater or lesser stress on internal social tensions, for instance. To arrive at a fully rounded view of your own you would need to read further the various authorities cited in this unit.

Finally, for another view of the desperate situation in which the European powers found themselves during the summer of 1914, let me remind you of the quote from the American historian, Paul Schroeder, which you read in Unit 1:

> [The] search for the fundamental cause of World War I is futile, while the argument that war simply happened is unhelpful. Is there no exit from the cul-de-sac? A different question may help: not why World War I? but why not? War was still *ultima ratio regnum*. World War I was a normal development in international relations; events had been building toward it

for a long time. There is no need to explain it as a deviation from the norm. In this sense, the question why not? answers the question Why? More important, it points to what is unexpected about the war and needs explanation: its long postponement. Why not until 1914? (P. W. Schroeder in D. W. Lee, ed., *The Outbreak of the First World War*, 1975, pp.148–69)

Think about these questions as you move on to study the war and its aftermath.

## References

Albertini, L. (1952) *The Origins of the War of 1914*, Oxford University Press (originally published as *Le origini della Guerra del 1914* in 1942–43).

Churchill, W. S. (1923–31) *The World Crisis 1911–18*, 1942 edition, Macmillan.

Fischer, F. (1974) *World Power or Decline: The Controversy over Germany's Aims in the First World War*, W. W. Norton (first published in 1965).

Fischer, F. (1986) *From Kaiserreich to Third Reich: Elements in Continuity in German History 1871–1945*, Allen and Unwin.

Gordon, M. R. (1974) 'Domestic conflict and the origins of the First World War: the British and the German cases', *Journal of Modern History*, vol.46, June, pp.191–226.

Mommsen, W. J. (1973) 'Domestic factors in German foreign policy', *Central European History*, vol.vi, no.1, pp.11–15.

Röhl, J. C. G. (ed.) (1973) *1914: Delusion or Design? The Testimony of Two German Diplomats*, Paul Elek.

Schroeder, P. W. (1972) 'World War I as Galloping Gertie' in Lee, D. W. (ed.) (1975) *The Outbreak of the First World War. Causes and Responsibilities*, D. C. Heath.

Taylor, A. J. P. (1969) *War by Timetable*, Macdonald.

## Bibliography

Berghahn, V. R. (1973) *Germany and the Approach of War in 1914*, Macmillan.

French, D. (1986) *British Strategy and War Aims 1914–1916*, Allen and Unwin.

Joll, J. (1984) *The Origins of the First World War*, Longman.

Koch, W. (ed.) (1972) *The Origins of the First World War: Great Power Rivalry and German War Aims*, Macmillan.

Lieven, D. (1983) *Russia and the Origins of the First World War*, Macmillan, chs 2 and 5.

McMillan, J. F. (1985) *Dreyfus to De Gaulle. Politics and Society in France 1898–1969*, Edward Arnold, ch.5.

Robbins, K. (1985) *The First World War*, Oxford University Press.

Röhl, J. C. G. (1970) *From Bismarck to Hitler: the Problem of Continuity in German History*, Longman.

Steiner, Z. S. (1977) *Britain and the Origins of the First World War*, Macmillan.

Stevenson, D. (1982) *French War Aims Against Germany 1914–1919*, Oxford University Press.

# INDEX